A Marine at Gallipoli and on The Western Front

To my wife

A Marine at Gallipoli and on The Western Front

First In, Last Out – The Diary of Harry Askin

Harry Askin

Edited by Jean Baker, Gaynor Newlyn and Nicola Woollaston

Pen & Sword
MILITARY

First published in Great Britain in 2015 by
Pen & Sword Military
an imprint of
Pen & Sword Books Ltd
47 Church Street
Barnsley
South Yorkshire
S70 2AS

ISBN 978 1 47382 784 4

Typeset in Ehrhardt by
Mac Style Ltd, Bridlington, East Yorkshire
Printed and bound in the UK by CPI Group (UK) Ltd,
Croydon, CRO 4YY

Pen & Sword Books Ltd incorporates the imprints of Pen & Sword
Archaeology, Atlas, Aviation, Battleground, Discovery, Family
History, History, Maritime, Military, Naval, Politics, Railways, Select,
Transport, True Crime, and Fiction, Frontline Books, Leo Cooper,
Praetorian Press, Seaforth Publishing and Wharncliffe.

For a complete list of Pen & Sword titles please contact
PEN & SWORD BOOKS LIMITED
47 Church Street, Barnsley, South Yorkshire, S70 2AS, England
E-mail: enquiries@pen-and-sword.co.uk
Website: www.pen-and-sword.co.uk

Contents

Introduction

I have tried in the following pages to give a true and unexaggerated account of my travels and of all that happened to me from leaving England, under orders with the MEF, to landing at Marseilles, where we were taken over by the BEF.

The first chapter of my book was actually written during the voyage, the rest I have taken from my memory, aided by my diaries, which I kept almost religiously, often entering notes under heavy fire but always sticking strictly to facts.

It is impossible to set down in writing just what those months on the Peninsula meant to me and to all the other fellows there and I have been content to write down the chief items of interest.

I may as well state here that I enlisted in the Royal Marines on 22 September 1914 at Nottingham and was sent from there to Portsmouth.

The interval between joining and leaving England was spent, on the whole, pleasantly, training at Portsmouth, Fareham, a three-day route march in glorious weather through the New Forest to Lyndhurst and Ringwood, finishing up at our final training place at Okeford Fitzpaine, a lovely little place in Dorset.

Blandford, about six miles away, was the training centre for the Royal Naval Division.

Here we got fit for the big move.

Harry Askin

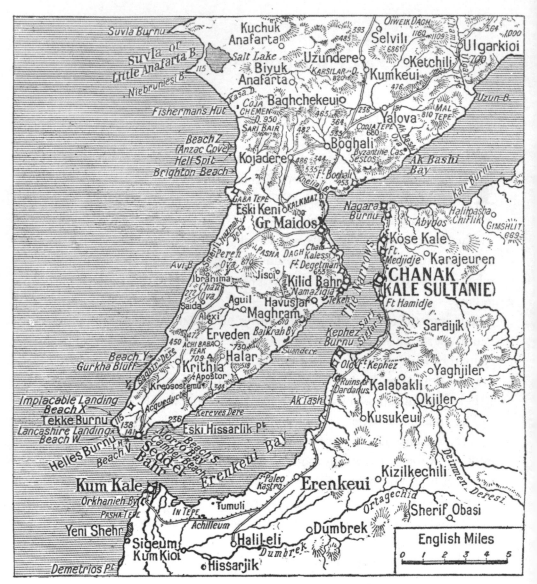

MAP OF THE GALLIPOLI PENINSULA

(By courtesy of the "Morning Post")

THIS MAP SHOWS ALL THE LANDING-PLACES MENTIONED IN MR. ASHMEAD-BARTLETT'S DESPATCHES, AND THE POSITIONS
OF KRITHIA, ACHI (OR AKI) BABA, SUVLA, ETC.

Chapter One

27 February 1915 – The Voyage

Portsmouth Battalion Royal Marines received orders to move from Okeford Fitzpaine. We had quite a busy time returning gear, bedding, ammunition and office material. I just had time to write two short letters and a few postcards home to let them know we were off at last. All our chaps were disappointed at having no leave, as some of the Naval battalions had been granted a few days at home and we quite expected the same before we left England.

We were all feeling excited and eager to be off, although we had no idea where we were bound. Several guesses were made as to our destination: France, Malta, Egypt, Serbia, German East and West Africa. It was certain to be somewhere hot as we had been served out with huge sun helmets. Marched down to Shillingstone station about 5.00pm, well stocked with food and drink and most of us with a few luxuries that the good people of Okeford had given us. All the village turned out to see us off and most went with us to the station.

It was 6.30pm when we got away, as most of the RN Division were in training there. Pushed right in a carriage, which was quite enough with full marching order. We managed to keep fairly lively on the journey, having plenty to eat and some jolly good cider to drink. We had a lively chap in our carriage who kept things going. 'Dolly' Gray was his name. All Grays in the marines are 'Dolly', the same as all Martins are 'Pincher' and all Bells are 'Daisy'. This Dolly was a 'bird'. He must have been, and so must all old soldiers who serve about twenty-one years in a regiment and finish up with the same rank that they started with. He had been with the division in the show at Antwerp and was the sole means whereby our battalion got back to safety with so few taken prisoner, so he told us. However, he could be good company and we passed the time fine. Went past Bath and finished up on the docks at Avonmouth about 11.30pm, scrambled out of the train and formed up in some sort of order on the quayside where several large troopships were berthed, lit up and taking troops and stores on board. Of course, everybody was dizzy which was only natural; officers and sergeant majors dashing about giving dozens of orders of which nobody took the slightest notice. We hung about for an hour and then got on board. Our company was allotted one mess deck just under the first-class saloon of our ship, the *Gloucester Castle*, about 7,000 tons. Had plenty of work to do once we got aboard, stowing rifles and bayonets in the armourer's shop, then getting kitbags and blankets aboard. Blankets were then served out and we turned in about 2.30am. I slept on deck with Jack Senior, a chap I met at the recruiting office in Sheffield. Did nothing but lounge round all Sunday and got thoroughly fed up. Saw a lot more ships in dock – *Franconia*, *Royal George*, *Alnwick Castle*, *Somali Crestian*, and *Grantully Castle*. Some had troops on board and others were taking them on; all were busy taking on stores. Saw the light cruiser *Duke of Cornwall* in dock for repairs. She had been damaged in the Falkland Islands battle. Everybody cheered up when the tugs came alongside and towed us out of harbour. We steamed down the Bristol Channel escorted by two TBDs.[1] It was blowing strong but the ship was steady and I thought then that I could stand sea life forever.

Things were pretty rough in the morning and I could hear the sea coming over on to the well deck, and when I got up I knew that the ship was pitching and rolling. Went up on deck and it was grand to watch the great waves as they dashed over the bows of the ship. It was jolly wet though and presently I began to feel a queer sensation inside me and also observed several chaps leaning over the side and others making a dash for it. I was soon over, and by the time breakfast was piped 80 per cent of the battalion were helpless. Men were just lying about anywhere, not caring whether the place under them was wet or dry. Mess orderlies, told off for the day, tried hard to carry out their duties but, when it came to manipulating dishes of sloppy porridge along the greasy shifting decks, they all seemed to fail. Porridge was everywhere and on nearly everyone. I'd nothing to eat that day and did nothing but lie about on deck. Felt better about 5.00pm and the sea had gone down a bit to help matters. I didn't feel well enough to fit my hammock up, so slept on the

---

1. TBD, or torpedo–boat destroyer, a title later abbreviated to destroyer.

mess deck. Conditions were much better in the morning, warm and bright, and everybody woke up with enormous appetites. It was bloater morning though, so I didn't get much chance to satisfy mine. I never was very partial to fish which had millions of bones in it. The only other course for breakfast was bread, rank margarine and very indifferent jam with some terrible tea out of a tin mug to wash it all down.

The meals were rotten. It was a bloater one morning and porridge made without sugar or milk the next. 'Try salt with it,' one old soldier said one morning. I did and nearly had a repetition of the first day. For dinner we had either stewed meat or a roast with small bad potatoes. Twice a week we had duff. The best meal was Saturday's dinner when we had corned beef, pickles and potatoes. The company was vaccinated on 3 March, but I managed to wriggle out of it. I had gone back to my old job of company clerk and had a pretty soft time with a nice deck cabin as an office.

We arrived at Gibraltar early on 5 March and everybody rushed up on deck to get a view. However, it was misty and all we could see was the dim outline of the big rock. Had it fresh all that day, but the next was fine and warm. We steamed close to the north coast of Africa that day and the next, and saw some of the most gorgeous scenery. We passed close to several towns, Algiers and Tunis being the largest. The coast appeared rocky and, far inland, we could see huge snowcapped mountains. The troops were having a tottering time on board, first drawing rifles from below, then returning them, drawing helmets and packs and doubling round the ship scores of times.

We sighted land on the morning of the 8th, the island of Gozo, a small place near Malta, and from what we could see of it, very barren. We saw a church, so I supposed people lived there. The next place we came to was Malta and we could see the *Royal George* entering harbour. We anchored in Grand Harbour about 2.00pm. It looked a lovely place, especially on the Valletta side. Weren't we all longing for a few hours ashore? The privilege was denied us and we had to contend with our view from the ship. Officers, of course, were allowed on shore and so were colour sergeants. Several more of our ships were in harbour and the *Grantully Castle* followed us in and anchored alongside. Their band struck up for about an hour and livened things up a bit. Several battleships were in, both British and French. It was amusing to watch the Maltese in their bumboats, simply swarming round the ship; some of them waited hours on the chance of rowing somebody ashore. Some tried to sell us things, but we weren't allowed to buy from them. As I had no money it didn't affect me much. I don't think anybody had much left; the canteen people had seen to that. I don't think it possible to find a more barefaced set of robbers or sharpers than that ship's company.

Kept awake nearly all night by Maltese boys coaling the ship; they were chattering like monkeys the whole time. Left Malta the next morning and sailed due east and again sighted land on the 10th. All that day we were amongst the islands of the Grecian Archipelago. Awfully desolate looking places, some of them just like huge barren rocks. It was a change from the open sea though. Packed our kitbags and stowed them away below. About 10 o'clock next morning we could see land straight ahead and soon after could make out the tripod masts of two battleships. We headed straight for them and arrived outside Mudros Bay, Lemnos, about noon. The harbour had a fine concealed entrance with a great submarine boom across it and was well protected by shore batteries. What a size the harbour was when we got inside and what scores of ships were in it! From great battleships and transports, both French and British, down to tiny Greek fishing-boats. The two battleships that we first sighted and passed were the *Nelson* and *Agamemnon*, both fine ships but considered old. We had a fine welcome from the crews of all the ships as we passed and the French troops and sailors nearly went frantic. We anchored close to the *Braemar* and *Cawdor Castle*, ships with our Plymouth and Chatham battalions on board. Australian and New Zealand ships were there too, all packed with troops; onshore at West Mudros was a huge camp of French colonial troops. We had a terrific thunderstorm at night and the lightning lit the whole place like day. I have never seen or heard anything like it in England. Ships were coming in all the next day, including the *Franconia* and *Royal George*. Boats were lowered from our ship during the day and so many told off from each company to man them. What a hash they made of boat pulling! They soon got a bit of shape into it though with the help of some active service marines.

The *Alnwick Castle* came in on the 13th with Deal Battalion on board. We had heard a strong rumour since arriving that she had been sunk with all on board. Two of our companies landed that day for drill, and troops were landing from other ships, some being engaged in making stone piers.

That night we could hear heavy gunfire but it was very distant. The *Queen Elizabeth* left next morning. She simply dwarfed every other ship in the bay. Our company (D) landed on Monday about 9.00am. We managed to pull halfway to the shore, then a picket boat took us in tow and finished a very scrappy job. Felt strange on shore for a time and I think Micky Sanders, our company second in command, was mad to try company drill. We did better at boat pulling. He sent each platoon off on its own after a time. Our platoon, with Mr Dougherty in charge, practised a patrol on a village. I think Dougherty was as curious as we were to see inside the place and to have a look at the people. As we approached we could see scores of women watching us from the outskirts, but as soon as we got about 100 yards of them they all fled inside and shut themselves up in their houses. As we passed through the village we could see them peeping at us through their windows. The most striking thing about the place was the smell, which was awful. No attempt was made at sanitation, refuse being thrown anywhere. Portiana is the name of the place, just a smattering of houses and hovels put up anyhow. A trench was dug round the whole place to prevent flooding during the rainy season. It must have been the rainy season then, for it started to pour and we were all drenched in a very short time. We saw some women and a few old men working on the land. It took one right back to the old Bible days. Saw one old chap, dressed in a sheepskin coat, turning the ground over with a wooden plough drawn by a couple of very ancient oxen. Windmills are stuck all over the place; as many as five and six in a row in places.

We had to row all the way back to the ship, everybody was fed up, wet and tired, and to crown matters we had to climb over the stern up rope ladders, not an easy task with full kit and rifle. One sergeant dropped his rifle as he got to the top. Straight down it went, gone forever.

Six large French troopships came in during the afternoon, one with General Amade and his staff on board. Heard about the little show that Plymouth Battalion had on 4 March.

There had been a big bombardment by our fleet about the end of February, which had silenced the two big forts at the entrance to the Dardanelles, at Sedd-el-Bahr on the European side and Kum Kale on the Asiatic shore. One company of marines landed at either place to finish off the forts. The Kum

Kale party came off without any casualties, having met with no opposition. The Sedd-el-Bahr party was less fortunate, however, and came in for a lot of sniping from the village behind the fort and had twenty-six killed and missing and twenty-six wounded. The demolition party had several casualties too. They returned to Lemnos and had done nothing further up to us joining them. One captain was in hospital in Malta; he had ventured too far ahead and the Turks had caught him, castrated him and left him lying in the village.

Our company landed again the following day but I didn't go with them. I'd had enough the previous day, so found some returns which wanted rendering. They consisted of reading and writing letters in the office. Heard news of the *Dresden* being sunk. The 17th saw a move on the part of our people. We had been wondering how long we were going to stick there and I think everybody was fed up with Lemnos.

The *Cawdor Castle* with Chatham Battalion on board left harbour at 7.00am. Had everybody guessing of course. Two of our companies went ashore again and by all accounts had a pretty rotten time, practising company drill and other queer evolutions that are not in the drill book, but exist only in the minds of ambitious subs. They made a mess of things generally and we were all glad when signals were made to leave shore and join the ship. The signal applied to all shore parties, but the water was too rough for amateur sailors, and tug-boats and lighters had to be sent for them. We quite thought our time for action had come and that it was to be Gallipoli.

We left Mudros at 6.00pm and most of the other RND ships followed us. We had an escort of battleships, cruisers and TBDs. We steamed until about 10 o'clock and then stopped. Next morning, when we got on deck, we were in sight of land but well away from it. The sea between us and the shore was full of warships, some of them firing. We steamed on again about 7.00am, keeping along the coast with all the ships in line. Destroyers kept racing past us giving us various signals by semaphore. One we made out was 'keep out of gun range of forts'. Nothing was fired at us, however. We could make out the entrance to the Dardanelles, but more by the number of our ships there than by the shape of the land. I found out from Major Clark's diary that the trip was arranged as a demonstration and lecture for officers on the defences of the Dardanelles.[2] Fancy putting the wind up the troops for that. In Lemnos again about 4.00pm.

Heard news on Sunday of our attempt to force the narrows and what it had cost us in ships and men. The *Ocean, Irresistible* and the French ship *Bouvet* had been sunk while nearly all the other ships that had taken part were more or less damaged. Scores of ships came in the next day and it gave us the impression that we had given up all idea of getting through the narrows.

Some of our sergeants rowed over to the *Queen Elizabeth* for a chat with some old shipmates and procured tobacco, books and papers, and glowing accounts of what the ship and her 15-inch guns had done to the Turks – smashed up all the forts and shelled the *Goeben* as she lay off Chanak. The *Lizzie* had been hit three times but none of the shells had done serious damage.

The 23rd saw more signs of moving and we left Lemnos at 4.30pm. Heard from some of the ship's crew that we were bound for Egypt. I hoped we had seen the last of Mudros. The place had got on my nerves. Had a lovely voyage and came in sight of the harbour works and lights of Alexandria about 5.00pm on the 25th.

Up early next morning, anxious to get a good view of the town. It looked a lovely place, some change from the dirty-looking places on Mudros. Lots of troopships there and not far away were eight German cargo boats. We were soon surrounded by native boats, most trying to sell us things but, as usual, we were not allowed to trade with them and, as usual, we had no money. Several well-off looking Arabs in flowing robes of brilliant colours tried hard to get on board. They pleaded urgent business with the captain or any old thing, but they couldn't bluff the quartermaster at the gangway. How they all scattered when the native police boat came on the scene. A few individuals were allowed on board just before lunch, amongst them a greasy-looking Arab lad selling Egyptian mails at 3d a time [1p]. Very few

---

2. Major Clark's diary stated that our trip to the entrance to the Dardanelles was in the nature of a lecture and demonstration on the defences of the place. Actually we were standing by to land and had the naval attack proved successful, we should have been rushed through and landed to take possession of the forts of Chanak, Kilid Bahr and Maidos etc.

of us were well enough off to sport 3d. Ready to sail again about 5.00pm. Just about then an American cruiser came into harbour; absolutely one of the latest, telescope masts and other fancy arrangements, but not half so business-like looking as our ships.

Said goodbye to Alex about 5.30pm and steamed due east, making for Port Said. Heaps of fishing boats were outside Alex and appeared to be having a pretty rough time with the weather. Arrived at Port Said at 7.30 next morning and had a very slow job getting berthed. The whole place was packed with shipping and most of our divisional ships came in about the same time as us. Some were already landing stores and troops and we were told to get everything ready for landing. Passed the day gazing at the drab and uninteresting surroundings. Arab kids came round us in boats, pestering us to throw pennies in the water. It was amusing at first to watch them diving for the money, bringing it up every time in their mouths, but it got tiring and we started slinging things at them. Granted shore leave from 5.00 to 8.00pm. Took advantage of it and had a walk round with two chums. Struck the native quarter first and what a smell. Worse even than Mudros. We were not allowed to enter the native quarter. Several soldiers had been killed there, so guards had been placed on the approaches. I hadn't the slightest desire for a closer inspection of the place.

Made our way to the English part of the town which was much better and cleaner, but which still had that horrible smell. Senior and I borrowed some money from Robinson and bought a few postcards and a bit of chocolate. Anything in the way of souvenirs was quite out of the question. There were plenty of good shops, cafes and hotels, all doing a roaring trade. Somebody must have had a payday. We got back to the ship alright, but some of the chaps had to be carried on board. Landed next day at 2.30pm and a proper good time we had. Although we had horses and mules on board we never used them but dragged everything ourselves. Limbers and GS[3] wagons full of stores tents, marquees, kitbags and ammunition had to be pulled from the ship to where we were to pitch our camp, half a mile from the ship with every inch over loose sand a foot deep. Several journeys like that, then to

---

3. General Service wagons.

pitch camp for our own company. It was done at last, but what a day's work. The hardest I ever remember. There was a small canal about 200 yards away and we had a bathe in it. What a relief!

All the naval division were encamped together and it made an enormous camp, thousands of tents pitched in order. We were put fourteen in a tent. It was hot but we all slept well, the first night on shore for a month. Had a change for breakfast – bacon, native cooked bread, jam and a drop of good tea. The lines of our camp didn't suit Colonel Luard and about 9.00am the whole battalion was at it stripping and re-pitching camp, all working to whistle signals. Micky Sanders was busy and dizzy as usual and Major Clark was like a mad bull. Leave in town again after tea but it was pretty miserable having no money. Parade next morning at 8.15am in full marching order for an inspection by General Trotman. Practised various stages of the attack after that, and in a sandstorm. We sank ankle deep in the sand every step we took and, with the wind getting up, clouds of sand buried us. We were full of sand and fed up to the teeth. Packed up at 12.30, had dinner, then a bathe in the canal. The water was dirty and the bottom slimy but it was lovely and cool inside. All the tired feeling disappeared and when we got to camp we were paid 10/- [50p] each, so were able to indulge a little after tea. Made ourselves ill eating Turkish delight and Jaffa oranges. Dirty-looking natives tried to take us down, wanting about 20 piastres for little trinkets worth about 2d [1p] and most probably made in Birmingham. There were heaps of lovely things in the shops, but the prices were too extortionate for a poor marine.

The next morning Micky Sanders picked on me to act as observer to Major Clark. Clever job. I had to stick to old Clark during the attack like a limpet and know exactly where everybody else was, read the thoughts and intentions of the colonel, and take note of all signals. It was a tricky little job, but far better than being a common ordinary soldier, having to make mad rushes at imaginary foes, flopping down in the sand and getting mouths, eyes and nose full of the stuff. I used to like the attack best when our company was on its own. We started off in artillery formation about 2,000 yards from the objective, deployed about 1,000 yards and then advanced by rushes, first by platoons, then sections, then a few men at a time. Everybody used to get dizzy and, as we came by each stage, dizzier still. About 100 yards from the objective, Major Clark and I would walk on and take up a position where we could see everything. He would then give the signal for the final stage of the attack. The lads would fix bayonets and, strange as it seems, would put lots of energy into that final charge, yelling like madmen the whole time. We had Divine Service on Good Friday in full marching order and after that carried on the attack, with the mercury in the glass at a hundred and something in the shade. We had night operations at 4 o'clock next morning, then at 9.00am fell in for an inspection by General Sir Ian Hamilton. About the hardest and most tiring time we've had for some time. Finished up with a march past, companies in line.

Granted leave from 2.00pm on Sunday, so had a good luck round. Went along the seafront and on one of the main breakwaters saw the statue to Ferdinand de Lesseps, the man who designed the Suez Canal. Went to a picture show after that, but it wasn't very interesting; all the titles were in French. Had tea at a French café and did ourselves well. Then back to camp early. Orders next day to stand by to embark at 2.00pm. Got all gear ready, gave in one blanket per man to go with kitbags to the base at Alex, and cleared up the lines. The order to move was cancelled, of course. Re-embarked at 10.00am on Wednesday 7 April, and found out we had mules and horses on board. The next day we took on board thousands of four-gallon tins of fresh water. The base party with Major Abrahall left us for Alex. We left Port Said at 9.30pm and anchored outside for the night. In the morning we took in tow a lighter full of the tins of water. We must be going somewhere hot and dry.

Set off at 10.00am on the 9th; the pace was just killing and at times we hardly appeared to be moving. We had to stop several times and some of the crew would have to chase after the lighter which kept breaking adrift. Sighted the Islands again on Sunday morning and shortly after received orders about submarine defence. We mounted machine guns round the ship and rigged telephones to them from the bridge but sighted nothing and came up to Mudros about 7.00pm on the Monday, too late to get into harbour as the boom closed at sunset.

Jack Senior and I made up our beds on the well deck as usual but had to turn in below as the weather was dirty. Awakened about 2.30am by the violent rocking of the ship and the noise of mess utensils as they flew from one side of the mess deck to the other. We could hear the water dashing over onto the decks and the crew dashing about. Then there were some frightful bumps and after that the noise and excitement died down and we dropped off to sleep again.

Heard in the morning that the ship had run her bows between two big rocks on the coast and the lighter kept bumping into the side, then she got in the way of the propellers which cut her in two. So ended the fresh water, and the only lighter out of dozens that actually reached Mudros. We were battened down below but the officers were all on deck with one of them on his knees, crying and praying. He oughtn't to have left his Mam. Got into harbour at 7.30 next morning and found it even more packed with shipping than before. Several more huge battleships were in, or so it appeared, but on close inspection we found them to be dummies, old tramps converted into modern first-class battleships and cruisers. General Trotman transferred to our ship from the *Braemar Castle* in the afternoon with all his staff. Our ship's company profited by that move. When we left the ship at Port Said a steward was supposed to come round to each mess table and take over all mess utensils, then make a list of any shortages. Some messes were complete and others were just short of a few oddments, perhaps a knife or spoon or a brush of some kind. What a surprise though when the bill was presented. It amounted to two or three shillings for each man. We kicked but only quietly and in consequence our officers took the matter through for us. Several of our senior officers had meetings with the ship's captain and purser and told them in the end that they must apply for the money through the Admiralty. It was settled at that until the general came on board and the question was then brought up again with the result that we had to pay. I think this ship carries about the rottenest lot of swindlers I've ever struck. They half starved us, then, at night, would sell us what was left over from the officers' dinner.

We were in the bay until Friday, during which time we got rid of our tins of water. A battleship took all ours. We left Mudros again at 7.30am on the Friday and, just outside, received a wireless message from the troopship *Minotaur* to the effect that she had been attacked. We put on steam and moved faster than we'd ever done before, steering a zigzag course to avoid being hit ourselves. Two companies were told off with their rifles, and machine guns posted round the ship again while everyone was told to keep a sharp lookout for periscopes. Sighted about half-a-dozen ships later on lying close together with the cruisers amongst them. Several ships' boats were passing from the ship we made out to be *Minotaur* to the *Royal George*. We could do nothing, and were told to clear off. We had no idea of what had happened but, while in Alex later, I had the story from a sergeant of the RFA in 29th Division who was on board at the time.

The *Minotaur* was on the way from Alex to Mudros with the 29th's field artillery. The guns were on deck but all ammunition was below and they had no means of defence. I expect they were like us and had forgotten all about the war. It was early in the morning when a torpedo boat came up alongside. Everyone thought it was British until she hoisted the Austrian flag and the captain spoke to the *Minotaur* and asked if she was carrying troops, but didn't wait for an answer: he just gave the order to fire. Three torpedoes were fired but, with the ships being so close together, they passed harmlessly under *Minotaur*. The Austrian boat then made off, making no attempt to shell the other. A panic started immediately on the *Minotaur* which the captain helped considerably by shouting 'Every man for himself'. There was a rush for the boats and two, lowered full of men, dropped in the water wrong side up. Between fifty and sixty soldiers were drowned as a result. That stopped the panic and no one else was eager to leave the ship. Our cruisers went in chase and eventually drove the Austrian onto a nearby island and shelled her into a complete wreck.

We carried on our way and presently came near to a large, rocky and mountainous island. The nearer we got to it, clearer and more blue the water appeared to get. It was a glorious day and a pleasure to be on the sea, and the knowledge that a little danger was near only added to our pleasure. We were all keeping a strict lookout for enemy craft and, as we approached the island, some of us got a shock. A boat of some kind left the coast and tore towards us at a terrific pace. I really thought we were in for it and, as it came nearer, could make out a gun in her bows. However, our hopes and fears were dashed as it turned out to be nothing more than a steam pinnace from HMS *Canopus* with a pilot on board to guide us into harbour. The island was Skyros, the most interesting and picturesque of the whole bunch that I had seen. It had a fine natural harbour, one side of the entrance being a steep cliff several hundred feet high and the other a great mountain rising steeply from the water's edge. All along the edge were huge rocks of pure marble. We anchored in umpteen fathoms of beautifully clear blue water and could follow the chain as it went down a long way. The old battleship *Canopus* was in, also a troopship. *Canopus* did look a pot mess; her crew were painting dazzle patterns on her. The light cruiser *Dartmouth* came in but didn't stay long and later we could see her patrolling the mouth of the harbour. Several more of our ships came in during the day, including the *Royal George*, which had brought in the dead from the *Minotaur*. A party went over to the *Franconia* next day and brought back our kitbags and the base party. The *Royal George* left during the morning with flag at half-mast but came back later with it flying full mast. The inference is obvious. We landed the next day but didn't stay long on shore. It was just to practise landing and then have a stand easy. The only signs of life ashore consisted of birds, lizards and snakes, with millions of insects of various kinds. Some of the lizards were lovely looking, one we saw being about twelve to fourteen inches long and a brilliant green. We chased several until they shed their tails through fright. Most of the vegetation consisted of herbs and the smell from them was lovely. What a contrast from Portiana and Port Said. Two French transports and a Red Cross ship came in. Things were looking more like business every day.

Several huge battleships and cruisers were patrolling about outside and one of them, according to some long-service men, had to be the *Princess Royal*, but as she was in the North Sea, this one must have been a dummy. So, I think, were the others. I wonder what the Turk thinks to all our ships? Landed again on the 19th in FMO[4] with cooking utensils and blankets. All officers' luggage was taken ashore too, and we expected to stay the night. Started off without anybody getting definite instructions about where to land.

All the boats formed a tow and we rowed about an hour and a half before we struck the proper place. Then we had to lump all our gear about 500 yards over rocks and rough ground to the place where we were to pitch our bivouacs. The first job was clearing the place of stones. There were millions of them. It must rain stones out here on the islands. Then we had a dizzy

---

4. Full marching order.

time putting the bivouacs up. They were our own blankets and we had spent hours on the ship making eyelets in them for this job. The officers had three bell tents between four. We had the bivouacs between six.

The usual stew for dinner. Always stew on land. We had a stand easy after that and could bathe and ramble about near the camp. I didn't fancy bathing, although the water was so cool and tempting. I saw two native fishermen in a boat and the fish they were catching were small octopus. Dozens of them they had stuck on long canes. The brigadier came along later on and inspected our camp and, shortly after tea, we received orders to pack up and get back to the ship.

Landed again next morning, every available man and full marching order. All the division were having a field day under the command of General Sir Archibald Paris. And what a field day. We were supposed to be making an attack on some objective six miles inland. Our battalion was supporting, and our route lay over a huge mountain, one huge mass of rocks and shifting stones.

The ships were supposed to bombard for half an hour, then we would advance half an hour and the ships would have another go, and so on. Our share apparently consisted of alternately crawling and stopping up this huge hill. It was a terribly hot day and, with about 80 or 90lb hanging onto us, we very soon got fed up and done up too.

Back again on the ship about 6.30pm. We had a severe thunderstorm at night but I slept through it, and on deck too. I found it much better on deck than down below in a hammock. All the ships were ready for sea on the 21st but nothing happened until Saturday the 24th. I could feel somehow that things were coming to a head, but wasn't it time they did? Six weeks on this rotten ship with a war on.

All the divisional ships left Skyros at 6.30pm with *Canopus*, *Doris*, *Dartmouth* and two destroyers as escort. Submarine and mine guards were mounted and everybody was worked up into a fever of excitement. Surely, something was going to happen now after all this time and preparation? We had lectures during the day on our conduct and general bearing towards the Turkish civilians during our victorious march to Constantinople, it being an assured fact that we should get there. We were to be sure to take off our boots before entering a mosque and on no account to lift a woman's yashmak. This and much more we were told.

Chapter Two

25 April 1915 – Action

Arrived somewhere off Gallipoli about 2.00am from our own calculations. We were about the NW part of the Gulf of Saros, lying somewhere off the Bulair Lines, the narrow neck of the peninsula, said to be heavily fortified.

About 5.00am *Canopus* and *Dartmouth* started a bombardment of the Turkish positions. This carried on for an hour, we being very interested spectators. This was the first touch of real warfare that most of us had experienced. We could see the bursts of most shells but, of course, not the effect. Nothing came at us in return and the two destroyers went close inshore and shelled the Turk. We got news about 3.00pm that 29th Division and our Plymouth Battalion had landed at Cape Helles, and the Australian Division at Gaba Tepe, and were getting on fine.

About 5.30pm we all moved about three miles nearer shore and some ships commenced lowering boats. We were only supposed to be making a landing here to keep so many thousand Turks from reinforcing their other positions. Heard that one officer, Captain Freyberg,[1] had volunteered to swim ashore after dusk, tow a small raft with him and then let off so many lights that were on the raft. He did it, though we didn't see the result as we received orders to steam south and stand by to land. As far as I could make out only the three marine battalions moved; the others carried on with the dummy landings,

I was fast asleep below when we stopped at Gaba Tepe and never heard the bombardment. Some chaps heard it, and the rattle of rifle and machine-gun fire too, so we must have been fairly close inshore. We were on the move again when I got on deck and I noticed that nearly all our boats had gone from the davits. They had been lent to help get the wounded off, and to

---

1. Later General Sir Bernard Freyberg VC.

land troops, as most of the other boats had been sunk when the Australians landed.

We were steaming very slowly and by noon came up to the armada lying off Cape Helles. There were about sixty more transports and scores of warships, both French and British, and every available gun on them was blazing away for all they were worth; from the 4-inch guns of the destroyers to the great 15-inch guns of the *Queen Elizabeth*. She was simply overwhelming in action and when she fired four of her 15-inch guns and then a broadside of 6-inch the concussion was terrific. We kept drifting about all that day and the next, sometimes finding ourselves close alongside a cruiser or a battleship just as she was firing, sometimes drifting close enough inshore to see the efforts of the landing parties, struggling to get guns and stores on shore, all the time under heavy shrapnel fire from the Turkish batteries.

We could see bunches of sixes and eights bursting every few seconds. It must be terrible there for our chaps, but what about poor Johnny Turk, with all our ships pumping HE[2] into them?

At times we should receive curt orders to clear out of it, but we kept drifting back every time. We could see the castle of Sedd-el-Bahr in a battered condition and behind it the village of the same name, almost flattened to the ground. Visible about twelve miles north-west was the big hill at Gaba Tepe, where the Australians were fighting. Towards dusk it presented a terrible appearance, the whole place one mass of flames, smoke and bursting shells. We had nothing to do but stand on deck and watch. I wondered what the people at home would think to it all, and how much some people with heaps of money would pay to see it all, with the same safety and comparative comfort with which we saw it? And if we had heaps of money, how much would we give to get out of it? Our turn ashore was sure to come, so it was no use kicking and, really, I think there were very few aboard the ship who were not anxious to have a turn. I slept on deck and slept sound. Up again on the 28th with the first streaks of dawn and found things just as busy. Both sides were blazing away and some of our ships appeared to be getting it hot. Great spurts of water kept shooting up into the air around them. They were the misses. We couldn't see the hits.

---

2. High Explosive.

We steamed up to Gaba Tepe at noon and watched the fun there, a repetition of Cape Helles. Were we only spectators in this game, or were we to take an active part in it? We were! Two destroyers came up alongside about 3.00pm and we received orders to get things ready for leaving. We had a jolly good meal about 4.30, the best we had had on the *Gloucester Castle* and then bade the ship's company a 'soldier's farewell'.

B and D Companies were taken off on the *Harpy*, A and C on the other destroyer. We heard lots of news from the sailors about the landings. The 29th Division was going strong and about five miles inland now. Our Plymouth Battalion had landed at Y beach with the KOSB[3] and had had no casualties. Their advanced guards had entered Krithia, but had not met with serious opposition; the whole lot were then rushed right off the peninsula again.

The Australians had lost heavily and were still losing heavily which, of course, was awfully bucking to us, as we were to join them. I had no forebodings, however, and felt nothing but a mild excitement and satisfaction at having something definite to do. I noticed that old Tom Watts, our company quartermaster sergeant major, and Joe Broster, our sergeant major, looked worried and anxious. They had seen service in China, South Africa and, recently, at Antwerp, and evidently expected something more than fun and a novel experience. I was still holding the position as observer to Major Clark, so had to stick to him and carry his periscope. The destroyers took us as far inshore as they dared, then we were transferred to tows (strings of boats towed by a steam pinnace) which took us to the beach. We had a quiet landing, not a shell being fired at us. The reason for that was obvious: every available ship was blazing away like mad, to keep down the fire of the Turkish batteries. Luckily for us they achieved their object. We got ashore but what a state of absolute chaos everything was in – stores, ammunition, guns and discarded equipment all mixed up together. Naval officers, from admirals downwards to stokers who had volunteered for work on the beach, mixed up with the Australian generals and staff officers. There was a dressing station just under the cliffs and the tarpaulin shelter was ripped in scores of places by shrapnel. There were strings of Australians and sailors who had been wounded waiting to be dressed, while just a few yards away under the shelter of the cliff were

---

3. King's Own Scottish Borderers.

scores of poor chaps who had passed beyond dressing. I seemed to realise then that it wasn't going to be all fun. I think I can rightly claim to have been the first one ashore out of our battalion, that is in the rank and file. I followed Major Clark onshore and had heaps of running about to do.

Old Clark immediately got dizzy and had me flying around in all directions. First to platoon commanders – 'Have your platoon got on shore yet and if not, why not?' – then to find the colonel, who was about half a mile away talking to General Birdwood of the Australians, and report D Company ashore. Then I had to chase after the company which had done a move and was about a mile along the beach. The Australians were jolly glad to see us and some told us what an awful time they had had, and were still having. The number of killed and wounded was awful and, as we moved along, fresh wounded were being carried down to the dressing station. Others were walking and all of them, if they were at all conscious, were swearing horribly and cursing the Turks.

We rested in a small open space by the sea until it was dark and were then guided by Australians up a deep gully for about half a mile. It was pouring with rain but we hardly noticed it, our minds being too much occupied with other things. First of all were the wounded, who were being carried past us faster than ever now that it was dark; then there was an incessant clatter of rifle and machine-gun fire from practically all round us, and it sounded jolly near too. We rested for about half an hour in the gully and while seated with Major Clark a runner came up to us. He was an Australian, caked with mud and almost speechless through running. He was gasping out for the officer commanding Portsmouth Marines, so I switched him on to Major Clark and he gave him this message: 'From Colonel Monash[4] of the Twelfth Australians, would Portsmouth Battalion follow the runner, as his troops were being heavily attacked by the Turks and can't hold them back much longer.' Of course, Major Clark couldn't do anything, but told the chap to wait until Colonel Luard came back. No one saw the runner after that; he just faded away into the night. One guide suggested that he was very likely a German who, had we followed him, would have led us into the Turkish lines.

---

4. Later General Sir John Monash, who commanded Australian forces on the Western Front.

We picked up two more guides after that and commenced a climb up the steep slope of the gully. The earth was slippery with the rain and it was a case of going up two and coming back one. I had the job of hauling up old Clark, then that fool Domville with his huge Barr and Stroud range-finder. Several times I felt like kicking him and his B & S to the bottom again. All around us lay signs of the fight, broken rifles, equipment and caps. We had on those great sun helmets and I took a sudden dislike to mine, so slung it away and picked up a cap, apparently lying on the ground, but when I came to touch it I found a head inside it belonging to a dead Australian. He had been shot through the head and there were the two holes in the cap where the bullet had passed through.

Our guides disappeared after a short time and we were left to wander about on our own. We had no idea where we were, or where we had to go, until somebody challenged us. It was an Australian officer who had just been attending to several wounded men who lay groaning in a hole nearby. This chap said he had been waiting for a relief for what had been his company, so he took us on. Just above us was a shallow communication trench and we passed up this for about fifty yards, then came to the firing line which was full of Australians. To avoid a crush we walked along the top and the other fellows began to file out. They had ceased fire as we came up, but not so the Turk. The sound of firing that we heard with comparative safety an hour ago was unpleasantly close now, and bullets were whizzing by us. I was walking ahead with Major Clark and the Aussie officer and when we came to the left of our company sector old Clark told me to get in. I was pleased to do so. I don't know if those Turkish bullets were close but they sounded so. The Australian I dropped in by told me to dig and keep on digging; said it was hell down there 'and don't be afraid of that chap in front of the parapet. He's dead and we've just thrown him out'. Then he went down the trench. I could see more than one dead one as I looked over the top. As they had got killed their chums had just rolled them over the top, firstly to form a parapet for cover and, secondly, to get them out of the way. One could hardly call this a trench; it was more like a series of holes, none more than three feet deep and with connections between them about a foot deep. On my left was a dead end but about six feet beyond I could see where the trench began again, but no signs of anyone in it. Found out that instead of being with my own platoon,

No. 15, I was with No. 13, Dornville's platoon. I had no idea who was on my left. I had only my entrenching tool to dig with but managed to get down a bit. The fellow next to me would insist on throwing most of his dirt down my neck. It was all chalky stuff and terrible to dig. What a night! Quietness on our part, then, after a time, quietness on Johnnie's part, a suspicious quietness, and the rain came pouring down. I was looking out whilst resting from digging and after a time felt certain that I could see someone moving out in front, so I did the expected – fired a round. Word flew up the line at once, from Domville I suppose: 'Who the devil fired that shot and why?' I sent word back, 'Private Askin fired', and 'what are we here for.' I thought our war had started. I claim that to be the first shot fired in our battalion. The excitement died down a little and I carried on digging again, but it was both back-aching and heartbreaking work. My hands were soon blistered and I was just about ready to throw the dammed tool over the top when an order came up the line 'Turks advancing, rapid fire', and we 'rapid fired' and blazed off enough ammunition on that occasion to blow all the Turks out of Europe. Then another order 'Turks retiring, cease fire.' Several times up to dawn we got those orders repeated and it was a continual change between digging and rapid fire.

It's a wonder we were able to fire at all, what with the muddy state of the ammunition and the red-hot rifles. Blaze away we did though, aim or no aim, Turks or no Turks. Sometimes we could see black masses moving towards us and could hear the yells of the Turks; other times we could see nothing but the black night.

With the first streaks of dawn came our first experience of being shelled. They started slinging shrapnel shells just over our lines, bursting nicely for them but awfully terrifying for us. Everybody had the wind up. I found the benefit of my digging then. I had dug low under the dead and had undercut it, so when I crouched low down in that, felt fairly safe.

The smell from the explosive was horrid and nearly choked us. We took it in turns to keep watch while the shelling was on, about one man in every six being up. As the first spasm of shelling died down we observed some men digging away to our right front, so sent word down to Major Clark to see if we could fire at them. He sent word back that they were our own men. I had my doubts. The sergeant in charge of No. 4 Platoon A Company had a good look at them through his glasses and said he thought they were Turks digging a machine-gun pit. We left them alone but had plenty of sport across to our front. The Turk had adorned his trench with green branches and small bushes but we spotted a few heads moving occasionally and tried hard to hit them. He could see ours too, I should imagine. We must have looked like a lot of Aunt Sallies sticking over the top of the trench. Every now and again a bullet would whizz just above our heads, then one would plonk into the parapet, knocking a shovel of earth over us. It was only the shells that made us take cover though, and as soon as we heard one coming down we got. About 7.00am I was feeling awfully dirty, and as my water bottle was full felt justified in using a little for a shave. Just as I started with the razor, the Turk started with his infernal shrapnel, but after the first violent duck I was able to carry on. Felt heaps better after a wash round with the brush and more like a feed than I had done before, so shared a tin of bully beef and jam with Smith, the chap next to me. A few hard biscuits and a drink of water furnished the repast. It wasn't very elaborate, but I felt like a new man after it and ready for anything. Got word up shortly afterwards that young Willoughby had been killed, sniped through the head while trying to get a Turk. Soon after we heard that Corporal Matthews had managed the same thing. Had several casualties a bit later with shrapnel. I didn't like those shells a little bit, although the first terrifying effect had gone off. The nose caps were the worst to me. They seemed to come whizzing down on their own long after the shell burst.

Our ships opened up about 10.00am and quietened the Turkish batteries a bit. I could see our huge shells bursting right up this great mountain and it made me think how little right we had to grumble. We are only getting about 12- or 16-pounders while they are getting anything up to 12-inch shells weighing about 240lb or more, lots of them filled with Lyddite; those shook us up considerably. Smith got up to have a shot. He spotted something, took a very careful aim and was just going to loose off, when something hit his rifle, smashing it in two and a splinter of the wood went into his arm. He thought he was hit and so did we. We got the splinter out and he carried on with an Aussie rifle; there were plenty knocking about. Dead Australians, and Turks too, were lying about in profusion and we could smell them when the sun got up. It got scorching hot towards midday and our water got low.

Major Clark sent word up for me to take his periscope down to him, but I didn't intend leaving my cosy spot, so sent him his silly old thing. I had found no use for it and could see heaps more by putting my head over the top.

I got in some decent sniping, with what result I wouldn't swear, but I'm not a bad shot and the targets at times were very fair and the range no more than 200 yards. Johnny got in some good sniping too. He made me duck a few times and filled my eyes and ears with dirt. We kept getting word up the line about different chaps getting killed and wounded. Colour Sergeant Blanchard of A Company, a Bisley man and one of the best shots in the marines, got sniped through the head; it would appear that the Turk had some fair shots too. Another rotten doing with shrapnel after dinner; more bully, jam and biscuits, not water. One fellow offered to take about ten bottles to the bottom of the gully and get them filled. He came back after about two hours and said he'd had to dig a hole and wait for the water to ooze in. It was more mud than water but it tasted good to us. I wonder where those thousands of tins of water were that we brought from Port Said? I hadn't seen one yet since landing. Some of our fellows had a scrounge round at the back of the trench and searched some dead Australians and Turks. They got plenty of souvenirs and luxuries in the way of food from the Aussies, but nothing from the Turks and the water in their bottles was warm and stale. Carried on improving my trench but I found that if I dug much more I should not be able to see or fire over the top.

Night came on again, cold and with a heavy dew that soaked through and through me but, thank heaven, no shelling. The Turks must have been afraid of hitting their own trenches. We could see a huge red glow in the sky all night and word was passed up that our ships had fired the fort and town of Great Maidos. We had a repetition of the previous night, attacks real and imaginary by the Turks, with wild bursts of firing by us. When the Turks came they came in thousands and we must have hit some, otherwise they would have reached us. I managed about an hour's sleep, the first since landing. I was awakened out of it by someone falling on to me. It turned out to be our doctor going along the trenches to attend to any wounded who couldn't be moved. He asked if we were alright and passed on his way. With the dawn came the shrapnel and more casualties. We had none. It must have been a lucky corner because we got plenty of shells. Threw my equipment on the back of the trench while I did a bit of digging and when I came to put it on again found that half my pouches had been blown away and most of my ammunition exploded. Something heavy must have hit them and it was a good job I hadn't them on at the time. Some big shells went over about noon and we could see them drop in the sea near one of our battleships. We surmised that they were 11-inch shells from the *Goeben*. What a terrible rushing sound they made as they went through the air.

Passed the day again sniping and digging. I cleaned my rifle a bit, oiled it and pulled it through. I was sick of digging; my hands were raw and my back nearly breaking. It was terribly hot all day with not a bit of cover from the sun and not a drop of water to drink. It was impossible to eat bully; it was just like salt. The smell from the dead bodies got sickening as the sun got stronger and when one of them got hit again by a shell or bullet the smell got worse. We got one or two guns into position during the day but as soon as they opened up the Turk replied and put them out of action.

We were relieved about 5.30pm by B Company, but only went back about a hundred yards to the top of the gully. There we had to start digging holes to sleep in, all loose and sandy earth, and as soon as one got a nice hole someone else would walk by and fill it in. I went to the bottom for some water but it was a long job, first digging down about two feet and then waiting for the water to come.

Turned in and had a sleep but was rudely awakened at 4.00am by shrapnel. Shells were bursting four at a time and, very often, right amongst us. Everybody dashed for cover, but there wasn't any. Fellows were dropping all around and others getting hit as they crouched down in their holes. Corporal Street got killed outright. Half a shell case hit him in the ribs, a nasty sight. An order was shouted out during the shelling 'Reinforce B Company in the line'. I made a dash with Sergeant Bob Chadwick to the little communication trench leading to the front line. My rifle and equipment were still in the hole, but I picked up another set and carried it so far then dropped it. The communication trench was full of our men taking cover from the shells. They had passed the order for reinforcements down the trench but were making no signs of moving. Bob Chadwick shouted to us to walk over the b******s. We did and what with the shells and curses the air was fairly blue. What a state the line was in when we reached it! The trench battered level in places, the dead and wounded lying two and three deep. Blood was all over and as we passed along to the right we had to crawl over these poor devils who had got hit and others were getting hit even as we passed. Some were groaning and crying, others were silent in their pain. One poor chap got hit just as I reached him; he never spoke when I asked him where he was hit, just pointed to the bottom of his back. I could tell by the colour of his face and his expression that he was dying fast. I was covered with blood and the taste of it was in my mouth. The smell of burning explosives and the smell and taste of blood was horrid. I picked a pair of field-glasses as I thought they might come in useful, but the chap they belonged to spotted me and told me to drop them. He was a colour sergeant, and, poor chap, he might have let me keep them; before I had gone two more yards he was killed outright. We ought never to have reinforced the line. It was too full already, with no cover for the men who were already in it. I finished up with Bob Chadwick and a few more men on the extreme right of our battalion sector with Deal Battalion on our right. It was a bit quieter there, with the trench in a better state. We had Lieutenant Erskine with us, one of our company officers and a real decent chap. He's the only officer I'd seen with the exception of the doctor since leaving old Clark.

I went shares with a rifle until the owner got sniped while using it, then I claimed it. He got shot through the head, just a tiny blue hole where the bullet entered but all the back of his head was blown away. His chum who was next to him went clean daft as soon as it happened and started dashing up and down the trench screaming. We had to sit on him till he had quietened down a bit. We threw a waterproof sheet on the dead fellow. I carried on sniping after that and spotted the Turk who I reckoned had caused the mischief and who kept throwing up showers of earth from our parapet. He was lying flat behind a bush and, as I watched, I saw the flash of his rifle and instantly a shower of dirt came into my face. Of course I ducked but got a good aim on the bush and fired. Another shower of earth and I fired again. This time the return bullet zipped wickedly by my ear, but I was on aim and pressed the trigger straight off. I saw a movement in the bush and had no reply, so concluded that I'd won.

Bob Chadwick was our next casualty. He came down to me and asked me to put a bandage on him. A shrapnel ball had gone through his left shoulder and I could see the thing halfway down his back under the skin. I wrapped him up as well as I could and he went down towards the CT [communication trench]. About 3.00pm we got the following message: 'From Colonel Luard, cease fire; Portsmouth Battalion will charge at 5 o'clock.' Five minutes later another order: 'Rapid fire; stand by to charge.' Lieutenant Erskine told us to blaze away and changed tunics with the daft chap, took his rifle and bayonet and told him that if he didn't come back he could have the few pounds in the pocket,

When the next order came 'From Colonel Luard, Charge', Erskine was over the top like a flash and so was Company Sergeant Major Joe Broster. There they stood on top yelling to everybody to get out and charge. I managed to get out, although it was a steep bit of trench and I wasn't very big. As far as I could see, instead of Portsmouth Battalion getting out to charge, there were about twenty of us, certainly no more. But we didn't wait, just chased off in the approved manner, yelling and cursing our breath away, so by the time we had gone fifty yards we were all exhausted and dropped down in a rough line. I dropped next to Erskine and we had a look round. There were no more than twenty of us and the rest of the battalion was in the trench behind, firing like mad and the Turk was in front blazing away like mad. Erskine observed, 'That must have been a fake message, nobody seems to be coming.' Then he yelled 'Get back to the trench lads', and we got back and even quicker than we came out. I jumped in at exactly the same spot that I'd got out and dropped with both feet on the dead fellow. Just as we reached the trench the Turk opened up with a machine gun and poor old Broster and another chap got killed. Broster was shot through the head and chest and died almost immediately. They were the only two that that mad dash cost us. We made enquiries down the trench as to who sent the message to charge but no one knew. We could only trace it about twenty or thirty yards down the trench; there, the only message they had had was 'From Colonel Luard, Portsmouth Battalion will be relieved at 5.00pm.' Either a Turk or a German had got in the trench or else one of our chaps had hashed the message up. We'd been back about twenty minutes when Lance Corporal Robinson struggled along the trench with what had been one of those big cans of water. He'd had about three bullets through it. We just managed a taste and no more, and we could all have drunk quarts.

We took things easy after that, letting one man look out for about every twenty yards. I was sitting down on the trench bottom having a nap when I was awakened by several of our chaps yelling and dashing past me. There were cries of 'They're here' and I saw a Turk jump into our trench about ten yards away from me. He made a jab at one man with his bayonet, but missed, then fired at another and nearly shot half his face off. A lance corporal of A [Company] then came up behind the Turk and shot him from about six yards, then rushed him with his bayonet as he was dropping. I was just an onlooker at the scene. I had only managed to scramble to my feet when the whole thing was over. I couldn't find a rifle anywhere. Someone had taken mine in the rush. The Turk was dead alright. He was only young, but tall and well-built, and his cap and clothing were adorned with grass and small branches of trees, no doubt a sniper who had been lying out in front of our trench and had lost his way. He was unlucky in his choice of direction, although he caused a panic. I heard after that the first one to bolt was Dolly Gray, the old soldier who used to give us such glowing accounts of his deeds at Antwerp. Heard that Captain Teague of A Company had been killed. I never used to think much of him during the time he had our company at Fareham but it seems he turned out trumps. He was walking along the top of the trench cheering his men when we got sniped. Lieutenant Erpson and heaps more got killed too. Mr Compton Dunville couldn't be found anywhere; I guess he's down at the beach or in some deep hole that someone else has dug. Had a walk to the extreme right again and found an officer of ours in a hole under the trench. The chaps said he'd been there since Thursday morning and wouldn't come out. It was the same officer who burst into tears and said his prayers when the old *Gloucester Castle* went ashore outside Mudros. Mr Erskine was away during the incident of the Turk. Major Clark sent for him to report on what had happened at our end and why we had charged.

Shrapnel and still more shrapnel. That big chap Smith got hit in the mouth with a nose cap. He always had his mouth wide open. Poor chap! It knocked his head right off. He was only a few yards from me when it happened.

Relieved at dusk by the Australians. As I came to the bottom of the CT there was a hold up. We couldn't move down and the Aussies couldn't get on. Everybody was talking to one another and I heard one Australian officer giving his men some final orders; 'Dig like hell,' he said, 'and not a shot to be fired until the Turks are twenty yards away, then let them have it hot.' If they dug much more they'd soon be back in Australia. All at once everybody went silent; somebody was creeping about in the bushes just on our right. Who was it and who would get the bullet if it was a Turk? No one moved except two Australians who were nearest the noise. They slipped their safety catches forward. Then someone stumbled out of the bushes and a sorrier-looking spectacle of a man I never saw. He was dressed in Australian clothes, torn and covered with mud and with a week's growth of beard. 'Shall I shoot him?' one of the Aussies asked. 'No, ask him some questions,' one of their officers said. Poor devil, he could hardly answer; he was speechless through fright and exhaustion. He just managed to mumble a name and the number of his battalion, so somebody took him down the gully to his battalion. We moved down to the bottom of the gully where I joined up with my own platoon, the first time since leaving the ship. What an age it seemed. We had a roll call as well as we could: Willoughby and Beechey dead, Senior, George, Robinson, Evans and Cooke wounded; Bob Hestor, old Seymour and myself alone left out of our section. The platoon was down to twelve instead of forty. Mr Dougherty was alright. More of the company officers were missing except Domville.

Our first issue of rum came along. What a Godsend! I don't think anybody refused it. I faded away a little later under a shallow bank with Bob Hestor for a bedmate and the song of a nightingale for a lullaby.

Breakfast at six on Sunday morning on Maconachie's and bully. Just got some water boiling for a drink of tea when a shrapnel burst plugged the tin. We had breakfast dry. The battalion moved nearer the beach about 10.00am to the sheltered side of a hill where we once more dug in. According to Major Clark the battalion had lost close on 500 men since landing. I shaved again, then had a wash in a pool of water, mud and dead men. Felt heaps better after it and had a walk to the beach to fill my bottle and, while at the pumping station, nearly got pipped with shrapnel. One chap got hit and another fell in the water through fright. Had to dash for cover several times on the way back. Found everybody dizzy when I got back to the battalion, standing to, ready to move. The Turk was making a big attack and already some Australian machine gunners were taking up fresh positions just on our left. It looked as though we were going to get chased off. B Company under Major Armstrong was told off to reinforce a weak part of the line, but came back after about two hours. They had not been wanted and the attack had fizzled out. It had been a near thing though. Went scrounging and fitted myself out with another set of equipment, rifle and shaving gear.

Volunteers were asked for at dusk to bury some dead and double tots of rum were offered as an inducement. A gallon wouldn't have tempted me. Some of the chaps said when they got back that very little burying had been possible. The smell was too awful for anything and some bodies fell to pieces when they tried to lift them.

Turned in and tried to sleep but it was too cold and I'd neither greatcoat nor waterproof sheet. We weren't given much opportunity for sleep though. Roused out by an order about 2.00am: 'Turn out, get rigged everybody.' We forgot everything we'd been taught about night operations and the first essential, quietness. What a din! Everybody cursing and picking up gear belonging to someone else. We got sorted out at the finish and filed down towards the beach, then made a turn to the right up another gully. What a tramp! Pace about half a mile an hour. Tripping over ground telephone wires, getting our rifles entangled in overhead wires and trees. We soon came upon signs of a stiff fight going on up the gully. Scores of wounded passed us going down to the beach. We appeared to be marching for miles, but it was the pace and the climb more than the distance. We heard we had to reinforce the Aussies and our Nelson Battalion, who had suffered heavily on the extreme left of the line. They had made an attack during the night but were hard pressed and found it difficult to hang on.

It seemed one continual climb from the beach and the farther we went the steeper it got until in places it resembled mountaineering and we had to help one another over the hard places. I found myself in front of the company again with old Clark. He did look a cut with a raincoat, Australian slouch hat and walking stick. (I heard after that while he was walking about in that attire the day following our attack, he was collared by some Australians who took him down to the beach and were going to shoot him straightaway but he prevailed on them to fetch somebody from the battalion to recognise him.) We came up with a part company of great massive Australians whose few remaining officers were vainly trying to urge them to reinforce the line in front. They wouldn't budge. 'Had enough of the blurry fighting,' they said, 'Let someone else have a go', meaning us of course. They thought we were straight off a big ship. There's a lot of truth in the remark that one of our chaps made, 'There's many a big potato rotten'. We passed them by and climbed, still some more. The noise from the front was getting deafening and the wounded more numerous; dawn had come and with it the shrapnel.

Evidence of the last night's advance was plain too. We passed partly-dug trenches, with lots of dead in them, then Turk trenches with even more dead. Rifles and equipment were littered all over the place. It was getting hot for us too. Shrapnel was getting unpleasantly close and bullets were whizzing just overhead. We came up to a trench full of Australians about thirty to forty yards from the top of the gully which spread out in the shape of a wide V. It was hot there. Major Clark shoved me into a hole and got in himself. 'It's pretty hot,' he said, 'We'd better wait here and see what's going to happen.' Things soon happened. Several Aussies left the trench and started going back down the hill. They'd had enough too, they said. Colonel Luard and their own colonel, a chap called Pope, tried to persuade them to go back to the trench but they wouldn't. They were the same sort of chaps we had passed below. Colonel Pope was a queer looking little chap, and had neither hat, equipment nor revolver, just a stick, and was walking about as though he didn't care what happened. He was certainly made of better stuff than his men. When our chaps saw these Aussies running back, they got the wind up and there was a general backward movement down the gully. It was easier I suppose than going up. Colonel Luard soon put a stop to that, though. He yelled out in his best parade voice (and he had a voice) 'Royal Marines, fix bayonets and charge'. And we charged. A Company under Captain Stockley was on our left, all bunched up anyhow, and the other two companies in rear. I dashed out of the hole with old Clark, yelling like mad. I got up to a smashed machine gun with its crew of Australians lying dead round it, and had a look round. I'd no idea where to charge to and I was pretty well in front. I could see our chaps dropping down all over the place and observed the expressions of pain and surprise on some as they got hit. Our battalion sergeant major got hit and rolled past me down the hill, then an officer who looked like Micky Sanders did the same thing, and they both went down as though they had been shot from a gun. Mr Erskine dashed past me to the front. I was just trying to decide where to go, when something hit me in the stomach.

Chapter Three

3 May – Out Of Action

Something hit me jolly hard too, right in the pit of the stomach, and I went down and gave myself up for dead. I daren't look at the place for a time as I was quite sure my bowels were scattered all over the machine gun. It wasn't as bad though; a bullet must have glanced off somewhere and hit me. There was a huge black lump and a nasty graze but I felt sure that nothing had gone in. I got up and staggered on a few more yards. All desire to get anywhere in particular had left me and I staggered on half dazed. Zonk! I received something else and down I went again.

I thought my left shoulder had been blown away and I also thought that two hits in one day was quite enough for anybody, so turned about and shuffled back down the hill. I don't know how I managed to get down. It was just hell there. The Turk was pitching shrapnel and bombs over the head of the gully and blazing away at us point-blank with his rifles and MGs. To help matters a bit, our ships were sending shrapnel and bursting it short, so it's really a wonder anybody came out alive at all. The place was just like a shambles, dead and dying all over. And chaps like me getting out of it as fast as ever they could. I scrambled down a bit to where it wasn't quite so bloody and came across Daisy Bell, one of our company stretcher-bearers. He asked me where I was hit and if I intended taking my equipment home as a souvenir, so I chucked it off and let him bandage me up. He cut the sleeve out of my tunic to begin with. A bullet had gone in at the front but had hardly managed to get right through. He could see it sticking up under the skin at the other side of my shoulder. Bell told me to get down to the beach dressing station, so I set off, and straightaway took the wrong way. I got into a riverbed or a pool with the water gone, but with about two feet of thick mud.

I got out of that and a bit farther down came across a big Australian with a water bottle full of rum. He gave me a good drink and I felt heaps better after and thought for a time that a wound or two was nothing. I felt no desire to turn back for another go, however. Another Aussie called me into a funk hole a bit later on and told me to rest a bit. There was another in the hole and I asked the first chap if he was asleep. 'No,' he said, 'he's dead.' I didn't stop there long.

I was followed all the way down the gully by shrapnel. The Turks were searching the whole place and, while dodging one shell, I tripped over a ground wire and fell onto my left shoulder. Farther down, while running from another, I ran my wound straight on to the branch of a tree. Swear? Never so much in my life. I never thought I should reach that dressing station alive. Just before I reached the bottom of the gully I saw an Indian leading two pack mules up the gully. He got about twenty yards from me when a shell burst and killed all three. I reached the dressing station at last but what a state it was in. The wounded were waiting in queues to be dressed and the station itself was full of wounded and dying men, most laid out on stretchers, all who could groaning out curses on the Turks. There were several doctors, naval and Australian, all of them performing their duties in a dazed manner. I don't think they had slept since landing. I looked round amongst the wounded and saw several of our chaps that I knew: Captain Stockley of A Company with one leg shattered; Sergeant Major Wingfield terribly mauled about and several others. One chap was brought in and as soon as the doctor looked at him he told them to take him outside and put him under the cliff with the others. The others were dead. Scores of them. My turn for dressing came and the doctor started probing and poking. I don't think he knew what he was doing. In the end he said he wouldn't bother taking the bullet out there, perhaps they'd take it out on the ship. Thank the Lord for that! I was eager to get away from that accursed place. I was sick of seeing dead and dying men, tired of hearing moans and cries, and sick with the smell of blood. I was covered with it and everything was covered with it in that dressing station at Gaba Tepe. Stretchers and men soaked with it and even the sand was red with blood.

I got in a boat at last with a crowd of others, not too badly wounded, but all utterly fed up and exhausted; not a smile in the whole boat. We were waiting for a picket boat to take us in tow but just before it arrived the Turk started shelling the beach and we got the contents of another shrapnel round in our boat. An Aussie sitting next to me was wounded again in the back.

'God!' some of us exclaimed, 'Aren't we to get away now?' We were towed away though, and the midshipman in charge of the tow didn't look more than sixteen years of age. Quite a boy, but I bet he and his mates had had a tottering time round the beach for a few days. They hadn't even the chance of hitting back. We reached the hospital ship *Gascon* and went on board. Sorted out at the top of the gangway according to the severity or otherwise of our wounds, we were told off to different wards.

I had my wound properly dressed and cleaned and then passed out. I hadn't even time to realise that I was on a soft clean spring bed and that a real Englishwoman, young and nice, had dressed my wound. I went right away and must have slept at least twenty hours. Woke up about noon on the 4th but felt far from well. We were still lying off Gallipoli and taking on stretcher cases. Had a stroll round the ship and found it full with lots of our chaps on board. Poor old Wingfield was there in the same ward. I had a talk to him and told him that I'd seen him roll past me down the side of the gully. He said a lump of case shelling had hit him in the ribs, smashing about four or five, and he had a few more wounds besides. It was difficult to see anything but bandage. He told me that it must have been Lieutenant Sanders who followed him, as he had been with him.

Heard that the colonel was wounded and on board the *Gloucester Castle*, Major Hoskyns Abrahall killed, Mr Erskine killed, Dougherty wounded, and several others killed and wounded. Majors Armstrong and Clark, and about three other officers, were left with about 150 men.

We had on board English nurses, doctors and Hindu attendants. We dropped about eight dead over the stern about 6.00pm. The *Gascon* sailed about 9.00am on the 5th. I felt much better and spent most of the day on deck reading. We had a lovely voyage to Alexandria and arrived on the Friday morning. Every evening about six the ship was stopped and several dead men were dropped into the sea. We buried forty-one men altogether on the voyage. Disembarked and entrained on a hospital train and had a steady run to Tanta, about halfway between Alex and Cairo. Batches of men were taken off at various towns down the line, according to the accommodation of the hospitals. About fifty of us were taken off at Tanta. We were taken in open carriages to the hospital and it looked as though the whole town had turned out to greet us. The streets we drove through were lined with natives and native soldiers were having a rough job keeping them back in places. Some people had a queer way of showing their feelings. As we passed up one narrow street we were pelted with stones.

Got to hospital about 7.15pm and gave our particulars for about the twentieth time since being hit. Seized immediately by two greasy-looking Arabs who fairly ripped the clothes off me, I was shoved under a hot shower and scrubbed with more energy than feeling. Wounds were treated as sound flesh and how the devils delighted in it. I felt an immediate and violent hatred for Egyptians from that time. Dressed in native clothes after the bath and waited my turn for the doctor, an Egyptian, fat and jovial, who had practised in Paris and London and spoke English fairly well. He had a look at the wound, then said 'Sit in that chair', so I sat in it. He got a knife and slashed me about an inch where the bullet was, then got a pair of forceps, gave a pull and the bullet was out. He informed me that it hadn't hurt. I can't say that it had hurt much, very much like having a tooth out. I wanted the bullet, which was a shrapnel ball, but the doctor wanted it too. He said it was the first he had taken out of an English soldier and he wanted it for a souvenir. 'We both have souvenirs,' he said, 'you have the wound, I have the bullet.'

Got to bed after a supper of goat meat and macaroni, served up by a French Sister of Mercy. The sisters were quite ancient and couldn't speak a word of English, but were very nice. A batch of French soldiers was already there; they had been wounded in the landing at Kum Kale on the Asiatic coast. There were two old marines and seven Australians in my ward, none seriously wounded.

We had lots of distinguished visitors to see us, including the Countess of Caernarvon, General Maxwell and Prince Alexander of Battenberg who was kind enough to say he hoped we should soon be back to help the others. I wondered if he'd any idea what sort of hell it was and if he'd like more than one dose.

I had a tottering time with the mosquitoes. They bit me in every possible place and my face was a mess. I was unable to shave for over a week and all that time I was anxious to try a new razor that a charming young lady had given to me. I had lost my own razor when I threw my gear away.

The English people were fine and would get us anything we wanted. They couldn't do much for us in the food line, though. The good people in charge of catering and cooking had some crude ideas about feeding Englishmen. Natives were more in their line. My wound healed up fine, but I didn't feel very grand. Perhaps the weather was too hot.

Sunday brought lots of visitors. The natives who were anybody were allowed inside and all the French people came. The town band came too, but I liked that best when they were smoking. I got very interested in one of our attendants: one of the worst-looking specimens of a low-class Arab that I've ever seen, he selected a spot in the garden in front of a little water-tap arrangement, took a prayer mat from his pocket and knelt down on it, then started salaaming to Allah. The performance included dabbling his hands in water and various other motions of 'tic-tac'. I suppose after that he would go round the wards and steal something. A photographer came one day and took each ward. Ours turned out a treat so I sent one home.

My wound was better by 19 May and I was able to dispense with bandages. I was fed up with hospital and eager for a glimpse of life other than that to be obtained from the roof of the hospital. A specialist came up from Cairo on the 21st and marked me off for convalescence at Alex. The draft was to go on the 21st, Whit Monday, but I managed to get a touch of fever on the 22nd and thought I should just about manage a draft for Heaven, or wherever marines go. I nearly knocked on the Saturday and the mercury nearly pushed the top off the thermometer. The old doctor came to see me several times during the day and, about 6.00pm, left me with a soft white tabloid of quinine. I had no idea how to take it so chewed it well, and I thought I should never forget it. What a change in the morning though! I was up and about and ready for the draft, but the old man wouldn't hear of it. A cinema show was arranged for us in the grounds at night with iced drinks and a few extras. That was to keep up the spirit of Whit Monday I suppose. One fellow died on the 29th. He had been wounded in the head and had then contracted Erysipelas. He had quite an impressive funeral. Another was taken away to the isolation hospital with the same complaint.

I had a fearfully monotonous time up to 2 June. Sat on the hospital wall that day, along with two big Australians, having an argument with some natives in the street below. The old major-domo, or whatever he was (boss of the native attendants), came along and told us to get off the wall. Of course we replied with something polite in plain English, upon which he seized the ladder which one of the Aussies was standing on and pulled it away. I never saw such a hit as that Australian gave him; he went down as though he was shot. Several more natives rolled up and we had a regular mix up for about ten minutes. Then we faded away. The doctor came round later and with help from some of the natives and some French soldiers, picked these two Aussies out. It wasn't difficult because their hospital clothes had been ripped off their backs and what they had on was covered in blood. There was hell to pay; both warned off for draft and a report sent to their depot. That didn't bother them any though. I don't know why I wasn't clicked; perhaps they thought I wasn't big enough to be awkward. I was down for draft though.

We drew our old clothes and left Tanta at 9.00am on the 3rd and arrived at Alex by 11.00am, then took the tram to Mustapha Barracks where nearly all base details were, about three miles from town but easy to get to. I was detailed off with the marines but didn't strike any old chums. Saw the MO in the morning and was passed A1, drew a rifle and a new set of equipment, clothes and other kit and was busy all morning getting it fired up. I had heaps of letters from home and hardly knew where to begin. Bob Hester joined up from Cairo. He hadn't been wounded and I don't think he knew how he'd got away. Said it was rheumatics or something like that. He had come away on the *Cestrian*, an old cattle-boat and had fed on bully beef and biscuits during the voyage. Poor old Billy George had come on the same ship but had died.

Paid 112 piastres (£1-3-0d/£1.15p) on the Saturday, so felt entitled to a run downtown. Alex is a lovely place with some splendid buildings and lovely shops, especially in Sherif Pasha Street, which seems to be the main thoroughfare. I found one shop where we could buy lovely French pastries, ices and cool drinks and I'm afraid I nearly made a beast of myself. I think I could be excused that though after the stuff I'd eaten lately. Did a two-hour route march on the Monday morning and wasn't it hot! Saw the MO afterward; he passed me fit for active service again. Went downtown again and had a last tuck in at the pastry shop and an hour in the casino.

Embarked the next day on the *Cardiganshire* with about 140 RN details, a decent solid-looking boat of about 8,000 tons. Lots of troops on board: details of the 29th Division, Australians and some Egyptian engineers. Steamed away about midnight. I made my bed up on deck as usual and enjoyed the voyage, although it was rough the whole way. It bucked me up fine and made me feel fit for anything.

Arrived outside Lemnos on 11 June but didn't get in until the following morning and found it full of ships and troops. Heard news of the Collingwood and Benbow Battalions, who had come out to complete the division. Two days after landing, they were used in a big attack on Achi Baba on 4 June. Collingwood had over 800 casualties and Benbow between 600 and 700. The battalions ceased to exist and those who were left reinforced the other naval battalions.

All our division had been transferred from Gaba Tepe to Cape Helles. The Australian details left us the first day for Gaba Tepe. Two hostile aeroplanes came over on the Sunday flying very high. Our ships blazed away at them with no visible effect, except that they soon made off. A transport berthed up alongside us, full of Sikhs and Gurkhas. The Sikhs are fine-looking men, tall and well built, and take as much pride in their hair and appearance as a woman. They even keep their beards in pins overnight. The Gurkhas are their opposites; short and stumpy and care for their appearance as much as a frog does. Ugly as sin they are. They did their own cooking on open fires on deck. Chapattis or pancakes were the chief article of diet. The Egyptians landed on the Sunday and on the Monday all the Indian troops left the *Ajax*. There appeared to be about 2,000 of them and they went up to Gaba Tepe.

Chapter Four

15 June – Cape Helles

Tuesday morning saw a move for us. We were transferred to the *Whitby Abbey*, a minesweeper, and left harbour about 8.00pm. Arriving off Cape Helles about midnight we were taken to the *River Clyde* by a trawler. My! Didn't she roll. She was just like a tub and I was glad to get on to the firm decks of the *River Clyde*. This was the ship that had been run ashore on 25 April, full of Dublins and Munsters. As soon as she grounded they were to pass through doors in the ship's side, down the gangways and onto the shore. It made shivers go down my spine as I thought of those poor devils cooped up on that ship with nothing but certain death before them. The venture would have been a complete success had it not been for the inevitable mistake. Just that little miscalculation, and instead of grounding on the beach ten yards from cover, she ran aground on a reef about fifty yards offshore in deep water that the Turks had wired. Some of the Irish wouldn't wait for lighters to be moved into position but jumped from the doors into the water, pack, rifle and everything else on. Their fate was obvious. What few reached shallow water got caught on the wire and simply shot down. We passed a grave on the beach with 200 Irishmen in it. There were lots more graves, and scores of bodies had not been recovered from the sea. What few were left from the two battalions were joined together and called the Dubsters.

We slept in an open air camp till dawn under the shelter of the fortress castle of Sedd-el-Bahr. Breakfasted on Maconochie's and biscuits, nothing to drink, and as soon as our respective guides came we moved away. Had a good view of the castle and village, all in ruins. We moved left along the beach, past the battery of 11-inch guns that our ships had smashed, then up to the first rise that had cost so many lives. There were piles of food, stores, ammunition and fodder for the horses, just stacked up anyhow. Hospitals and clearing stations were rigged up on the beach, too. On top of the rise was a new cemetery with hundreds of fresh graves neatly laid out, all British. Nearby was an old Turkish burial ground with a few stone crosses and pillars standing up. A splendid view of the country could be obtained from the top. About eight miles to the front could be seen the Achi Baba ridge running from coast to coast and looking more like the head and shoulders of a man. In between was a valley or a basin with olive groves, vineyards and old-fashioned wells dotted about all over the place. On the right by Morto Bay could be seen the remains of several big houses and an aqueduct, and to the left, about five miles away, was the village of Rhothia, looking from here fairly intact. The very conspicuous thing was a row of six windmills to the right of the village. The Dardanelles flowed on the right and on the left was the Aegean.

Over the straits one could see the coast of Asia and the plain of Troy where a battle was fought a few thousand years ago for the beautiful Helen. I didn't see many beautiful Helens knocking around. It appeared far more civilised than the country round Gaba Tepe; the whole place looked peaceful, with no sounds or signs of fighting.

Walked about a mile and a half across country, over bits of trenches, funk holes and wide dugouts for stabling the horses. Passed hundreds of troops bivouacked in holes in the ground about three-feet deep and large enough to hold from two to six men. Found Portsmouth Battalion at last and reported at the orderly room, a dugout rather larger than the others and covered with a tarpaulin.

Told off to No. 8 Platoon (Sergeant Spicer) No. 2 Company with Captain Gowney in charge. The battalion was down to two weak companies, but had just been reinforced by a new company from England under Major Grover. Major Clark was in charge of the battalion with Captain Chandler, just out, as adjutant. Had invitations from several of the chaps to dig in with them, so Bob Hester and I dropped into the hole that required least digging. There was old soldier Robinson and two more fellows in it. Everybody was feeling downy. It appeared that a big gun from the Asiatic side kept sending big shells over, something like a 10-inch, and only the previous day had dropped one amongst seven of our fellows. Tom Watts (an old friend), filthy Joe Hartley, the cook, who had never washed since leaving the ship, an MG corporal and four more men were all talking about twenty yards from the galley.

Tom had an arm blown clean off, one chap was killed by the concussion, hadn't a scratch on him, the MG corporal and another were blown to bits, which were picked up from all over the camp and put in sandbags. Only Joe Hartley escaped unhurt. The fellows told me that old Tom Watts walked straight over to the doctors carrying his other arm. He just said something cheerful, 'Could he stick the blurry thing on again', and then went off into unconsciousness. He was hit about the head too. That little turn, along with a few more 10-inch shells, had shaken the chaps up a bit.

Up to about 9.00am I had heard no signs of fighting but I hadn't much longer to wait. The chaps in our hole had told me that our place was the worst in the camp. A road ran through our camp and all the transport from the beach to battalion dumps and batteries passed along it. Our dugout was right alongside the road and just at the spot where the Turk dropped most of his stuff. I was crossing the road intending to find some old chums, when I heard the old familiar sound of shells rushing through the air. Action left me, I couldn't move, and took no notice of the other chaps yelling to me to run and get down. The bursting of four shrapnels put action into me, though, and I could feel the bullets whizzing past me as I dived across the roadway. I have hazy recollections of turning about three somersaults, then finishing up in a small dugout on top of Harris, an old roommate at Forton. Talk about 'atmosphere vertical'. I had it.

We had a hot five minutes, then quiet again and one began to observe signs of life appearing on the face of the earth. I had a chat to Harris, then returned home. The slightest sign of a shell and I became terrified and immediately went to earth or, in other words, burrowed my head as far into the front of my hole as I could get it.

Hadn't I been a dammed fool, eager to get back to the lads? And what lads, why they were more like old men. Everybody had grown a beard. There was old Percival, one of the dandies, looking more like a cheap representation of John the Baptist than anything else; and Stuart, just like an old sea pirate. They are a scruffy lot, and they tell me that everybody is lousy and that I shan't be long before I am.

I watched the de-lousing process after dinner. All the men took off their shirts and made an exhaustive search along the seams, paying particular attention to the ones under the arms. Some used a lighted match to burn out huge clusters of eggs.

I slept well that night lulled off to sleep by the distant clatter of rifle fire.

Fell in between the lines at 8.00 next morning for a rifle inspection. As soon as Johnny spotted us, and he could see our every move, he sent over a few shells. Nobody got hit, so we carried on with the inspection. I was beginning to feel at home and on quite familiar terms with the shrapnel, (when I was in, or very near, a hole) when 'Asiatic Annie' started. She slung about six great shells over which dropped right into our camp. They didn't come all at once or even quickly. But one every few minutes, and we could hear the blighted things as they travelled across the water. It was as though an express train was rushing down on one at an angle of 60 degrees. The noise was tremendous and the explosion on contact frightful, but I'd far rather have the explosion than the rushing through the air. With that the danger is still to come; with the sound of the explosion comes the assurance that you are safe from immediate annihilation. With the rushing of the next shell comes the fear of death. Cries for stretcher-bearers came from No.1 Company's lines. Someone had been hit with a lump of casing. Lumps could be heard whizzing down long after the explosion.

I went digging after dinner. Each man drew a pick and shovel and we walked to within 1,500 yards of the firing line. Our task was widening and deepening the Oxford Street CT; higher up it was called Regent Street and where the two met at Brown House, a ruined farm, was Piccadilly Circus.

Heard some heavy fighting at night and we heard that a small stretch of trench had been lost, but regained at dawn. Friday was the hundredth anniversary of Waterloo and things were expected from the fleet. However, they didn't turn up. We had a lecture in the morning, followed by a demonstration on 'Troops, moving into artillery formation'. Captain Gowney's idea of it. Brilliant man!

The Turk spotted us and thought he would make the show realistic, so sent over a few salvoes of shrapnel. All formation ended with the sound of the first shell, men diving head-first into any hole they happened to be near. No casualties, although there ought to have been. Even that didn't satisfy our gallant captain. He had us out soon afterwards with our towels, formed us up and set us off in artillery formation to the beach for a bathe. As we reached the top of the cliffs I could see the remains of the battleship *Majestic* lying about 600 yards from shore. She just looked like some huge stranded whale.

Another result of British superiority. At the time it happened, there were scores of ships lying offshore, feeling, I suppose, quite safe from the Turks' ships. None of the lookouts noticed a destroyer come down the straits, make for the *Majestic* and let fly with a couple of torpedoes. They both got home, and in the confusion which followed, the Turkish destroyer got back home safely.

We bathed down by the ASC[1] beach and it was a treat to get into the water. A dead mule or two floating about in the water didn't take away much of the pleasure, although the stench from them was frightful. The ASC people bake bread down on the beach and about there it ran half a loaf a man. Up where we were it was a loaf between five or six and up the line a loaf between ten, when it landed. The loaves were about a pound in weight. They tell us the Turk gets no bread at all, so I suppose we are lucky really.

A lovely strafe at dusk, both sides going 'Hell for leather'. We couldn't see Achi Baba for dust and smoke. There was a battery of field guns, manned by Australians and the noise when they fired was deafening. The Aussies looked like blacks and I don't think any of them had worn shirts for ages. Went over with Bob Hester to watch them firing, then went farther over and watched a battery of French 75s. One of their guns was doing as much work as the whole battery of Australian guns. And weren't the Frenchies a lively lot too. One chap (I think he was directing the fire) was entertaining the gunners by reciting, dancing and singing. He had them nearly rolling off their guns with laughter, but there was no mistake about the firing.

We were certainly at the most pleasant end of the gun. I suppose poor old Johnny Turk was crouched down in his trenches, praying to Allah if he was a good man, cursing everybody if he was only a soldier. Poor devils! I reckoned they had a worse time than us. I wondered if they laughed as we did when a shell nearly hit them? And the nearer the shell the louder we laughed.

---

1. Army Service Corps, later Royal Army Service Corps.

Up by 4.30 next morning and digging up Oxford Street till dinner time. The food was rotten. The stew, whew! – corned beef and dried vegetables with far too much water. Here and there, floating about in the scum on top, were dead flies. Sometimes an issue of fresh meat would come along. First the IM gets his share, then all his satellites would dig in, then the various officers and sergeants' messes, cooks, servants etc., then what's left goes to the men. And there one can see, floating about on top of the dixies, huge greenish looking pieces of fat, with all the sand and dirt and flies that have accumulated on its journey from the beach. It was impossible to eat jam until the sun had gone to rest and with it the millions of flies. Biscuits and a bit of cheese were the only possible things.

Had a pretty rough time after tea. The Turk started shelling our road at one of its busiest times. It was full of horses and transport. One limber was blown to bits just outside our dugout, both horses killed but the men unhurt. About half a dozen horses were killed near us and once or twice we heard thuds and knew that something had gone in our parapet. We dug three empty shell-cases out of the front of our dugout in the morning.

The road on the left was getting shelled too, just on the rise up to the beach. There was a clear stretch of about 500 yards in full view of the Turk and it was a mad dash to get over it. I saw two direct hits there. The first was a GS wagon. The Turk sent over one shell just too late, the next just in front and the third between the two horses. He knocked off shelling then until the road was cleared, then started again. His first shot blew a limber with its horses and driver to bits. He was unlucky after that. Our guns started and they simply overwhelmed the Turk. Of course he had to start with Asiatic Annie and her friends. Their chief objective appeared to be the guns on our right.

Sunday was a repetition of the other days. We had Divine Service in two of the biggest holes. The Reverend Moore took the service. He seems a sticker.

Went digging, of course. Asiatic Annie confined her attentions to the beach and aerodrome. News came up towards dusk that there had been over a hundred casualties on the beach and that one of our aeroplanes had been hit. We only had a few shells over, but one of them reckoned: it went in the officers' mess dugout. Captain Gowney was sitting there between the doctor and a sub when the shell burst. It badly wounded the two but never touched Gowney.

Our guns were at it all night, especially on the right. Heard on Monday that the French had made an attack and taken the trenches on a front of about 800 yards. Saw scores of Turks pass down our road. They did look a filthy lot. The Turks counter-attacked after tea and we stood by to reinforce, but were not called. Saw a scrap in the air Tuesday. A German aeroplane came over and one of our planes chased it away. Some of our chaps said it was Commander Sampson, but I'm hanged if I could see who it was from where I stood. I suppose they liked to think it was. The Taube came back in about half an hour and dropped three bombs very near our camp. Put the wind up us nicely but did no damage.

Got ready after for a trip up the line. Stowed our packs in a big dugout and took what we wanted with us in our haversacks. By the time we were ready for starting we looked more like Christmas trees than soldiers. All manner of strange things were hanging from us. Sandbags full of rations, greatcoats, firewood (if we were lucky), parcels (with the same remark applying), 200 rounds of ammunition and various other little items including our best friend, the blurry rifle. Then came the walk, developing at times into a run and all the way like an obstacle race. Actually, there were about two miles of CT to traverse, but with the way it twisted and turned it was more like five. Telephone wires kept falling from the side and got entangled in our rifles and legs.

Arrived at Trotman Road at last. This was a new firing line, dug the last time up by our battalion, under the supervision of the engineers and without any casualties, and named after our brigadier, General Trotman. It was quite a decent affair, with fire-bays, traverses and fire-steps. Relieved the Hawke Battalion, RND, and got nicely settled down about 7.00pm. Nothing happened during the night beyond a bit of rifle firing. Worked watches of one hour up and one down till dawn when everybody 'stood to'. A chap called Charlie Hamilton asked me to take an orderly to Lieutenant Harden our platoon officer, so I did. He said it was a good number.

Had some good sport on Wednesday, sniping and being sniped. The Turks were about 200 yards away and he fired from loopholes in the bottom of his parapet. We fired from over the top of ours. Both our trench and his were supposed to be wired in front, but I'm sorry for the wire. It wouldn't stop much of a rush. Two French 75s started skimming shells just over our trench and right into the Turk's front line. He replied with one gun but couldn't get us.

Had a pretty rough time at night. No. 3 Company, the reinforcements, made an attack on a Turk bombing sap in front. They took it easily; in fact, they only found about six Turks in it who were killed without putting up a fight. One of our chaps, only young and very new, got his bayonet into one of the Turks, but couldn't pull it out and his nerve gave way completely. He started crying and screaming. Someone brought him back to our trench. We used to be told, by those who knew or thought they did, that once you draw the bayonet out of a man and feel the suck of blood and flesh on it, you see red and can go on killing indefinitely. Evidently this chap must have stuck his Turk in the wind; consequently there was no suck to feel. They got in this sap, very narrow and about six- to eight-feet deep, and found it full of dead, Turks and RND fellows who had taken the trench before. Everything was quiet for half an hour and our chaps managed to clear the trench a bit. Then Johnny started lobbing bombs into it as hard as he could go. Of course a panic started straightaway. Major Grover tried to organise a rush to the next Turkish trench but was killed by a bomb. Then one of the subs got killed and the other led a small party of men to get the Turks out. None came back. The company had fifty-five casualties, mostly killed and missing. We could hear one poor devil crying out all night 'stretcher-bearer' and 'Oh my God, fetch me in'. They found him about dawn, only slightly hit but as daft as anyone could be. The last striking impression I had of that fight was Captain Gowney standing up in front of our parapet, oblivious to danger and swinging a huge stick hand grenade. He intended it for the Turks, but it landed about ten yards from himself and burst on contact; he wasn't even scratched. He must have had the luck of the devil. He came in at that and gave the order for five rounds rapid. It was funny to see some of the chaps firing. They were simply terrified of being hit and made no attempt to put their heads over the top. They were crouched down on the fire-step with their rifles pointing up into the air at an angle of 75 degrees, blazing away as fast as they could work the bolt. They would very likely hit the top of Achi Baba. One chap next to me had two fingers shot away by a return bullet.

I turned in soon after and managed a sleep till 'stand to'. Had a stroll round the firing line after breakfast and as far up Sap 9 as they had dug. Saw Major Grover laid out on one of the fire-steps and two or three more of the chaps who had been brought in. Did a bit of sniping from Sap 9, but it was pretty dangerous as the Turks were only fifty yards away in most places. Had a fairly quiet day but another little spasm at night. A party went out digging in front to connect Sap 9 with Sap 8 on the right. Everything went well until one of the scouts in front got the wind up and blazed off a couple of rounds. Of course everybody did what they shouldn't have done; dropped their tools and bolted back to our trench. Johnny Turk woke up with the row and blazed away. Another twenty or thirty casualties, mostly wounds, several caused by jumping on to bayonets in the trench. I missed that little lot as Captain Gowney had put me on guard over his dugout, which was full of bombs and detonators.

Had a scare on Friday. Two or three of our shells burst over our line but luckily did no damage.

The Turk shelled our trench on Saturday but no one was hit. Two of our 6-inch howitzers replied and the shells as they burst fairly shook the earth. They put the wind up Johnny and we could see several of them nipping away from this trench. Nobody fired at them; why I don't know, except that it might not have crossed anybody's mind.

Sunday was a quiet day except for some shrapnel towards sunset. Saw about eight of our aeroplanes go over Achi Baba and could hear them until after midnight. The French got busy on our right at dawn.

Expected relief at noon on Monday by the Hawkes but the order was washed out. A terrific bombardment started on the left about 2.00pm. The fleet turned up and every available gun on land blazed away. It seemed impossible that anyone could live in those Turkish trenches. The artillery lifted their range about 4.00pm and we could see the troops advancing from our lines. Then Johnny opened up with shrapnel, bursting right amongst those groups of advancing men. They just disappeared. More followed through and we could see them advancing beyond the belt of Turkish fire. Then we could see the Turks leaving their trenches and nipping back into the cover of their positions in rear. We heard later that the 29th Division and 29 Indian Brigade had advanced about 1,000 yards, taken four lines of trenches, one battalion of field guns, five machine guns and 250 prisoners. Relieved about 8.30pm by the Hawkes.

I thought we should never get down to that rest camp. It was bad enough walking up in the light but it proved a thousand times worse going back in the dark. Going up we were fresh, but on the down journey everybody was exhausted and worn out through having no sleep, very little to eat and two pretty rough nights. Went off to sleep immediately on arrival and in the morning had a refreshing bathe in the sea. I went in with my shirt on, got it wet and then slashed it well on a rock. It dried in the sun in less than half an hour and all the lice that I thought would be dead came to life again. A Taube came over later and dropped a bomb near us, but did no damage.

Our guns put up a heavy bombardment at night but not the slightest sound of it could we hear. The night was awfully dark with a strong wind blowing towards Achi Baba, which no doubt carried the sound away from us. The sight was wonderful. The whole three miles of front at times was one huge burst of red flame. The strafe carried on all Wednesday and the French made an attack on the right which met with a certain amount of success.

We set off to dig some new trenches but only got as far as Sandbag Corner (the entrance to the CT) when the order was washed out. We waited there about half an hour and the whole time bullets were whistling and whining amongst us. They had a quiet, tired sort of sound as though they were fed up and wanted to get to rest. It must have been two miles from the Turks' firing line so I expect Johnny rapid fired in the same way that some of our chaps did. Two or three of our chaps got hit while we were waiting but only slightly. The bullets had no penetrating power. Sergeant Milne was one who got hit and it got him in the back of the neck, but only went in about half an inch. He carried on, worse luck. Word passed round like wild fire: 'Old Milne is wounded.' Everybody was delighted till they knew it was only slight and that there was no chance of him dying or being sent away. I think he was the most hated man in the whole battalion and, long before we left England or during the voyage out, chaps were threatening to shoot him when we got into action. However, he carried on and lots of the chaps who made the threats would never be able to carry them out.

Had a few quiet days after that. Thursday and Friday, I don't think our guns opened up at all. Went digging Friday afternoon and, just as we were passing Port Arthur, a big shell dropped amongst us, killing three and wounding six. Had a lot of rain in the night, cooling but very uncomfortable. The roof of our dugout leaked and we were wet though in a few minutes.

Had a pretty bad doing with heavy shells in the morning and to make things more cheerful I started with sickness and diarrhoea. This carried on Saturday and Sunday and I thought I should start with dysentery. There was a fearful lot of it knocking about then. Went down to the beach for a bathe on Sunday and saw a big French troopship lying off V beach. By the time we reached camp again she was under the sea, torpedoed. Saw a big French SAA[2] dump blown up on the right. It was just like a huge firework display and lasted about two hours. Heavy fighting all Monday morning. The Turks appeared to have a lot more guns now. Had a Taube over three times dropping bombs.

Towards tea-time twelve of our planes went over Achi Baba in one bunch. It was fun watching the Turks' frantic efforts to stop them getting over his lines. Hundreds of shells were pumped at them but not one turned back.

We were supposed to be standing by for the line, but only in case of a stunt. The Anson Battalion on our right got shelled heavily just before dusk. I could see groups of them standing about their dugouts, and a big shell came over from Asia and pitched amongst the dugouts. Then followed nine more in quick succession, one alone accounting for twenty casualties. Lots of men were wounded by stones and splinters of rock which were scattered about at a terrific speed.

Orders for the line were cancelled on Tuesday as the 52nd Lowland Division was taking over our lines and headquarters. They hadn't been on the peninsula long and hadn't had a trip up the line. They seemed fairly eager to get up and referred to Achi Baba as 'as wee bit muck'. They had an idea that they were going to walk right over it that trip up the line. Let 'em try, we'd had some.

Lieutenant Harden's servant was away sick so Charlie Hamilton asked me to look after him for a time. There didn't appear to be much to do for him, except share his parcels, borrow his books and field-glasses and make

---

2. Small arms ammunition.

his bed down at night. The advantages attached to the job were numerous, some of them being no digging, no fatigues, no rotten stew, and a good meal with Hamilton, usually steak and chips, and that when the sun and flies had gone to rest.

The colonel joined us up again from Egypt, looking spruce and fit, and with the rank of full colonel. Mr Dougherty came back too, also with another pip up and a brand new rig-out. Went for a bathe in the sea on Wednesday but got shelled out of it. Got back to camp safely and found two lovely parcels from home. Had a good feed and felt quite ill after it.

Things were very quiet up to Saturday, hardly anything doing at all. The Scotties don't appear to be shifting that 'wee bit muck'. Water was awfully scarce and the quality of it poor. Nearly all the wells were dried up and it was no use digging for water. It meant a trip to the beach for a drop of decent drinking water.

Some days we washed, some days we didn't, and the flies! Scores to the square inch, and the vermin! One can strip and have a rub-down, search minutely amongst one's clothes and, five minutes after dressing again, there they are again. Hundreds of troops were being taken from the peninsula every day with dysentery and jaundice.

Chapter Five

10 July 1915 – That 'wee bit muck'

The observation balloon went up from *Ark Royal* on the Saturday and our guns opened up on the Turkish trenches and positions behind Achi Baba. I had a lovely view of it all through Mr Harden's glasses. Saw a cruiser sending some heavy shells over. We were standing by as immediate reserves to 52nd Division who were expected to attack at any time.

Sunday the 11th was quiet until about 5.00pm when both sides opened up with the guns.

Orders at 4.00am on Monday to stand by with gear ready for the line. A terrific bombardment opened up at the same time and the Turk replied with far more guns than we thought he possessed. It was impossible to see Achi Baba at all for the smoke and dust of the bursting shells. The 52nd Division attacked early in the morning and took four lines of trenches but, later, had to retire from one. They had taken about 400 prisoners but had lost heavily themselves. About 300 of the Turks passed our camp about dinner time. Orders to get rigged at 3.00pm and we set off for the line at half past. We were stuck in the CT the whole day. Hundreds of Scotties passed us. In fact it was one long procession of groaning, cursing and crying, wounded men.

It was surprising how many of them cried. They were nearly all very young though, and everyone was utterly fed up and miserable with thirst and exhaustion. Lots of wounded Turks went down too, but they seemed a much older and staid set of men. Every one of them looked afraid though, as though they were thinking they had escaped one death, only to be going straight into a more certain and more horrible death. In one or two cases a wounded Scottie and a Turk were helping one another down the trench. The RAMC people were having a tottering time. It was a blazing hot day and they were doing nothing but carry the more serious cases on stretchers from the line to the aid station at the bottom of the CT. The procession eased off a little towards dusk and just odd batches of wounded men and water carriers would pass us.

We were able to get forward a few yards every half hour or so and, by one o'clock on the morning of the 13th, had reached Trotman Road, our old firing line. It was now a back number, the firing line being two or three trenches in front. Nobody knew for certain. Very few signs of fighting came from the front, just now and again a spasm of rapid fire with its complement of Very lights. Away on our right we could see the French lights. They hung in the air for quite a minute, suspended by a parachute. We found the trench deserted except for a few spare Scotties. They appeared to be walking aimlessly about, as though they belonged to nobody and had no object in view. Some were half daft, the others quite daft. We found one, a quartermaster sergeant, blind to the world and everything that was going on around him. He was full of rum.

The Scotties didn't appear to have done so well in this sector and the line was a little behind the ones on the flanks. No doubt a little straightening job for us. I managed a couple of hours sleep till 'stand to'. About 7.00am I was talking to Sergeant Spicer, and several more chaps were in the bay, including Bill Finch and Lance Corporal Robinson. All of a sudden, Robinson gave a yell and, as we looked, both he and Finch were on the ground. A bullet had come from somewhere, hit Finch between the eyes, knocked the back of his head out and then ploughed its way through Robinson's shoulder and shoulder blade. Finch was a big powerful chap and it was at least two hours before he died. The stretcher-bearers had just time to get him to the dressing station before he died. Robinson was pretty bad too.

All that morning Scotties kept coming down from the two trenches in front and everyone appeared to be going down to Brown House to fill his own water bottle. They never thought about taking half a dozen or so. They said they had no officers or NCOs left with them and everybody was doing as he liked. No one on watch, no one consolidating the new trenches. Colonel Luard put sentries on the CT and stopped the Scotties going down. Although scores had gone down for water, none returned.

About 10.30am I set off to fetch two rum jars full of water from Brown House. As I reached the top of the CT I heard a terrific din from the front, men yelling and shouting, then a sharp burst of rifle fire. As I looked over the top I saw a horde of Scotties and Turks all mixed up, running like mad for Trotman Road. It appeared that the Scotties had been in the firing line all night with the Turkish prisoners and something happened to cause a panic. Perhaps they had all lost their nerve. Anyhow, they deserted their trench and the prisoners followed on like so many sheep. Things looked pretty serious for a time. It just depended who got there first, our party or the Turks. Major Sketchly of divisional HQ, who happened to be up the line, grasped the situation and led a party of Plymouth marines over the top and took possession again, for which he received the DSO. Things were pretty quiet after that until 3.40pm. I had got back from fetching the water, feeling half dead and wet through with perspiration, when Captain Gowney nailed me. 'Find Mr Harden,' he lisped, 'and tell him to report at the Colonel's place at once.' Found him, asleep of course, mouth wide open and full of flies. Woke him up and delivered my message, then went down with him to the Colonel's shack. All our officers were there and the pow-wow was well on the way. I couldn't hear a word of what was said but knew the substance of it as soon as Mr Harden came out. We were to go over at 4.30 and take three lines of trenches. Our artillery would bombard from 4 to 4.30. As soon as they stopped we were to go over.

They had been exactly half an hour talking and that's all the information we got. Some didn't even get to know that much. It was 4.20 when Harden came out and by the time we reached the platoon, which was on the extreme right, it was time to go over. Our artillery had stopped and were then no doubt preparing to lift. Mr Harden said to Sergeant Spicer, 'Get the platoon to follow me', and off he went up a narrow little CT, two feet deep at the best place. The rest of the platoon followed us, just like sheep. Our next trench was on top of a rise about 120 to 160 yards away and we were then out of sight of the Turk. I passed an order down from Harden that we were to get down behind the parados of the next trench and fix bayonets. We passed several rotten, stinking, dead Turks as we went up, swollen to about three times their normal size by the heat, and the stench from them was simply awful, something absolutely unforgettable.

We reached the trench and did as ordered, or perhaps about half a dozen of our platoon did, when the order came to charge. Nothing so far had happened from the Turk, but as soon as the order to charge came along, things happened all at once and all over. It was though he had been biding his time until we said

'Go'. Shrapnel came at us like a hailstorm, bullets were whizzing by and a few odd bombs and grenades were bursting about. Our own artillery had opened up again and it was just like Hell let loose (or so I should imagine).

I had grabbed up a pick or a shovel, I couldn't say which it was; I know I carried my rifle in my left hand and the other thing in my right. I jumped across the trench with Mr Harden, yelling like mad as usual, but didn't get very far. A shrapnel round burst just in front of me and something seemed to hit me all over at once. Down I went, and the force of the thing that hit me sent me over and over backwards for about six yards. I realised two or three things immediately. One was: I'd had enough; another was: inside a trench is safer than outside; they are made for cover; and another: I shouldn't get court-martialled if I had lost my rifle. I didn't stop to look for it, but made a hop, skip and a jump and was inside the trench. It was more like a road. An old Turkish trench it was, about eight-feet wide and very shallow. Several of our chaps were already there, wounded, one of them just about going out. A couple of Scotties were looking to him. There was a machine gun just where I jumped in, manned by RNAS fellows, with an officer in charge. He did look a mess too, clothes all torn and filthy and eyes nearly closed through want of sleep. His gun's crew looked no better and half of them were asleep under the lee of the trench. There were several Scotties too, lying about, but none taking an active part in the stunt, or making any effort to help bind our wounds up. 'What about that wee bit muck now, Jock?' I asked one. 'Arraway to Hell with yer wee bit muck,' he growled. Our fellows kept coming back, hit in all sorts of places. Mr Harden followed me in after about five minutes. He asked me where I was hit and I told him through the left knee. He looked like a butcher's shop for blood, but it was another chap's blood, or most of it was. He thought a bomb had burst by him filling him full of splinters, but nothing very serious. He showed me his chest and it was cut and scratched all over. He said he was going to get down to the dressing station, he didn't fancy that trench. I dressed my own wound when he was gone. I had to cut my left trouser leg off about the knee to get at it. I could see where the bullet had gone in, just on the inside of the left knee, but it hadn't managed to get right through. I could see the big blue lump at the back where the bullet had lodged. Another cutting job for someone! My wound wasn't bleeding much and wasn't particularly painful while I sat down. I intended sitting down for a time too. The amount of stuff that was hitting the trench was enormous. Showers of dirt and stone kept coming in and everybody was covered with it. Shells and bombs were hitting the front and back of the trench but nothing actually came in it. One fellow came rushing along the trench, yelling at the top of his voice 'Oh my God, I'm hit!' I told him he'd get hit again if he didn't get down. I wanted to dress his wound, but no, he wouldn't stop. Said he was dying but he appeared pretty lusty about it, and dashed down the little CT as though he was in a race. They kept coming along, some going straight down, some stopping where I was, and nearly all bringing fresh news of the battle. Heard that Mr Dougherty was killed, Captain Chandler, the adjutant, badly wounded, and lots of other chaps I knew killed or badly hit. The battalion had taken all the trenches and some were still pushing on to the first slopes of Achi Baba. One poor devil came staggering along the trench muttering and mumbling in a fearful manner. Blood was pouring from his mouth and where his left cheek had been was a gaping, ragged hole. A bullet had gone in his mouth and out through the side of his face, taking the whole of the cheek with it. He did look awful. After about half an hour and when our bit of trench was packed tight with wounded and dying, Captain Gowney came in from the front and dashed off down the CT, brandishing his revolver. After about ten minutes he came back with a crowd of our chaps at his heels. He had been rounding the shirkers up and had made a good haul. 'Who are you?' he yelled at us. 'Wounded,' I replied. 'Be careful.' 'Be dammed,' he said, 'come on, walk over 'em', to the shirkers and hangers back. And he stood there until they had all clambered out of the trench. He looked just like a raving maniac as he stood and kept waving his revolver about in a most alarming manner. I felt quite relieved when he followed the crowd. And to think that only last August he was serving out buns and coffee in the canteen at Pompey.

I think nearly every one of those chaps had trod on my wound in passing. I think they were too scared to have any feeling for us. They had hung back and skulked until their hearts were the size of peas. I had been there about an hour when the chap in charge of the MG yelled to his crew to stand by. He said the Turks were attacking on the right and coming towards us in thousands. He slewed his gun round and was just going to loose off when he noticed that they were French colonial troops making an attack half left. I made my way down shortly after that and found that I could walk, although the wound was very painful and the left knee joint had gone stiff. Got halfway down the CT to Trotman Road, just where three of those rotten Turks were lying, when I came across Bob Hester crouching down on the trench bottom. 'Hello Bob,' I said, 'are you hit?' 'No, but I can't see,' he replied. He said a shell had burst as he was going up the trench and blinded him. I'd an idea that he had been rubbing dirt into his eyes. He was trembling like a leaf and it was plain to see he had a pretty bad funk on. He wouldn't go down with me. Said he'd wait and see how he went on.

There was an aid station at the top of Oxford Street and I had my wound dressed and a ticket given to me. They told me there that if I could walk at all, I'd better set off as I wouldn't get a stretcher for hours. Got about halfway down and had to make way for a stretcher. Major Clark was on it, groaning and moaning. He had been shot through the wrist. I'd been shot in the knee but had to walk. He must have been pretty bad though. I got down by Brown House and came across Sergeants Milne and Squib, both drunk on rum. 'How's the boys getting on up there, Askin?' Milne asked me. 'Go up and see, you drunken pig,' I answered sweetly. There was a bit of excuse for Squiby. He didn't lay claim to having 'guts'. He came out with the reinforcements and, since landing, had lost a stomach weighing about three stone. Milne was a worm though, with a big mouth and scrawling nature.

It took me hours to get down. I kept calling at different dressing stations in the hope of getting a lift but there was nothing doing. 'Make your way down to the First Field Ambulance,' they all said. That was in Fleming Gully, nearly at the beach and quite four miles from where I'd been hit. I got about half a mile away and sat down, beat to the world. I couldn't have gone another ten yards if all the Turks on the peninsula had been after me. I was nearly sick with the pain of my leg and everything kept going black in front of my eyes. Two big Australian gunners came along after a time and carried me the rest of the way. I had a good drink of tea and a rest and felt heaps better. There were crowds of our fellows there, some laid out on stretchers, others sitting round drinking tea and munching hard biscuits. I had my wound attended to again and was told to hang around until they were ready to take the bullet out. They roused me up about midnight. I'd fallen fast asleep on the floor outside the marquee. I went inside this marquee that acted as operating theatre and waited until the doctor was ready. There were dozens of fellows laid out on stretchers, some waiting to be operated on, some coming round and others just dying. There were no lights in the place except the electric torches carried by the sick-bay staff. It looked awfully weird but worse than the appearance was the sickening stench of blood and antiseptics.

My turn came at last, one of the attendants asking me if I was the chap who wanted a shrapnel ball taking out of the knee. I made him wise and followed him to the doctor. He put me face down on a stretcher and commenced poking and probing about. He shone a light on my face after a bit and asked if I could stand the knife. I told him I could stand anything if only he was quick about it. He got busy then while his chap shone his light on the back of my leg. I think the doctor must have used his knife to sharpen pencils with, or as a tin-opener. Anyway he was a deuce of a time, minutes at least, before he had cut me enough. He swore a few times, then gave a grunt of satisfaction as the ball came away. After that he pushed a tube of antiseptic paste in the hole. In at the front and out through the back, then worked it backwards and forwards a few times, something after the manner of cleaning out the bore of a gun. He complimented me on the way I'd stuck it and said he thought I had fainted with making no noise. I told him I was getting quite used to it now. Had the wound properly dressed, another drink of 'maz' (tea) and sat down outside to wait for the next wagon to the beach. What a terrible journey it was too in that GS wagon. Along a road, or what had been a road, we went, past the village and castle of Sedd-el-Bahr, past the fort at Cape Helles, and on to the clearing station on the beach. It was a succession of jolts and bumps from start to finish and we were thrown out almost. I could have laughed when we got in one of the marquees at the CCS. We were waiting for blankets when a chap came in. He wanted a tooth out. It struck me as being funny, that amongst all that suffering there should be one with common toothache. And poor devil, I bet he was suffering as much as any of us. The doctor didn't waste much time with him. Sat him in a chair, asked him which it was and out it came.

We turned in after that, but not for long. They were soon out. 'Hospital ship party, make your way down to the beach.' More hopping for about 500 yards, and it was no joke hopping with a game leg and an empty stomach. I was hungry, and it seemed ages since I'd had anything to eat.

We were taken to the hospital ship *Rewa* and given three straw biscuits[1] and two blankets and told to find a place somewhere on the top decks. The ship was about full. There must have been hundreds on board. All the wards below were full of serious cases and the covered-in places on the decks were hung with cradle cots, which were nearly all full of rather less serious cases, and then there were about 200 walking cases, hanging about just anywhere. I thought I ought not to grumble at being a walking case with a bullet through the knee, as there were some on board (walking cases) who had been shot through both legs. Heard scraps of news regarding our little stunt. It appears that only our battalion and Nelson Battalion took part in the advance and Nelson lost even more heavily than we did. We went up the line on the 12th about 300 strong (or weak) with ten officers, and by the end of the 13th had lost nine officers and about 200 men. Four officers, including the Colonel, were killed and five wounded. Only old Dave Gowney is left and he'll be like a dog with two tails now that he's got a battalion, even if it is a skeleton. The Colonel and his servant were killed together. They were wounded together by the same sniper at Gaba Tepe on 3 May and now had both been killed together by the same shell. I heard how Mr Dougherty died too. He had got over the first Turk trench, finding it practically empty but when about fifty yards from the next found it full of Turks, with a couple of German officers standing on top urging the Turks to get out and charge. Mr Dougherty dropped down, took aim with a rifle that he had carried with him and put out one of the Germans. Then he got sniped through the head and died almost at once. He was a game little chap.

Cases were coming on all day and as night came on they brought a lot more serious stretcher cases on board.

Captain Gowney came on board, wounded. He was having the Colonel buried, when a shell burst over the party and the wonderful thing, or part of it, hit Dave.

Thursday morning a Taube came over and dropped three bombs on the beach, with what effect I couldn't say as I wasn't a little bit interested.

---

1. A biscuit in this case is a third part of a mattress.

Chapter Six

15 July – Hopes For England

Just before noon 240 minor cases were sorted out and transferred to another boat which took them straight away to Mudros. They were to get better in the hospitals there. I stayed on the *Rewa*, thank God! And we steamed off about 3.30pm. What a relief to see Achi Baba fade away with the distance and with it the noise of battle and the fear of death. There was plenty of death knocking about though; most of the cot cases were in frightful agony and kept crying out in their pain. I got into conversation with one of the ship's company. 'Oh yes,' he said, 'we are straight for England.' Their contract was up, or something of the sort.

However at 7.00pm we sighted the entrance to Mudros and steamed straight in. The bay looked more full of shipping than I'd seen it before. Perhaps the size of the ships had something to do with that though. The *Aquitania*, *Mauritania* and *Franconia* were all in, full to the top with fresh troops from home. Three new divisions were out for a fresh stunt.

Left harbour on Friday afternoon but only to bury about a dozen dead, then back again. Left Mudros on the Saturday about 6.00pm and, after a quick smooth journey, took up our berth at Alex on the Monday. My wound had healed well but was still painful. The sea voyage had bucked me up wonderfully though and I felt more like going back again than going to hospital. We had an old chaplain on board and he had set us all hoping for England. He knew for certain that the ship was going straight there. Perhaps so, but not with us. However, some of us might get sent home from hospital and, in any case, our division was to be withdrawn from the peninsula because we'd lost so heavily. So the latest 'buzz' went. As it had been buzzing round ever since 3 May, it was hardly worth taking notice of.

Entrained about 1.00pm, arrived at Cairo at 7.00pm and were then taken by motor to Kasr-el-Aini hospital, on the banks of the Nile, the same old river that watered the bull rushes where they found Moses a few generations ago. My word! Weren't things happening these days? And weren't we seeing things? And to think, that the most exciting thing that happened to me before the war was to get in the same smoke room as 'Mooney's' and 'Mad Jack's' gangs. I was soon rigged out again as a native and told off to a decent bed, of which I took an immediate advantage. A strange bed never kept me awake those days.

I felt A1 after a good night's sleep and decent breakfast. Kasr-el-Aini is a pleasant hospital, a great big place with large lofty wards and great open windows and, all day through, pretty birds would fly in and out. The view from some of the windows was lovely, a large stretch of the Nile was visible, and the banks on either side were covered with palms of various descriptions with, here and there, beautiful houses and mosques. The river itself was dotted with all manner of boats. A few miles away on the bank of the river were three huge pyramids.

The doctors and attendants were Egyptian, but there were several English nurses who seemed to put a more homely air on the place. On the Wednesday about 11.00am a score or so of local medical students were let loose on us and treated us as so much material to practise on, not taking the slightest interest in us personally; if our wounds were nothing new or strange to them they would just treat that with indifference, slap a bandage on and walk away.

One fastened on to me and found something in my wound to interest him. He opened it back and front and, after much prodding and poking about, fished a few bits of lead from where I'd had it taken out on Gallipoli. It felt much easier after that and healed up fine so that by the 26th I was convalescent.

A big clearance was made from Kasr-el-Aini then, and a crowd of us moved to a big school about five minutes' walk nearer the city. They were just converting it into a hospital. Nasrich was the name of the place. The feeding was good but the medical and comforts departments were rotten. I was there from 26 July to 7 August and in that time had my wound dressed twice. The thing started discharging and I thought it was going to turn awkward. There was absolutely nothing there with which to occupy our minds; no visitors, no books or papers and just one concert which was decent.

They must have been making us fed-up so that we should be glad to get back to our battalions. They succeeded with me. I couldn't but envy the fellows who were wounded in France, their quick journey home to Blighty and the splendid time in hospital that they had.

We were not allowed to put our noses outside the place and used to spend hours sitting on the wall overlooking the main road into Cairo. We watched the cars and the people as they passed by. Our dress consisted of pyjamas and a bright red tie, not very conventional dress for walking out, but I went out on two occasions with three more of the fellows. We dropped over the wall after tea one day and wandered into one of the suburbs, and felt lucky when we got out of it. At one time we must have had a hundred kiddies yelling and screeching at us, some flying round and round, some spitting, some throwing mud or worse, and others just being mildly curious. We jumped on a car once to avoid them but about a score stuck. As we neared the hospital again, each of us darted at one of the imps and they received sufficient beating to go round the whole lot who had followed us.

The next time out we stuck to more civilised parts, watching the Arab men, women and kiddies bathing in the Nile. It was a treat to see them until an Egyptian policeman came on the scene. They dashed out of the water, picked up their small bundles of clothing and ran as fast as they could for cover. It was hard lines for whoever the policeman caught. He asked for no names and addresses but just laid about them with a big stick.

I saw several local funerals and found them awfully amusing. If it was a man getting buried, all his wives would follow behind carrying on most alarmingly, tearing their hair and dresses and letting off the most weird cries. The men friends and relations went on in front, letting off a terribly monotonous chant. The corpse was well stowed away in an orange-box coffin, carried by four hefty villains.

We could smell burning very strongly on the night of the 31st. It appeared to come from the city and we heard afterwards that the Australians had run amok in the Wazza, setting fire to some of the houses as they did before. One or two were killed and a few Red Caps who interfered were badly mauled by the Aussies. No wonder troops run amok. I felt like doing the same. I was never so fed up before in all my life. Our next move was to Abbassia Barracks but before leaving Nasrich we were fitted out with a khaki suit. I said fitted, but they were just thrown at us. My tunic measured forty inches round the chest and the trousers had been made for a guardsman. It took me hours at Abbassia to ensure that it wouldn't fit me about three times. Conditions in barracks were even worse than at Nasrich. Attention to our wounds or various ailments was minus. We used to draw our food in bulk from the IM and take it to the cookhouse. After that it was a fight as to who got any.

Two or three of us saw the MO on Monday about some pay, and he told us to go to Hell. We said that was where we had come from.

I was strolling across the parade one morning minus my hat and tunic and was pulled up by a big fat officer. 'Where's your hat?' and 'Don't you usually salute an officer when you pass him?' he said. I told him they taught us in the Royal Marines not to salute an officer if we were improperly dressed. Things like that just helped make us more and more fed up and anxious to get back to the fighting. All hopes of England had fled. We saw nearly everybody about some pay and at last the garrison adjutant roused himself and said he'd see us on Saturday morning. He did, and we drew 8/- (40p). We were allowed out in town but it wasn't much use going without any money.

On the Saturday night I went for a stroll round Heliopolis, one of the swell suburbs of Cairo, and found it awfully interesting. Several lovely buildings and one huge palace that was being used as a hospital. I found very few chances of spending my 8/- there.

I saw the doctor next morning and volunteered to go back to duty. He said my leg wasn't better yet, but would be before I got back to Gallipoli, so, seeing that I wanted to go, he marked me for the base. Left Cairo at 9.30am on Monday 16 August and arrived once more in Alex. What a treat to smell the sea again. Joined up with RMLI details at Mustapha and fitted out again with all the clothes and gear necessary for another spell of fighting. Saw the doctor on Tuesday morning who put me on seven days' light duty. That made no difference because when I got back to camp my name was being read out for the next draft.

About 500 survivors had just arrived from the *Royal Edward*, a big troopship that was torpedoed about twelve hours' sail from Mudros. She went down in three minutes with more than 800 onboard.

We were roused out every morning at 5.30 for bathing parade and it was lovely in the sea. I have never seen anything so lovely as the sea and sky at Alex. I was paid 30 piastres (6/2d/31p) on the Wednesday. I put in for more but had my request refused. Some of the chaps had been getting too drunk in town, so they had stopped paying so much money out.

I had a couple of nights down in town, but was quite ready for the draft on Friday morning. Found out that Captain Gowney was in charge of all RND details. We went straight to the docks in electric cars, to within 500 yards of our ship. No one knew that, of course, least of all Gowney who marched us for at least two miles before he thought of enquiring for the ship. Full marching order, rifle and 220 rounds of the best, under a tropical sun, then all the way to march back again. He ought never to have left Pompey parade and canteen.

The ship was the *Derfflinger*, a big German prize-boat and a fine-looking thing. Hundreds of all kinds of troops were on board, including a lot of the survivors from the *Royal Edward*. The OC Troops was a colonel who had survived and we knew it. He made Gowney ship's adjutant and a more dizzy pair it would be impossible to imagine. They had submarine guards all over the ship and everybody had to eat and sleep in lifebelts.

We left Alex at 5.00pm Friday and had it awfully rough until the Sunday afternoon. We arrived in Lemnos harbour just on sunset and I don't think I've ever seen anything so grand and lovely as the hills and rugged cliffs of Mudros. They were just like piles of soft velvet in every conceivable shade of brown. It turned awfully cold at night and I had to move between decks to sleep.

Transferred to the *Hythe*, a big minesweeper, on the 26th and cleared off for Gallipoli about 4.30. The battalion was still there but about to be withdrawn to Imbros for a rest. We had a forty-mile voyage of rough sea, wind, thunder and lightning and arrived at W Beach Gallipoli at 10.30pm.

Chapter Seven

August 1915 – Dragging On

Stayed on board the *Hythe* all night and of course I touched unlucky. Did a seven-hour watch on the ship while a working party of Egyptians unloaded a few thousand bombs. We landed at 5.30 on the Friday morning and marched up to the new dugouts where I joined up with A Company 2nd Battalion RM. Deal and Chatham Battalions had been amalgamated and called the 1st Battalion, and Plymouth and Portsmouth called the 2nd Battalion. The four battalions only numbered about 800 men in total. Very few of the Pompey boys were left. Bob Heston still hung on. I pigged in with Mick Smith, a North Country lad, and a friend of Billy Georges, who died in May. Sergeant Owen was in charge of our platoon (No. 1). He was an old Pompey man and pretty easygoing.

Very little fighting was going on. The chaps said that Johnny never shelled now. He was too occupied with the new landing at Suvla Bay, where those three new divisions landed. Orders on Monday for the trenches and we moved at 1.00pm. Went up the gully ravine on the left, which ran from Y beach to the left of Krithia and was about 200 feet deep in places. It was a hot and dusty journey and our Lance Corporal Bill Love seemed to think that our legs were as long and as fresh as his. We had some rare lads in our platoon, all nationalities: Jock Baird from Motherwell, Cooper from Wales, very entertaining when he sang in Welsh, Jimmy Rimmer from Ireland, and real Irish, and Tommy Bolan, a corner boy from Middlesbrough. All 'birds' and they soon shouted if Bill Love opened out.

The gully twisted and turned so that it appeared never ending and had it not been for the little springs of fresh water trickling out of the rocks, the journey would have been absolute torture. We came to a zigzag path at the finish that led right up the face of the gully and at the top was the CT leading to the firing line.

We relieved the Hawkes and were in the firing line until Wednesday. Very little firing but plenty of work. I was attached to some miners and did six hours on and eighteen off. The work consisted of dragging bags of chalk along the bottom of an underground sap that two miners were making, and this thing was a foot deep in water. The eighteen hours off consisted of doing odd watches, fetching rations and SAA from the zigzag and clearing up the trench. When we could we slept. The RGA[1] were very busy just then, bringing up some heavy trench mortars and land torpedoes that the French had lent us. The torpedoes are great things with fins on and have about 60lbs of high explosive in them. Thoughts and visions of another stunt flashed across my mind. We moved down into support about 4.00pm on the Wednesday and, about that time, our guns opened up on the Turks' trenches in front of our position. I was on a sapping party from 1.00 to 4.00am, digging a little sap from our front lines towards the Turks' trench. We were just about forty yards from the Turk and it was awfully lonely. Just Mick Smith and I with not a scrap of wire in front of us and a Turkish wiring party only thirty yards away. Mick and I took it in turns to dig and while one was on his knees digging the other would be filling sandbags with the loose earth and lifting them up on top to form a parapet. All at once someone dashed up the sap (on hands and knees) and told us to keep down as our chaps in the line were going to give Johnny's party five rounds rapid. They did but I don't think they did much damage beyond scaring them back into their trench. I was jolly glad when our four hours were up. About 250 reinforcements joined the battalion on 2 September with several new officers. Our company got a new OC, a Captain Cordnor, and two subs, Weeks and McCready. Captain Cordnor appeared dizzy, but I suppose that was only natural and to be expected.

Our ships and guns bombarded in the morning and the Turk replied with a few guns on our trenches. We moved up into the firing line at 3.00pm but received orders soon after to stand by to leave again at 5.00pm. There was to be a big strafe with the trench mortars, bombs and field guns from 5.30 to 6.30pm and we had to move down the CT, with the exception of two men in each bay who would keep watch. It was a strafe, and if Johnny Turk got it worse than we did, then I'm sorry for him. Great lumps of those torpedoes came flying back,

---

1. Royal Garrison Artillery.

bombs dropped short and the Turk opened up with whizz-bangs on the CT, where we were all crouched. Two or three fellows were killed about ten yards below me and when the order came at 6.30 to fix bayonets and man the firing line at the double several more chaps got stuck with bayonets. Our trench was in a shocking condition when we arrived there, sandbags knocked in and torn, all the parapet battered in and the whole place littered with lumps of iron, pieces of bombs and lumps of earth.

There was a chap called Shackleton grovelling about on the floor of the trench, moaning and groaning out that he was hit. No wound could be seen and only a small bruise on his hip told us that a stone or a splinter had caught him. It caused a laugh and relieved the tension which was pretty high just then. Poor old Shackleton, he was a funny little fellow and I often thought about the times I'd hammered him into a state of sleep in our room at Forton Barracks. He came from decent people, had had a decent education but something was wrong in his mental box. He used to get frightfully drunk every night at Forton and after 'lights out' would start tormenting the other chaps. I used to get first attention from him as my bed was next to his and as soon as he got to my bed I would knock him back into his own. He was then under a suspended sentence of two years for cowardice at Gaba Tepe. Somebody found him wandering about on the beach when he should have been in the trenches.

An officer and six men of the Manchesters came along at night and went out at North Barricade to fetch in one of their men who had been killed some time ago. He did stink! Standing by for another bombardment, but thank the Lord, the wind was too strong. We sent off a few bombs from the barricade, but the wind carried them back almost into our own trench.

Stood to arms at 4.30 Sunday morning and think we might have been 'standing to' for a week, had not two chaps, one in our bay and one in the next, been killed. We were all stuck up on that fire-step for two hours and we must have looked like Aunt Sallies to the Turk. It got to a nice shooting light and one smart Turk took advantage and popped both these fellows off. They were dead as they fell off the step. Sergeant Owen came along, found out what had happened and played war with Captain Gardner, who should have passed word along to 'stand down, carry on daily routine' an hour and a half before. The captain went down the line next day sick. We got our own back next morning at 'stand to'. Two or three of us waited with our rifles at the ready and just before it got really light a Turk climbed over the back of his trench. I fired and Jack Spencer fired. Perhaps we both hit him, we shall never really know that but I'm certain he never climbed out of another trench. Later in the day we picked out another nice spot for sniping. We could see where the Turks' CT ran into his firing line and about twenty yards down was a bend where anyone passing was visible to us for about three yards. We spotted a big fat Turk and something caused him to pause at that bend. He paused just long enough for Jock Baird to hit him. He must have yelled because two more dashed down and tried to get him away. We got one of those and the other one dashed away again. I guess all the other Turks who used that trench went up and down it on hands and knees.

We were relieved at 5.00pm and went down to the reserve trench, which was blessed with the name of College Green. This was an old Turkish trench battered into the semblance of a sunken road and wide enough in places to turn a horse and cart round. There was plenty of room for a comfy sleep though, different from the firing line where the fire-step was anything from a foot to eighteen inches wide and that with an outward slope on it. I had a walk with Jack Spencer along this trench to the left and, about a hundred yards past our sector, came into a maze of old Turkish trenches, which had been shelled and battered until they looked like anything else on earth but trenches.

They had been taken by 29th Division on 28 June and had suffered terribly in the bombardment. The remains of Turks were still lying about all over the place, no attempt being made to clear them away or bury them. The whole place was littered with broken rifles, equipment, telephone wires, blankets and greatcoats. I shouldn't like a revetting job with his sandbags; they held anything from one to two hundredweight of earth and it must have been an awful job getting them into position. All the print on the bags was in German. In some parts of the trenches he had run short of bags and had used blankets and greatcoats to fill up. Safety before comfort was his motto.

We could see where the poor old Turk had been crouching down under the parapet and in his little funk-hole during the bombardment and a shell had burst, filling up the trench and burying the lot. Arms and legs were sticking out from the sides and bottom of the trench, and if we touched them the clothing would drop off, revealing just a horrid-looking bone. Jack

Spencer spotted a pair of very good boots on a Turk. 'I'm having them,' he said, 'they don't need boots in heaven', and he took them off and changed them for his own. He was a queer chap. A short time before coming out here, he was an orderly to Admiral Jellicoe on the *Iron Duke* and got kicked out for being in a frightful state of intoxication whilst escorting the Admiral's wife to somewhere in a motor car.

I was jolly pleased to get away from that hell hole. The whole place stank of death and disease and everything was swarming with horrid black files and grass-hoppers. We were really hunting for firewood but had no luck. We spotted some barbed-wire stakes just over the top and went out to pull a few up and could see where several dead Turks had been hastily dragged into a heap, oil poured on them and fired. They were only half-burnt though and the stench from them was awful. We lingered out there a little too long and a Turkish sniper got busy. Two or three bullets whistled unpleasantly close to us so we got back at the double.

Went out again on the sapping job at night, for four hours, and had a few bursts of rapid while working. We had nothing to do the following day so had another walk through the 'shambles'. Thought I might get a few souvenirs, but couldn't bring myself to touch those dead Turks. C Company, who had relieved us, sent a few bombs over at night from the Northern Barricade and one burst in the catapult, wounding five of our men. Relieved by the Hawkes early on Tuesday the 7th and went down to Rest Camp. Had a bathe in the sea, a clean change and felt A1.

We did fatigues for four days, first making winter quarters for the corps staff on the beach, second building a pier on Y beach, the third and fourth days with a sanitary squad at divisional HQ, shovelling a big stack of dry horse manure into a deep pit. Both those days were very windy and I think I swallowed nearly as much manure as I put into the pit. Anyhow, on Sunday I felt bad and thought I was going to touch for dysentery or jaundice. Both complaints were prevalent and it was pitiful to see the men with dysentery. They could hardly crawl about and had no hopes of getting sent away from the peninsula or even to field ambulance unless they were just about dying. There appeared to be absolutely no method of preventing or treating the disease in that awful place. It was a sickening sight to see the poor devils as they crawled on hands and knees to the latrines, lying there for hours, in many cases all through the night. My chum Mick Smith had had it bad, but the doctor sent him away on the Sunday. I never expected him to get better.

I felt bad on Monday, but didn't report sick as there were no fatigues on. We went over to 3rd Field Ambulance (3 FA) in the afternoon to be inoculated again for cholera. When we got back the company was being paid out and I drew 10/- (50p). What on earth they paid us for I don't know and didn't care much then. Fancy giving us 10/- in that wilderness?

I crawled down to the doctor's shop on Tuesday morning. I had a temperature of 101.2, so I suppose Jimmy Ross (that's our pet name for the doctor) thought I was ill. He excused me duty and ordered me milk diet. I didn't waste any energy thinking where I was to get the milk from. All I wanted to do was get down and sleep. Some of the chaps bought some eggs from a Greek on the beach and tried to tempt me with them but I couldn't face anything. The doctor put my complaint down as pyrexia[2] on Wednesday. Don't know what that is. The battalion went up the line after tea but I stayed down along with about fifty more sick, lame and lazy. We all had orders to report at 3 FA in the morning for treatment. There was a frightful storm all night, rain, thunder and lightning but I slept through it all. I was lying in about two inches of water in the morning and, as soon as I made to get up, all the water that had collected in my waterproof sheet – and there was at least a gallon – came down on me, drenching me through. Nothing mattered. They packed me off to the beach CCS from 3 FA and from there to the hospital ship *Valtivia*, where, thank the Lord, I was able to undress and get into a clean bed. And there I stayed until we reached Lemnos on the Saturday afternoon. I felt a bit better then and went up on deck. I had something to eat on Sunday, the first for a week and then managed a shave.

I was taken on the 21st to the 1st Canadian Field Hospital and stayed there till the 29th, receiving better attention and food than on either occasion in Egypt. There were some real jolly Canadian nurses there and I felt sorry when the time came to move to convalescent camp. Once there the hardening process commenced and I was pushed with seven more chaps into a bell tent. It certainly had floorboards but they were damned hard after

---

2. Fever of unknown origin.

a soft bed. All the other fellows in the tent were of different regiments and absolutely different natures and, although arguments got rather fierce about the merits of our respective regiments, we got on very well together. Most of our time we spent playing bridge but life there was rotten. I think that convalescent camps are instituted by GHQ solely for the purpose of making wounded and sick men so fed up that they are only too glad to rush back to the fighting. I know that my short stay in the camp had been far too long. I was put on sanitary squad fatigue from getting in camp to leaving it. The work consisted chiefly of emptying latrine buckets twice a day, and digging great pits in the hard ground to bury the contents. Quite a nice steady job for a chap who had just been dragged from the 'edge of beyond'.

I had a few letters the day before leaving convalescent camp. As a matter of fact there were forty-three and I hardly knew how to begin on them. One night, while in camp, we had a violent wind and rain storm and had to dash outside with only our shirts on. We could feel all our tent pegs giving and by the time we got outside they had given and we had to hang on like grim death. Half the camp was down by morning.

It was 15 October when I went to the RND detail camp and it was no easy job getting away from there. There was plenty of work but we had a certain amount of freedom and a little pay, so I managed a run through one or two of the villages. These half-Turks-half-Greeks were realising one of the effects of the war – easy money by fleecing the British Tommy.

I left Detail Camp on 21 October and embarked on the *Brighton*, a big minesweeper. The voyage to Cape Helles was awfully rough, waves washing right over the boat nearly the whole way. The weather seems to have broken up and I reckoned we were in for a rotten winter.

Landed at dawn on W beach and went straight to the battalion. Joined up with the same section and found them in new quarters. They were supposed to be winter quarters but the dugouts were only partly finished. All the camp was laid out on proper lines and all work carried out under supervision of the engineers. Dugouts were twelve feet long, six feet wide and four feet deep, and we were to have sheets of iron to put on the top. I wonder! No one was allowed to walk about on top as we had five-feet trenches connecting up all the dugouts and lines. The Turk might know we were here if he saw us walking about.

Just a few words about the section. Captain Pilgrim in charge, a real decent chap and a first reinforcement. He was wounded pretty badly in their little stunt on 25 June and had only lately rejoined.

Private Daniels, long-service marine and just reverted from corporal. He had just done seven days' field punishment and couldn't get over it. He got wrong with Major Tetley over some Turkish binoculars and of course went under. He was talking about getting back on the signal staff again and good luck to him. We all hoped he would get back; he always had a moan on.

There were Jock Baird and Tommy Barlow, old chums, and a bird by the name of Clayton. All the chaps nicknamed him Kelly and he was the dirtiest specimen of a marine that I had ever struck. He was lousy. They say a chap is never really lousy till they come out of his lace holes. Kelly was beyond that. He made me shudder when he came near me. He was one of the original Plymouths and was badly bayoneted in the scramble to get off the peninsula on 26 April. The back of his neck was covered in wounds, some of which kept discharging, owing, I supposed, to the filthy state in which he kept himself.

I shook down alright with them all and they shared rations and parcels for the first day. They said it was a lucky dugout for parcels and hoped now it would be more lucky.

It rained all the first day and my new WP sheet came in handy. It kept the dugout fairly dry.

Up at 6.30 next morning, improving dugouts and drains. At it till noon, then from 1.30 to 6.30 on fatigues at the bomb school at the beach. We only had two shells over all day and they pitched about ten yards from our line. About ten men were leaving the battalion every day through sickness, some of them just worked to death. It was nothing but dig from getting up to getting down. Our new CO, Colonel Hutchinson seemed keen on it. If we weren't digging our own camp, we were doing for divisional HQ or brigade HQ.

We were all inoculated on the 26th for cholera and the following day went up the line. I was let in for the section as Corporal Daniels had picked up his two stripes and had rejoined his signal section (for which Allah be praised). A platoon of London Fusiliers was attached to our company for instruction in the line. As they were unable to bring their big sisters with them from Malta (where they had been since 14 August) we had to carry their blankets, fetch them water, let them have our funk-holes to sleep in, and carry them about generally.

We were filling sandbags all the first morning, in the M Barricade and revetting fresh traverses in the F line. Told off for duty in Sap 9 at night. This was the new firing line and ran from N[orth] Barricade to the Manchesters on our left. This was the little sap that Mick Smith and I worked in before I was bad. It was a fine trench now but awfully near the Turks, only about sixty yards in some places. We had a new chap with us, Sergeant Jeffries, a pre-war Bisley man and crack shot of Plymouth Division. He arrived with two rifles, one fitted with telescopic sights for fine sniping. He came in Sap 9 the first morning, got on the fire-step and took a few pot shots at nothing in particular. A good shot he may have been, but he had a lot to learn about the kind of shooting that was done out there. It's a case of one round, one position. It was about his fourth shot and as soon as he had pressed the trigger his hat flew off. One of Johnny's fairly decent shots had beaten him. The bullet went clean through the front and back of his cap, taking with it a few of Jeffries' remaining hairs. He never sniped from Sap 9 again.

We had a crazy way of working things at night, Captain Gowney's idea again. Everybody did half an hour on watch, and was down half an hour, and every man during his half hour on watch had to fire at least five rounds. Most of the bullets, from the sound of them, would just about hit the top of Achi Baba, about two miles away. Usually the half hour up would seem like hours, our heads nodding, our eyes half closed and our minds a complete blank. Had it not been for the five rounds we had to fire we should have gone to sleep standing up.

The half hour down went like a flash. We no sooner appeared to drop off than our opposite number was shaking us, 'your turn up'. 'Go on, I've only just got down,' we would say. Sometimes it would need the corporal or sergeant on watch to induce some of the fellows to get up. They were awfully long nights too, and it was frightfully cold, especially the hour before the dawn and 'stand to'.

We had a Sergeant Major Cutcher in charge of our platoon, and a dizzier old bird I've never struck. He just daren't put his head above the top and he went off something alarming at me for looking over the top without using the periscope.

We went down to the reserves on the Friday afternoon and at night went out digging a new trench. It was all top work and the whole time bullets were whizzing by us or going plop, into the ground by us. No one was hit. The whole area of ground that we were working on was littered with dead men, and we had to move several of them before we could get on with the work. All sorts were there, Scotties, English, Indians and Turks. One chap we moved was a major. Gowney got another brilliant idea: we were to have a big party out, collect all these dead and burn them with some sprayers and chemical stuff. One party did go out, but all they collected was souvenirs. As soon as they tried to lift the dead they dropped to pieces.

Johnny shelled our line pretty heavily on 31 October. He had got some 4-inch howitzers by then and was getting pretty accurate with them. We moved to Sap 8 on 1 November. It was very decent there, and about 150 yards from the Turk. A dead man was lying just in front of our parapet and when Johnny kept hitting him with a bullet, which was pretty often, the stench was awful.

We had a few spasms of rapid and on Tuesday night the Turk shelled us with shrapnel and sent over a lot of bombs. Old Bob Trevot, our sanitary sergeant, woke up at 'stand to' in the supports and found out that he was wounded. A shrapnel ball had gone through his leg. Volunteers were wanted for a wiring party at night. Jock Baird and I went out with Sergeant Douglas and pulled a few coils of concertina wire out and pegged it down. Then there were a few *chevaux-de-frise* to be put into position. It was a queer sensation being out in no man's land at night with firing going on all around and lights going up suddenly from the Turks' trench. Everything was like day then and it was policy to stand still. It made me feel like dropping down for cover and you felt certain a Turk only fifty yards away had just got a fine sight on you. I expect the Turks were like most of our fellows though; as soon as a light went up, they got down.

The 1st RM Battalion put some wire out one night – just chevaux-de-frise – and never anchored them to the ground. Next morning the wire was in front of the Turks trench instead of their own. We were relieved at 5.30pm on the 3rd and went down to camp again. We had a stand-off on the first day to get cleaned up and I ran into a square number as company clerk again. There was no clerking to do, I just had to fetch the company's mail every day if there was any, serve rations out to platoons and keep the CSM's and QM Sergeant's rifles clean; they were a drunken pair, especially CSM Chapman. He came out with us in Portsmouth Battalion, as a bugler, was made corporal of the band at Port Said (where it died) and colour sergeant after Gaba Tepe. He won't get much beyond that because his best friend, Jacky Luard our old colonel, has gone west. The Hawkes had a little stunt on the Saturday night. They advanced from both barricades, but only succeeded in making headway from the Southern. From there they advanced about twenty-five yards and dug in. They had several casualties.

The weather changed again and on the Sunday it was just like summer. Terrible hot. We were served out with winter clothing. Jerkins, cardigan jackets and big waterproof capes.

Three monitors and the *Swiftsure* turned up on Sunday afternoon and bombarded behind Krithia. Some of the shells from the monitors, 12- or 14-inch, sounded just like express trains as they rushed through the air. They did kick some dust up behind the village. I felt bad all Monday and Tuesday but managed to drag myself to the battalion order board when someone told me I had been made lance corporal. I couldn't believe it at first but didn't feel very keen, only that it meant another 4d (1.5p) a day more, and that's a consideration, especially if this silly war lasts many years. I reckoned my pay now to be about 1/9d (8.5p) a day. And 6d (2.5p) a day field allowance if it materialised.

Up at 5.00am Wednesday morning, everything to be ready for moving up the line by 9. We only went as far as Eski Lines, the general reserve trench. This was a strongly-built trench, stretching right across the peninsula from one coast to the other. Everything was ankle deep in mud and it rained every bit of the day. Nothing to do until 7.30 at night when we went digging a new trench.

Rations were poor and water was scarce, and when we got water we could find no wood or heather for a fire. I felt bad all Thursday and, after returning from a ration party to the front line, I turned in. And it started raining again, and raining harder than I'd ever known it rain before. It kept up for the best part of the night and washed everybody off the fire-step. We were all walking about until dawn knee deep in water and mud. I went scrounging down the gully later in the day and found enough wood to boil a canteen of tea and one of stew. Cutcher excused me rations at night, so I turned in early and felt heaps better on the Saturday. I had to go up to the battalion sergeant major's dump at Marble Arch on the Saturday morning and on the way had a narrow escape. Three whizz-bangs came over and I bet none of them burst more than five yards from me. I got a move on then.

Heard at Brigade Dump that Kitchener had been on the peninsula and was very pleased with the troops. More heavy rain on Monday morning and I made things cheerful again.

Exactly at 3.00pm, two monitors sent over two heavy shells, two mines went up and part of 52nd Division advanced and took two lines of trenches in a place called the Vine Yard. All this with sixteen casualties, mostly wounded. The whole thing was an absolute surprise to the Turk and the Scotties were all over him before he knew there was a stunt on. All our guns opened up after that and gave the Turk no time to concentrate or re-organise for a counter-attack. This was kept up at full force for an hour and a half, but of course it wasn't all one-sided. He had some guns and he used them. He shelled Goki Lines pretty heavily and our battalion had several casualties.

More thunder and rain at night and everybody was walking about like lumps of wet mud. I was caked from head to foot with the beastly stuff. We were working hard all Tuesday trying to clear the trenches of water, but there was nowhere to run it to. There was heavy fighting in the Vine Yard all night, but in his several counter-attacks the Turk never once got beyond his own wire.

Up and about by 5.30 Wednesday morning getting things ready for moving down. Most of the way down the CT we were over the knees in water. We drifted back to the same camp that we had left and found it in a state of flood. Most of the dugouts were dry, but the connecting trenches were a foot deep in water. We rigged our WP sheets over the dugouts in case the weather changed and we had some rain. Rain it did, and the water gradually came in through the trench and crept up round our feet as we lay down. It came in through the top and down the sides and we were jolly soon washed out and were walking about to keep warm. What a hole in winter! I wonder what happened to our iron sheets for the dug-outs? Somebody said that the ship that was bringing them out had been torpedoed in the Mediterranean. My section was down to five including myself.

We did nothing all Thursday but clear our dugouts and drains and try to make them a little more waterproof. We had no mail up that day. The sea was so rough in the night, it washed the pier away from W beach.

All the company went over to 1 FA on Friday to be fumigated, but when we got there they were unable to put us through. If we liked we could take all our clothes off and put them through the steaming arrangement. There they had to stop for thirty to forty minutes and in the meantime we were stood outside with absolutely nothing on and November too. Very few availed themselves of the generous offer, but were content to put in two blankets which we had taken with us.

Somebody who knew wrote an article about the winter in Gallipoli. 'Usually,' it said, 'it is very mild, with some rain but very little snow. Not at all severe, but similar to those experienced in the South of France and Italy.' We had already had *some* rain and over the way we can see the island of Samothraki with its great mountain, the top of which was already snow covered.

Three men were wounded in the camp on Saturday night by stray rifle bullets (Turkish) and two more on Sunday night, one of them being Corporal Daniels. For some reason, no doubt a good one for himself, he refused to leave the battalion and was content to put up with the crude attentions of our sick-bay. One chap in the next dugout was shot through the arm and another, a little farther away, through the nose. Those bullets must have come at least four miles. The Turks bombarded our trenches heavily on Sunday morning and followed it by an infantry attack which fizzled out at his own barbed wire. We heard on the Monday that they had lost about 800 men in that attack and gained nothing.

The Turks tried every day to get at two of our 6-inch guns just on the left of our camp, but usually managed to drop their shells amongst us. Up the line again on Wednesday 24 November. Our platoon was to work the Northern Barricade. The bombers under Corporal Grindy worked a catapult from there and sent over bombs. These were made on the beach, from jam tins, nails, bits of barbed wire and ammonal, with a six-second length of time fuse. Sometimes they worked alright and the bombs got over into the Turks' trenches and sometimes they didn't work. This was the case on the Thursday morning. I was in North Face, just opposite the little entrance to the Barricade, and had watched Grindy send over a few bombs. Captain

Gowney was there, Cutcher was there (which was surprising) and Sergeant Major Chapman was there along with a few more. All at once there was a rush for the entrance. Cutcher got there first but fell over himself and Chapman dropped on top of him, completely blocking up the entrance. I heard a bomb go off in the barricade, but no one was hurt. It seems the bomb left the catapult but struck the parapet and instead of going over the top dropped back into our trench and exploded. There was a repetition of this about an hour after, only Cutcher wasn't there. I think he'd gone to change. This time the bomb didn't leave the catapult and no one noticed it but Holt, the bomber. He told Grindy, who just nipped the fuse with his fingers. No doubt he saved some lives by doing that. (Grindy afterwards received the Conspicuous Gallantry Medal for that bit of work.)

Company cooks were up the line with us this time with dixies and a good supply of wood, and all our tea and food was cooked for us. We were not allowed to light fires in the firing line.

The Turks were busy at night putting out wire and building a machine gun emplacement. We had quite a lively night trying to hit a few. Two more chaps joined up with my section. Both 'Birds' – Houlet, a jailbird and Griggs, a Yank. Houlet fired at least 200 rounds at those Turks and all through his watches he kept calling to me, 'Corporal, I can see a blurry Turk.' It was no use telling him that what he could see were our own wire stakes. Everybody saw Turks advancing until they'd been up a few times. His last half hour up before 'stand to' he let off a yell and dropped off the step. He swore he was hit – and he could swear too – and he was hit. One of the other chaps, I think it was Jock Baird, had thrown a lump of shrapnel at him.

As soon as it got light the bombers got on to his emplacement and knocked it flat. He had rigged an artillery ranging flag up just opposite us and we had a good hour's sport shooting it to bits.

Down to Chelmsford Street in support at 1.30 pm. Had a most awful night, thunder and heavy rain and afterwards a wind storm that nearly blew us out of the trenches. Our capes came in jolly handy. They were the only means of shelter that we had. I was on patrol round the supports and up to the front line most of the night but I enjoyed the whole storm. I felt better than I had done for weeks, and trudging knee deep through the sloppy mud was no hardship.

Saturday was a decent day but awfully cold and about 8.00pm it commenced snowing and went at it hard until it was a foot deep; then it froze. No one could sleep at night, it was so bitterly cold and most of the fellows had to keep walking about to keep warm. It was awful for those on watch on the fire-step. We had to relieve them every twenty minutes, otherwise they would have been frozen stiff. I was on the same patrol again and when I reached the line found that none of the chaps could use their rifles. The oil on the bolts had frozen and locked the rifles. I expect Johnny was in the same plight, so it wouldn't matter much.

Somebody said it had been fifty years since it snowed there before Christmas. It was freezing keen all Sunday and lots of our fellows went away with frostbite. One young lad in No.2 Platoon took off his shoes and stockings and started running up and down the trench in his bare feet. He was taken away that day and by the time he had got to Malta had lost both his feet.

Rations were very poor that time up the line. We got tea and stew, but it isn't like being able to make your own tea. With that arrangement we only got tea twice a day; with our own method we always had a canteen on the go.

All supplies of water were frozen up except the engineers' well in the gully, and that's a nice old tramp. Up in Sap 9 again on Monday morning. I had a new chum now, Billy Hurrell from Woodhouse, and quite a decent chap. He was a first reinforcement and was badly wounded in the back in their stunt. He was now doing runner to old Cutcher. Charlie Hamilton was cooking for Cutcher and we all three got on jolly well together. There was always a drop of real tea ready and we often managed a decent feed out of old Cutcher's rations. One or two shells were quite sufficient to put him past his meals.

Plenty of whizz-bangs on our trench and north face on Monday. The buzz came round that Turkey wanted peace, but it took a lot of swallowing. He had more guns by then than he ever had and was making good use of them. There wasn't much actual fighting and we were pretty sick of things by Wednesday. The most interesting thing that happened was a Turk singing every morning from the trench opposite the Northern Barricade. He had a lovely voice. We used to give him a cheer when he'd finished, but he would never oblige with an encore. Bob Hacking, an Oldham fellow, obliged twice with a song in return but we never got any appreciation from Abdulla, as we named the Turk.

We were relieved on the Wednesday and went down to camp again and started the next day down on five hours digging. Most of the digging was done for the sake of keeping us occupied. Having lost or given away their cap-badges, most of the fellows drew a crossed pick and spade in blue pencil on their caps which led to a Divisional Order that 'practice of disfiguring the uniform with indelible ink must cease forthwith'. A big bombardment started on 4 December on the left of the line, monitors, cruisers and destroyers taking part and about twenty land mines were exploded. Very little was done by the infantry, however and the whole thing died away about 5.00pm.

On work in the battalion area on Sunday, each man with a double task; dig 108 cubic feet in hard brittle clay. It was a most awful job, especially on the rations we had been having lately. Bread twice a week and then a pound loaf between five or six men, biscuits, and not many – five days – and fresh meat, three days. Even the apricot jam was being knocked off and some of the fellows were scrounging round trying to find some of the stuff we had slung away in the summer. Every day in the hot weather we got apricot jam, and every day we slung it as far as we could sling it. Sometimes it would run a pound tin per man. Now we were lucky to get one between the section three times a week.

I watched a curious experiment after tea on the 7th. Two destroyers were cruising about off Y beach and sending off clouds of thick black smoke. It looked almost solid as it left the funnels. This gradually drifted right across the peninsula and moved slowly towards Achi Baba until not a scrap of the hill could be seen. We heard that day that the next time up the line we were to take over the old July sector up Achi Baba nullah and relieve the French Senegalese troops who were leaving the peninsula. We went up on 10 December and our company stayed in supports. A small stream flowed down the nullah just by the right of our sector and over it the engineers had put a wooden bridge with a five-foot wall of sandbags towards the front line.

The firing line was similar too but the nullah was deeper there. There were still numbers of Turkish dead about, and in the stream just by was the hand of one, shot or cut off clean by the wrist. We used the stream for washing and sometimes for drinking and cooking. The Lord knows what came down it from the Turkish trenches.

A change for dinner on the Saturday – steak and chips cooked in butter. Real butter too, not marg. Billy and I went with Cutcher after dinner up to the front line to look over the sector we would occupy when we moved up. In places the line was only forty yards away from the Turk and bombing and listening saps had been run out so that the distance in some places was only about twenty yards. There was no wire, or not enough to deter a blind man.

The Turks were now sending over some heavy shells and shelling the rest camps again every day. It was getting quite like old times, except that his stuff was much heavier and hotter. The Asiatic guns appeared to have got a new lease of life and were warming things up on the beaches. I saw a decent fight in the air on Sunday.

A Taube came over our lines flying fairly low and we opened up on it with rifles and machine guns, but without any apparent success, then one of our planes came along and chased it away, finally bringing it down in flames. Got word along about eleven on Sunday morning that the Turkish support trenches were full of troops and that they were expected to attack at noon on our sector. Everybody wished they would come as we were all bored stiff. Nothing exciting seemed to happen these days.

The attack came off alright but not on our sector; the French had all the fun and glory, what bit there was. Exactly at noon the Turkish batteries opened up on the back areas and CTs and their infantry got out over the top. And that was the Turks' share in that attack. Not one reached the French lines. The French were in readiness for them the same as we were and they opened up with rapid fire, machine guns, 75s and their big land torpedoes. Half an hour of incessant hammering and the Turkish attack fizzled completely out.

We got plenty of shrapnel after that, but I think everybody is more or less used to that now, under the cover of a trench, that is. Of course there are exceptions, Cutcher and 'Kelly' Clayton for two. We moved up to the front line at 3.00pm, when the stunt had just about died away, and our platoon took over a trench just on the left of the 'Horseshoe'. We were in a funny position, only eighty yards from the Turk but with not a sight of his trench to our front or left. There was a dip just beyond our wire and the Turk was down there. However, we had a grand view up Achi Baba nullah and could see the whole front slope of the hill about 1,500 to 2,000 yards away.

Had a good bit of sport on Tuesday. Micky Ash was on watch in my bay and all at once he called to me that he had spotted a Turk moving about up the nullah. He put me on to the spot and I told him to fire and I'd watch the shot. It brought a big dog out of a trench about 300 yards away and after it had stretched itself it walked slowly up the nullah. Micky fired fourteen rounds at it and never even made it hurry. Just as it jumped into another trench, one of our shrapnels burst behind us and Micky fell off the fire-step. It was nothing serious, just a shrapnel ball on the head. It hit his cap first and made a good old bump but didn't go inside. He went down to the doctor's shop and we expected him back any time, but he never came. (I heard afterwards that complications set in and a dose of enteric at the same time and Micky Ash nearly went under.)

About an hour after that, I was looking out for something to snipe and spotted the dog in the same place. I fired about ten shots and only succeeded in making it jump once. I think I must have hit its tail. Others were firing at it too from the Horseshoe, but it dropped safely into its trench again. We hadn't a shot in reply to all this from the Turk. I passed the time on spotting loopholes in the Turkish trenches and could always tell when I hit them by the metallic ring they gave off. No Turk took up my challenge, so after a time I got fed up with shooting at inanimate objects, and turned in for an hour's nap.

Went down into reserve at 6.45pm and our platoon manned Port Arthur Redoubt. There were plenty of good places to turn in for a sleep but no chance. It was work from going in to getting out. We were working all night on Wednesday and from 4 to 6 in the morning I took two men (Kelly Clayton and a lad called Smith) down the approach trench and starting revetting the parapets. All the work was on top, the two men filling and carrying the sandbags from about a dozen yards away and I fixing them. We had been out about an hour and were getting on fine when I heard two yells and Clayton dashed up to me yelling 'he's hit'. He tripped over a sandbag and disappeared into the trench. I shouted to him to fetch the stretcher-bearers but he got up and set off for the redoubt as fast as he could go. I looked round for Smith and was just in time to stop him falling into the trench. A stray bullet from the line had got him through the knee, smashing the bone badly and, seeing Clayton dash in, he thought the Turks were on us and so tried to get into the trench. I dressed his wound as well as I could and, just as I was getting him fairly comfortable, Cutcher and Sergeant Douglas came along and soon after we got him away with the stretcher-bearers. (The lad lost his leg in hospital later.) Kelly got strafed by Cutcher and chaffed by the lads about the way he'd got the wind up. I could quite understand how he'd got all those bayonet wounds in his neck.

We had a fine view of Krithia from the redoubt and it appeared quite near. A monitor was lying off in the Gulf of Saros on Wednesday, sending 14-inch shells right into the village. It was possible to see what a mass of ruins the village was. Not a single house remained complete, some being just heaps of charred wood and stone, others just mere skeletons of houses. The lines of windmills were badly battered and I should imagine it most unhealthy for the Turks in occupation of the place. The ground all around the place was a maze of trenches and wire. The Turk evidently intended to stick to that place as long as he could.

Digging again all night and about 11.30pm we had to take cover. The French exploded a big mine and both sides went at it ding-dong for the crater. Shrapnel and bullets flew about and we got quite a lot of both. This lasted about an hour and when it was over we carried on digging.

This redoubt had been built in case we were pushed back at any time. Several had been constructed across the peninsula and manning them would enable the troops from the firing line to retreat in an orderly manner with an opportunity to construct another line of defence. Our redoubt was about twenty yards square and consisted of a broad fire trench on all four sides, thus obtaining an all-round field of fire. It was well wired towards the front and flanks and the only entrance was by the trench leading from the left. This trench was protected by a loophole in the redoubt which commanded a stretch of straight trench for twenty-five yards. The chunk of earth in the middle of the redoubt was cut into three gun positions but were not occupied, except by Cutcher and Sergeant Douglas for sleeping quarters.

Chapter Eight

December 1915 – The Evacuation

We heard on 16 December that our troops had evacuated the Suvla district. That was a nasty smack for us. Heard too that the Turks had given us seven days to clear a big field ambulance from above W beach as they intended bombarding. Very sporting of them. Up in the firing line again by 6.30pm and manning a part of the Horseshoe fifty yards from the Turk. We had orders to keep a strict watch as the Turks had been observed massing for an attack in that sector.

The French were reported to be leaving the peninsula and we were to take over their line and rest camp. Troops appeared to be getting fairly thin in numbers this side of our line. The Turks in our sector got it hot on Saturday. Our 10-inch guns and heavy trench mortars bumped them all morning. I reckoned that would upset his plans for an attack.

Everyone felt pretty well done up. I think it was the worst time we had had for sleep. It was dig or hump rations from going up to getting relieved. Everybody felt thankful when the 2nd Londons came wandering up about 7.00pm. They were only two hours late, but they came. We all collapsed on reaching our camp. The journey down had been awful. Heard that the Scotties were attacking again the following day, bombardment to start at 2.00pm and every gun to fire 300 rounds.

Eggs and bacon for breakfast on Sunday morning. The eggs were supposed to have come off a Turkish prize but they looked like Egyptians. I was lucky and got two good ones. We were to move at 11.00pm to take over the French rest camp. Of course it was 2.00pm when we actually did move, just as all our guns opened up on the Turkish lines and Achi Baba. It was by far the finest bombardment I had witnessed since the landing. Every ship and every gun was going at it 'hell for leather' and the whole front of Achi Baba was blotted out by dust and smoke. This was kept up until 4.00pm and we heard afterwards that all our troops and nearly every gun had got safely away from Anzac.

What was going to happen to us?

I expected that, in a few days' time, we would all be swept or blown into the sea.

The Scots advanced and managed to take two trenches, H.11a and H.12a, but failed to get their real objective. The opposition was too strong. One would have imagined that after such a terrific bombardment there would be no living thing left to oppose an advance. There was so much of the ground to hit though, and a trench really takes up so little of the space, and the individual man is a mere speck and an invisible one.

To be in a bombardment though, one's feelings are entirely different to that of observation. It is as though you and your bit of trench are standing out absolutely alone like some huge landmark and that all the enemy's guns are concentrated on you and your particular trench.

We found our new dugouts fine. The French were certainly more thorough in their efforts at comfort than we were. Each dugout could accommodate a platoon and was fitted with splinter-proof roofs and shell-proof backs. Weren't they busy!

Lice, big fat white ones, continually dropped on us from the roof and walls, and if there's one kind of louse that I particularly detest more than another, it's a white one. This camp was occupied before us by French colonial troops and I didn't think they were very clean at the best of times. All the French troops except some artillery were leaving the peninsula in a few days' time.

On Tuesday we had a heavy rainstorm which carried on all night and swamped the whole camp. Poor old Cutcher was washed out of his little place and, later on, the whole thing collapsed, burying all his gear. He seemed absolutely out of place and quite unable to adapt himself to his surroundings. The troops up on the line were having a lively time by the sound of things. The Turk was sending over some great black shells, and, for down in the rest camps he had a special thing, something specially invented to put the wind up hardened troops. I suppose the Turk knew that, after a time, troops lose all fear of shrapnel, providing of course that we had cover handy, so he or the Bosch had thought out something new. This new one was like two shells in one. First, they burst in the air like an ordinary shell, then again on contact with the ground or whatever it hit. Real devilish things. One went right into one of C Company's dugouts, nearly wiping out No. 11 Platoon. Griggs had a fright on Wednesday morning. He was taking an empty dixie back to the galley when one of these things went off, part of it hitting the dixie and knocking it yards away. He came dashing back to the dugout, shaking like a leaf and nothing would induce him to go out again that day. I had the wind up for about two days but on the Thursday morning Billy Hurrell and I were outside, throwing some more earth on our roof, when two of these things burst a matter of feet away. We could feel the concussion as they burst and could hear the bits of casing as they whizzed by, but we were both safe. I lost all fear of them from then, and felt confident as I had done all the time that I should pull through alright.

On digging fatigues on Thursday morning with the engineers who are drilling and blasting rock. The Turk was sending over heavy black stuff all day, some of it unpleasantly close to us.

Promoted to full corporal on Christmas Eve, a nice present for Christmas, especially the pay part. I immediately proceeded to put myself another stripe on either shoulder strap by the aid of indelible pencil. That was where we wore our stripes. Early on in the campaign, all NCOs ripped off their stripes and became, in all outward appearance, as ordinary soldiers. By doing so they stood so many chances less of being picked off by a sniper. Later on, and when the fear of the sniper had diminished somewhat, they wished for their stripes back, but they were unobtainable in that heathen land; hence the indelible.

The Turks bombarded our trenches heavily all morning and then made a very weak-hearted attempt at an infantry attack, but our guns were waiting and immediately squashed it.

I believe Johnny was guessing all he could as to what our game was; if we were going to hit him in a new place, or clear off as we had done at Suvla and Anzac. The 29th Division came round here again from Suvla and the troops appeared to be getting thick again. We had three Taubes over all day Christmas Eve and after tea they dropped three fairly big bombs in Fleming Gully, just on our right. There were several casualties, one of our transport men being blown to bits with his three mules.

No fatigues on Christmas day. Peace and goodwill towards men. I don't think.

We had plenty of sport and games and I came off with a prize of 5/- (25p). My luck must have been in. We had a change for dinner. It should have been fresh meat but we had bully stew with dried veg and a sweet, half a pound of deadly Christmas pudding out of a tin. We were on half rations, the reason being the new adventure at Salonika. All our supply ships were being diverted to Greece instead of Turkey. We heard the cheerful news, too, that the ship that was bringing our Christmas mail and parcels had been turned back to Egypt or Mudros. A fresh batch of reinforcements were on her too, but were not allowed to land. A Taube came over and three of our planes tried to catch it but with no success. It was a sight worth watching though.

I clicked for a nice little job. Clayton was up before Captain Gowney for having a dirty rifle and when Gowney set eyes on Kelly he straightaway went off. 'Send for Corporal Askin,' he yelled. I went, 'Get two men and take Private Clayton to the nearest well and have him scrubbed.' Poor old Kelly howled but he got the scrubbing. I wouldn't touch him though. His legs were awful, one mass of septic sores where he had scratched himself. I made him report sick as soon as we got back and he got another good drubbing from Jimmy Ross.

Parade 9.15am on the 26th for the line. Captain Gowney had had a party up to the firing line to see which and what was the best method of getting up. Practically the whole way up the CT was knee deep in mud and water. He told us we could either take off our boots and stockings and roll our trousers above our knees, or put sandbags over them. The majority favoured sandbags, but I think the others were better off. It was a terrible journey and Gowney led off like a racehorse. The rear of the company didn't get up till the following morning. We had a pretty rough time leaving camp. The Turk must have spotted us as we were lined up for inspection for he shelled us heavily with those double-event HE things.

There were several casualties in the battalion and we were all fairly glad to get up the line. We were to do two days in support, first in the old Trotman Road sector. Our platoon was on the extreme right of the battalion sector, in an old Turkish trench. We had a most cheerful night for a kick off, a severe thunderstorm with a heavy downpour of rain. The rain carried on till the Monday noon and the state of the trench was something to remember forever. The mud almost dragged our boots off our feet.

I thought that I had lost all fear of shells. Those two days completely changed my views and put a fresh fear of death and mutilation into me, and in everybody else. From noon when the rain ceased to 3.00pm we were subjected to the worst bombardment that I had ever been in. Shrapnel Saturday – 1 May – was nothing compared with this three hours. It wasn't the quantity of the shells that mattered so much; it was the quality and weight.

Great big howitzer shells that came down on us at an angle of about 60 degrees and which made a noise similar to an express train dashing at full speed through a station. Every other noise was swallowed up in that great terrifying roar. Whizz-bangs kept bursting on the parapet but we never heard them and then, when these big ones burst, it was more like an earthquake and an eruption at the same time. The earth would tremble and shake and where the shell had burst a great column of earth and smoke would shoot up a hundred feet into the air. Long after they had burst, huge lumps of earth and iron casing kept whizzing down to earth at a terrific speed. There were one or two shelters in our trench capable of holding about twenty men. No. 2 Platoon had crowded into one – a mad thing to do – and one of these shells went right through the top and burst in the ground underneath, blowing the whole thing high in the air. There was a huge crater where it had been, and sheets of iron, beams of wood and boxes of ammunition were blown for scores of yards. Most of the fellows were buried, and when got out had to be taken away suffering from shellshock as well as wounds. Two men were blown to little bits. No matter who you looked at they all had fear on their faces. Some chaps who before this were apparently nerveless were now shaking with fear and everybody had a tendency to bunch together and keep moving up and down a trench. I was terrified but tried hard not to show it and if there was one thing I hated in a bombardment it was a crowd. As I heard a shell coming I got down in the bottom of the trench and turned my face towards the roar. I saw about four of those shells just before they pitched into the ground. Once after I'd seen one pitch in I saw a mass of wreckage, lumps of wood, sandbags, sheets of iron, men and parts of men go up in the air. It was in the Anson lines on our right and we heard after that fifteen men had been blown to bits in one shelter. The concussion was enough to kill anybody. Rations went begging that first day. Charlie Hamilton came along the trench with a plate full of dinner. He was asking for Cutcher, but I told him we hadn't seen him since the shelling started and it wasn't much use walking that dinner round. Even if we found Cutcher, he wouldn't want his dinner. No doubt he would be at Company HQ where the shells weren't going. Billy and I had his dinner and it was good; Charlie can cook!

Everybody started cursing the fleet and our heavy artillery for not opening. Not a shell went over from our side until 2.30. Two of our aeroplanes went over there and spotted for the heavies. The last big shell came over about 3.00pm and we began to sort things out a bit and got back a few of our good spirits.

The second fire-bay from me on the left was filled in, and some of the chaps were busy digging it into shape again. No one was underneath, luckily, but a bit farther on, where No. 2 Platoon had caught it, the trench was in a frightful state. Sheets of corrugated iron and huge logs of wood were torn to shreds and the whole place smelt of burnt chemicals and smouldering rag. Bits of uniform and equipment and broken rifles were all over the place. On what was left of the fire-step stood an old and semi-deformed man called David. He had been on watch the whole strafe and refused to be relieved. He had been blown off the step twice with the concussion and knocked off once with a huge lump of earth, but still he stuck it. Word was passed along at 3.30 to reinforce the front line as the Turk showed signs of an attack. We weren't wanted, however, and C Company, who were in the line, didn't thank us for going up. They could manage all the blurry Turks who came their way. No doubt, but they hadn't had a shell. In fact, our company was the only one in the battalion to catch those big ones. Got back to our own trench after about an hour and carried on clearing up.

Our company had had about twenty to twenty-five casualties during the afternoon. Later on we found out the apparent reason for the shelling. About twenty yards behind our trench was another very narrow, deep trench and cut off from it were covered-in places full of big French land torpedoes, demoiselles they called them. That's most likely what the Turks over at Chanak or Kilid Bahr were trying to hit. If he did hit a dump, I reckoned everyone within a hundred yards would be killed straight off.

News came along later that one of the Turks' submarines had been netted by the Fleet at the mouth of the Dardanelles.

We had another dizzy time on Tuesday. It started with a Taube flying low over our lines about 7.00am, very likely spotting for the result of the previous day's shelling. We opened up on it with our rifles but with no result. He flew about until he was ready to go. There was no interference from our planes or anti-aircraft guns.

Later on, I watched some shells from a French battery bursting behind Krithia and we heard later that they had put out two Turkish siege guns. The uppermost thought in the mind of every man in A Company was 'will he start again with those accursed shells?' Start he did and the fun commenced in our bay. We were all sitting on the fire-step eating stew – which was rather better than usual – myself, Billy, Jimmy Rimmer, Baird and Bolan. All at once a whizz-bang burst on the parapet and Bolan sprang up with a wild yell. His canteen went over the back of the trench, stew and all, and he dashed off down the trench yelling 'stretcher-bearers'. All our dinners were spoilt and the big dixie was full of dirt, and it wasn't nice dirt. Of course everybody laughed; we had to, as we always did when anything just missed us.

Presently Bolan came back looking rather shamefaced. A piece of hard earth had hit him on the back of the neck, not even making a lump. We hadn't much chance to laugh at him, because we heard one of those big devils coming. Everybody got down and said a little prayer. 'Oh God don't let this thing hit me and I'll be good for ever,' or something to that effect. The shell burst about twenty yards in front and Captain Gowney's runner, Micky, got two fair portions of casing in his ribs.

The shells came pretty thick and fast after that and the company got quite panicky. The men started, first moving to the right, then to the left, getting as far as possible from the place where the last shell burst. 'Why can't we reinforce the firing line?' chaps kept asking. No shells were dropping there. I tried to find Cutcher. I thought if he kept knocking about among his own platoon it would tend to quieten the men a bit. I knew that if many more shells came over, some of the chaps would be bolting. I couldn't find him though. Perhaps he had gone to find someone else in the firing line.

A corporal and several more men went away from No. 2 Platoon suffering from shellshock. Six more were killed in the company and eighteen wounded.

One shell pitched in the back of our parados. Everybody in the bay was down flat thinking that the next second we should all be twenty feet in the air. It was a dud and we all laughed like idiots. We heard that our chaplain, the Reverend Moore, was up at Company Headquarters burying the dead in the open behind the trench.

Everybody was thankful when we saw our aeroplanes come over about 4.00pm. About a dozen went over at once and the Turks' big guns 'piped down'. We could hear our aeroplanes shortly after, dropping bombs on the forts across the narrows I suppose.

Some of the chaps found a base belonging to one of the big shells, a great piece of steel, ten inches across, and on the bottom was stamped the British War Department's stamp and the date of manufacture. They must have been shells that were sent to Bulgaria before she turned against us. How nice to be blown up and shaken up by your own shells.

We moved up to the firing line at 6.00pm and relieved C Company. We gave them our deepest sympathy and fully thought they would need it on the morrow. C Company always were unlucky. The Turks were about 150 yards away and very lively. We had a new stunt on. From midnight to 3.00am everything in our line was silent. Not a shot or a light to be fired and if anybody wanted to sneeze or cough they must do it in a sandbag or go down to the CT.

The Turk was very lively at first, then he too grew quiet and we could see the dim shadowy forms of his patrols as they walked up and down. They kept very near to their own wire and no one ventured very near to our trench. Even had they done so we would not have fired. Only in case of an attack in force were we to fire. Three o'clock came and Gowney came with it: 'Every man in A Company up on the fire-step and fire five rounds rapid.' That woke Johnny up with a vengeance and he replied with rapid and bombs. When that had died away, he was on with something else. Gowney was certainly thorough in his efforts to annoy and harass the Turk.

He told me to fetch a pick and a shovel and had Billy and me tapping this shovel with the pick. The shovel had to be as far over the parapet as we could get it, so, of course, there were plenty of us to hit. Cutcher was there but he watched us from the bottom. Gowney said, 'Perhaps they'll think it's a wiring party.' Perhaps they did. Anyhow, they soon shifted us and our pick and shovel. Bullets were flying past, making that wicked *zipp*, that tells you they have missed, but not by much. Even Gowney thought it was policy to get down.

Saw a Taube brought down on Wednesday morning and, just before noon, both sides opened up on the back areas with artillery.

The Turk never sent a shell anywhere near C Company in support. Stood to arms at 12.45. Two mines were exploded on the left and the Scotties advanced again. We could see plenty of movement in the Turks' trenches opposite to our own. We could see their bayonets flashing over the top and there appeared to be a general move to the left, or to his right.

We had a little spasm at night in our sector. Johnny slung quite a lot of bombs over and opened up with rapid fire several times. We were silent again from 1 to 3.30am. It was awfully weird to be stuck in that trench in such utter silence.

Captain Gowney came round again during my watch and told me to follow him round. He questioned all the sentries and everything was alright until he came to a lad called King. Poor kid, he'd been wounded twice and this was his first time up since coming back from hospital, and those two days in support had shaken him up badly. He was shivering like a leaf when we got up to him and his head was sunk onto his chest. He was making no attempt to keep watch and evidently hadn't heard us as we came along. Gowney got on the step alongside him and watched him for about half a minute without speaking. Then all at once he hit him on the jaw and knocked him into the bottom of the trench. 'I'll give you go to sleep on watch,' he yapped. Poor old King thought the Turks had come. He got it the better way though. It was either that or a court martial, and several chaps had been sentenced to be shot for being asleep whilst on watch.

Just before the silent hours ended, Gowney came along again. He had thought of two fresh numbers. One was to send a French *demoiselle* over and the other to imitate a machine gun with all the rifles of the company. All this on the stroke of 3.30. The *demoiselle* was almost disastrous to us. It only went ten yards over our parapet and exploded with a terrific roar. At the same time the man on the right of our company – poor old King again – had to fire one round. The man on his left had to fire almost immediately and so on to the left of the company. David was quite delighted with us all and with the effect it had on the Turk. He immediately sent up scores of lights, red, white and green, and opened up rapid.

We got official news on 30 December that IX Army Corps – that is, the people from Suvla and Anzac – would relieve VIII Corps – us – in a few days' time. Bunkum!

IX Army Corps that relieves us will be comprised of Turks from around Achi Baba, and if we don't clear soon he will push us off. Friday was a quiet day and we were relieved at 6.00pm by D Company, and went down in reserve. The CTs were in a shocking state, still up to the knees in mud and more stickier mud than we've had before.

We had a frightful time in Trotman Road, shelled the whole day and covered in dirt several times. Relieved at 6.00pm and set off for rest camp at Cypress Grove. I think that trip down was the most awful I've ever experienced. Soon after starting, the mud dragged one of my sandbag leggings down over my boot, and I could neither pull it off nor cut it. It soon got like a ton weight dragging behind in the mud, and every now and again the man behind me kept treading on it. Just before I got to the bottom of the CT, I trod on the chap's sandbags in front of me. He was in a like plight to myself. Down I went, flop into about eighteen inches of mud, and about three of the chaps trod on me before I could get up. What a relief when we reached Sandbag Corner and got our feet on to a fairly clean track.

We passed a battalion of the HLI going up the line. 'Lucky devils', some of them shouted, 'you're going straight off the peninsula.' I believe they really thought we were. Farther down we passed some more chaps who looked fairly new. 'Who are you?' someone shouted. 'Nine Army Corps' came back, but with it came a laugh that put 'blotto' to the truth. What a New Year's Day! Found out when we reached camp that all our field kitchens were embarked and all our transport gone. We seemed all alone on the peninsula. Practically all the French troops had gone and about 10,000 of our own troops had already left, including most of the artillery.

Had a fairly quiet day on the Sunday, getting or trying to get clean.

Had to go to ration party at night up to the front line. Picked up the rations in bags at Eski Line and had to take them to the 1st Battalion. The route was quite new to all of us and when we struck the CT it took us right along the cliffs overlooking the narrows. Right ahead we could see a

powerful searchlight playing from Chanak which at times flashed right on to
us, almost blinding us with its powerful glare. It seemed awfully weird to me
as we neared the firing line; everything was still, except for an occasional rifle
shot from the Turk. It was our silent hours, and the darkness and silence was
so intense it could almost be felt. That, and the knowledge of how few troops
were on there and how little support we had, fairly gave me the impression
that we were 'up in the air'. Just below us on the right were the waters of
the Dardanelles, behind us was the Aegean and barely three miles away on
our left was the Gulf of Saros. Water all round, except in front where only
a matter of 300 yards or so away were thousands of Turks eager to smash
us before we could slink away. All we had to prevent them smashing us and
chasing us into the sea were a few battalions of weary, fed-up troops where
the other day we had divisions. In support were a few worn-out guns. How
many of us would get off?

We reached the support trench which ran along the top of a steep hill,
and down below in the valley was the firing line. Just across on another hill
was the Turks' firing line, easily discernible when he sent up a light. There
wasn't a soul in our support line and when we got down into the firing line
found about one man on watch every twenty yards or so. In places, the trench
consisted of a barricade of stones in which were hundreds of places where a
bullet could come through. The officer of the watch passed us. 'Drop your
rations in the next bay,' he said, 'and clear out of this without making a row.'
One of the chaps told us that their company had only been there for two days
and had already had over twenty casualties. The French had been there for
four months before them and had only had about four men wounded.

In the daytime each side could see the other moving about and before the
1st Battalion took over there was a sort of mutual arrangement between the
French and the Turks: 'Don't shoot at us and we won't shoot at you.' Our
chaps soon upset that arrangement and although our chaps were dressed as
Frenchmen I don't suppose it took the Turks in. We got out over the back
of the support trench and went back to camp, again without touching the
coast. Just on top above the support trench we passed a party of engineers
laying landmines. They were busy too in the FL and supports, setting traps
in the shape of huge trench mortar bombs placed gingerly on top of shelter

doors. Orders to move up to Eski Lines on the Monday afternoon in case of anything happening in front and to be handy for rations.

Our platoon was housed comfortably in a big shelter and for two days we had the time of our lives. Rations were in abundance. There was a big dump just below the trench with no one in charge except the RSM of 1 RM and he didn't care what we took, so long as we didn't interfere with his battalion rations. We had three braziers in that shelter with coal fires burning day and night. Tea was mashed every half hour. We had a chest of tea, a few sides of bacon, bags of sugar, cheese and milk and several cases of the best jam, hot plum and apples, and not ticklers but the best makes of strawberry, damson and blackcurrant, a sure sign that the ASC and most of the staff had left.

Just below us in a deep gully was a pond and we went down in the afternoon for a wash and a swim. The Turk was continually dropping big shells in the gully though and it wasn't the safest of places.

On Tuesday night all our company under Captain Gowney went on the headland above Morts Bay and did about four hours wiring in front of De Tott's battery. We put out scores of barbed-wire coils and about sixty coils of French concertina wire. I couldn't imagine the intention; perhaps it was to delay the Turk in pursuit or to divert him into a mined road, or perhaps it was to use up some of the surplus gear and break up our idea of a picnic.

Went down to Cypress Grove again on the 5th about 6.00pm. We fell in outside Eski Lines about 5.00pm and called the roll. Houlet was missing and no one knew where he was, nor had anybody seen him for hours. Gowney fumed. Said he'd see him when he turned up. We set off without him at the finish and he landed down at camp about midnight loaded with souvenirs of all descriptions. He had been with a few French artillerymen who had been left with an 8-inch howitzer and had managed to touch them for these things.

Direction boards were up all over the place bearing an arrow and the words 'This way down'. At certain places in the CTs chevaux-de-frise were placed in readiness, so that when the last man was down they could be pulled into position to delay the Turks and to make him take to the open. The work of destruction had begun and fatigue parties were put to destroying small dumps of stores. One party I saw were ripping up leather jackets, waterproof capes and clothing of all kinds. Our quartermaster did what to some of the fellows was an unforgivable act, in fact a deadly sin. He had all the rum emptied into a ditch. Not a drop was served out, not a drop saved, and a crowd of old marines gathered round, cursing as they watched the precious fluid soaking into the ground.

We had a good loot on the Thursday morning in the ASC dump. Great stacks of stuff were still there. Hundreds of boxes of bacon and hams, milk, jam, bully and butter etc. The milk interested us most. One tin of Ideal mixed with half a tin of Nestlé's made a lively drink. Most of the chaps were sick afterwards. Hundreds of horses and mules had been shot and left lying where they had dropped. Limbers and GS wagons were smashed to bits, and the whole area looked in a state of utter chaos.

At dusk the whole battalion went up to the hill above V, X and W beaches and commenced digging a new trench. We dug our way on this place and were having to dig it off again. We were up there from 6.30 to midnight and got down about three feet. No wiring was attempted, except on the road from Sedd-el-Bahr to Krithia. We put a couple of chevaux-de-frise in readiness for when the last troops were down. Had another good loot on the Friday, but picked up nothing of value.

All the big dumps were mined ready to go up. Orders came round in the afternoon to stand by in camp and destroy everything that had to be left. The Turk was bombarding our line all morning with heavy black stuff and, just after dinner, he let off two mines, shook his bayonets over the trench but only attacked the Staffords on the extreme left. I don't think half a dozen Turks reached our front line, most of them never even passing their own wire. The Turks' courage is certainly not in proportion to his military strength.

Two monitors and a few destroyers were lying off in the Gulf of Saros and played the deuce with Johnny until dusk.

We went up to the new trench again after tea and stayed till midnight, finishing all we had to do at it. It was only a rough trench, no fire-step or sandbag parapet, but we only had to hold it until the troops from the line had passed through. On Saturday 8 January we received orders to destroy the camp. We obeyed that order thoroughly. Tins of jam and milk were opened and spread all over the floors of our dugouts. Every tin of eatables was punctured and all the roofs of the dugouts were knocked in. In fact everything was messed up a treat. During the last week we buried hundreds of boxes of SAA. After dinner, several sergeants and corporals went down to Sedd-el-Bahr to see where we were to embark and where we were to rendezvous in the village. Everything on V beach was a wreck. Hundreds of wagons and ammunition limbers had been smashed to bits, and several motor ambulances were lying about shattered.

Orders at 6.00pm to get rigged ready for moving and we were all in position at 7.00pm in the new trench. Patrols were sent out to the front and a piquet was posted on the road about ten yards to the right of where I was. All troops embarking from V beach would pass down that road.

The last of the guns went down about 8.00pm. Mr Adamson was in charge of the piquet, ably assisted by Sergeant Douglas. Old Douglas couldn't speak French though, and when he got a mouthful of French in reply to his challenge he had to call on Mr Adamson. 'Qui est la?' he roared. 'Les artilleurs français, monsieur," came back. Then came the checking of horses and men and on they rumbled, giving us as they passed several loaves of French bread. We hadn't seen bread for a fortnight.

The Asiatic guns were busy the whole time, one big gun playing just in front of our trench and another battery shelling the *River Clyde* and V beach. Two heavy guns from behind Krithia were shelling W beach. We could see the flash of the Asiatic guns as they fired and a bugler was placed on the top of the fort at Cape Helles to give warning at every flash. The shell could be heard in its thirty-second flight over the water, growing from a faint whine into a deafening crescendo. Then came the explosion of the shell; it would burst harmlessly in the sea and sometimes fall with a shattering crash in the heaps of wreckage that littered the beach.

We had reports up from the beach that the sea was awfully rough and that embarkation was slow and difficult. All embarkation had been stopped from Y beach as the piers had been washed away and, later, the same thing happened at W beach. About 11.30 all the troops were diverted to V beach. Parties from the front trenches kept passing down the road and we could hear the sharp challenge of the sentry as they approached. We kept wondering, 'Who is it this time, our chaps or the Turks?' and 'How long will the Turk be before he's down here?'

All attachments were in parties of a hundred, and they had all to be numbered and checked before passing the piquet. We got word along about one o'clock that the last party had passed through and we knew then that the next man who came along would be a Turk. Long after our line was deserted, Very lights kept going up, rifle shots went off and occasionally we should hear a sharp burst of rapid. All these from our now deserted trench.

Of course, everybody was on the lookout and I think everybody's nerves were all on edge. It was a weird anxious time. No end of chaps could see Turks advancing, there were plenty of posts and small trees that could be mistaken for men if stared at long enough in the dark. Houlet was very persistent. He knew he could see a man. 'Alright,' we said, 'fetch him in.' Griggs said he'd go with him and they got over the top. They had got about ten yards when one of the big shells dropped about 200 yards in front. Griggs jumped in the trench, Houlet fell in and lay where he fell until it was time to move. We got orders about 2.30am to call in the patrol and piquet and to file out of the trench and make our way down to the rendezvous in the village. No one spoke a word as we walked down, no one felt like speaking or listening to speech. We kept turning round to the line, watching for some signal from the Turk that he had missed us. Everything was as usual though. Just a few lights going up from either side. We uncharged our magazines in the village and formed up as a battalion en masse. Colonel Hutchinson gave an order. It must have been to retire because D Company led off and were all embarked before we had reached the beach.

For reasons of safety the *River Clyde* was not being used as a pier. Most of the shells that had come over had been directed at her, so they were using an old French battleship as the embarkation pier. The Asiatic guns had slowed down a little as we reached the beach, the reason being fairly obvious. Two of our monitors were blazing away with 14-inch guns and I expect Johnny had taken cover.

It was 3.30am on 9 January 1916 when our platoon left the peninsula, the last platoon of the last battalion to leave Gallipoli. All we left behind was the demolition party. I can vouch for that, for as we went up the gangway of the old French ship the officer in charge of affairs yelled to someone on shore, 'How many more on shore now?' The answer came back, 'Only the demolition party, Sir.' Just on our left we could see the dark hulk of the

River Clyde and could almost see in one's imagination the ghosts of those dead Dublins and Munsters watching us with derisive grins on their faces as we slunk away.

We were a miserable lot, cold, hungry and tired, to say nothing of being utterly fed up. No one was pleased at the thought of going away as we were going. We fought our way on, we ought to have fought it off. I think if volunteers had been asked for, for some final stunt, not one of our chaps would have refused. As I went up the gangway of the battleship I noticed somebody in front struggling with a motorbike. All at once a nasty seafaring voice broke out, 'Throw that dammed thing overboard' and 'get through this ship.' And over it went.

We passed through the ship and boarded HMS *Grasshopper*, a destroyer. There were hundreds packed on her and the only room we could find was right outboard on the starboard side. I could make out Captain Gowney, Cutcher, Mr Mitchell, Chapman and a few more of the leading lights stowed away fairly comfortably between the funnels.

Charlie Hamilton and Billy Hurrell were with me and we decided to drop our gear and sit on it. It was almost an impossible task to do, but we managed it and, just as we got down, the ship shoved off and we left Gallipoli with its thousands of dead to the Turk. As we got about 400 yards from the shore a terrific explosion occurred on V beach. The demolition party had done their work. With that, and the enormous blaze that followed, all the warships standing by opened up. They all had something definite to shell: dumps and camps, trenches and dugouts, both ours and the Turks. We heard as we got on the destroyer that the Turks were already on Y beach and one of our ships had shelled them. Fires broke out all over the place and very soon the whole place was light as day, casting a ruddy glow over the rough surging sea.

We soon realised what life on a destroyer must be. Every few minutes a huge sea would sweep the boat from end to end, making us hang on to anything like grim death. Only a yard separated me from the side of the ship and there was nothing more solid between the sea and me than a steel rope that ran round the ship. We found it impossible to sit down and as soon as we stood up our gear was washed away. I managed to keep hold of my rifle. It acted as a support. We kept wondering where they were taking us and when we should get there. They took us nowhere in particular but up and down the coast of Gallipoli.

The fires on shore were visible the whole time, but nobody was in the least interested. We were all soaked, of course, and starved through and through. About 4.30am cocoa made its appearance on deck, but it was kept strictly to the regions of the funnels. I don't think I ever remember such a cold, long and miserable hour as the one before the dawn on the 9th. Just as dawn broke we steamed into the harbour at Imbros where the water was calm and still. The place was crowded with ships and our floating palace took us alongside HMS *Mars*, an old battleship. We were transferred to her and lushed up immediately with hot tea and biscuits.

I found my gear right astern of the destroyer but Charlie had lost everything and so had several more of the chaps. A nine-month collection of souvenirs had gone to Davy Jones. Charlie knew his way about a ship so we followed him and he took us down below where it was hot and we dried in about half an hour. It was impossible for me to sleep. I felt after a time that if I didn't get out of it into the fresh air I should have about as much nature left in me as a tin of bully.

Everywhere I went on that ship I saw fellows lying about absolutely dead to everything about them. All sorts of regiments were represented onboard and it was a proper scrap to get a wash and nearly a riot when the canteen opened. All they had when they did open were tins of rabbit and biscuits. We ate two tins and a score or so of biscuits between the three of us and then turned in on an iron hatch cover in the NOs' quarters astern.

We left Imbros at 5.30pm in company of a monitor and arrived once again in Mudros, at dawn next morning.

Chapter Nine

10 January 1916 – Mudros

L anded at 1.00pm and marched to a canvas camp that had been erected for us. Base parties, returned sick and wounded, reinforcements, scroungers and swingers of the lead were awaiting us in large numbers. The number of NCOs that had sprung up from apparently nowhere was surprising. We had Sergeant Owen back again, but looked like losing old Douglas who had swelled to about three times his usual size through dropsy or some such thing.

Tuesday was supposed to be a 'stand-off' but, as we happened to be duty platoon of the duty company, it didn't affect us much. It was graft from Reveille to Lights Out, lumping rations, mails and putting up more tents and marquees. Some 'stand-off'.

We had a rough week. Three nights we were almost washed and blown out of our camp. It could rain out there. We were lumping mail from the beach for two days. I don't think there has ever been such a collection before of mail. The mail for the whole division had been dumped there since a week before Christmas. Nearly everybody had a parcel, some two or three, but everything that could go bad was rotten. Scores of bags of parcels had been in the sea and the whole of it had been left lying about in the open.

The 15th was a bitterly cold day with a cutting wind. Kelly Clayton was up before Gowney again for something. A dirty shirt I think it was. Poor old Kelly caught it hot again. I had to take him down to the beach, have him stripped and scrubbed in the sea. It nearly froze me stiff, even with my greatcoat on, but Kelly had to go in. Neither of my two men would touch him; he was too filthy for words and covered with sores where he had scratched himself.

A big party went on leave to England about two days after, Gowney being amongst them. Men who had spent longest on the peninsula were given preference and we poor devils who had been wounded through not shirking our bit were left on the rotten island. Our noble Sergeant Major Chapman went. So did Milne and several more whose attempts at duty got so far as drinking the rum of we poor fools who yelled and shouted and charged. However, we had a fairly decent time on the island drawing a fair amount of money, which went like water in the villages, and having plenty of concerts and football. We stayed under canvas about ten days then moved into hutments about half a mile from the village of Portiano.

Word came round on the 26th that leave to Malta was to be granted, but very few of the eligible men would volunteer. It was perhaps in lieu of English leave. I was confirmed as corporal on the 27th and on the following day had my notice drawn to orders again, where I saw that I had reverted to private again, owing, it said, to over-establishment. That in plain language meant that so many NCOs who had been holding square numbers had come back now that the fighting was over that we poor devils who had fought for our promotion had to stand down.

Captain Williams, our new OC, was very nice about it. He sent for me and another chap who had gone down and told us he was sorry, but it was the custom and he didn't think we should be very long before we picked up our stripes again. As soon as fighting was mentioned again those same fellows would fade away like snow in a fire, he said. In the same day's orders we were both appointed paid lance corporals, so that it wasn't too bad. It appears that that is another custom. We couldn't revert to lance corporal but must be made private first, then appointed to the lance rank.

Roll on my duration!

The RND took over the whole control of Mudros on 1 February, all the army having cleared off.

Chapter Ten

12 February 1916 – Malta

Volunteered along with Charlie, Billy and Bob Bayliss to go to Malta on leave. About a hundred went from the division and we all embarked on the *Aragon*, a RMSP [Royal Mail Steam Packet] boat at 3.30pm on the 13th. All through the Gallipoli stunt she had been anchored in Mudros Bay and was used as a staff ship. Her bottom must have been thick with barnacles. Several civilian spies were on board, brought in from Salonika and more were brought on next day. We left Mudros the same day about 4.00pm and, after three awful rough days, entered the Grand Harbour at Malta on the 17th about noon. We landed about 4.30pm and marched to Spinola where a huge camp had been erected for the reception of the hundreds of casualties expected from the evacuation. They had decided not to give us a few of the comforts that we had missed by not getting wounded.

Lieutenant Colonel 'Joe' Mullins was in charge of the camp and, as soon as we got there, he delivered a few kind words to us all. One thing he told us was that if any of us abused the privileges that were granted us we should all be confined to camp for a week. The first night in town and seven men were adrift. A nice start and old Joe fumed. We were sent out downtown in groups of three to hunt these men up and it took us all day to find them. I found one chap down the 'rag' in a little drinking house absolutely 'blotto'. He had been there all night and the old girl in charge of the show said he wouldn't leave. We got him back to camp, and when the sergeant major saw him he told us to take him away and keep him quiet. He hadn't been reported adrift.

I went down Valletta after with my three chums and had a good spruce up. For one thing we had our lance corporals' chevrons stitched on our tunics, our buttons cleaned and boots cleaned, the first time I'd felt smart in khaki. Charlie wasn't a lance corporal so had his two GC[1] badges sewn on.

---

1. Inverted chevrons worn on the left forearm by privates and lance corporals.

I found Malta a lovely little place, but one that anyone would quickly get fed up with. There seems to be an overabundance of priests and goats here, and an all-pervading smell of garlic. The people are a pretty greasy lot on the whole, nearly all speaking English and all intent on robbing the English. The whole place seems overrun with sailors and mariners, both English and French, but they have apparently nothing better to do than spend their time in the drinking and eating houses in the various 'rags'. I'll pass over a description of a 'rag' and be content to let it gradually fade from my memory, if it ever will.

The first draft back to the battalion went on the 23rd and the next on 1 March, Billy and Bob amongst them. Colonel Mullins went back too and Colonel Noble took over the camp. The carnival started on 4 March and carried on for three days; three days and nights of drunken foolery. All the people got up in fancy dress and masks and ran mad generally. Charlie and I had a terrific time while it lasted. Most of our time apart from the carnival was passed in rowing ourselves round the little bays that indent the coast.

The weather the whole three weeks was perfect and I felt in a better state of health than ever before. Charlie and I were warned off for draft on 7 March and embarked on the *Wahine*, a swift, small boat, used for carrying mails between Malta and Mudros. Before the war she'd been a passenger carrier between the north and south Islands of New Zealand. She simply swarmed with cockroaches and there was no provision whatever for troops. Food was just scrambled and the only thing that was served out at all decently was the rum. We left Malta at 7.00am on the 9th in a rough, heavy sea. That boat did roll, and nearly every time her gunwales touched the water.

A sharp lookout was kept the whole way for submarines, but none were spotted. I think we went too fast for them, keeping up a speed the whole way of 18 to 20 knots.

We entered Mudros again at dawn on 11 March, just twelve months after I first entered there. Landed and marched to the RND Detail camp, Colonel Mullins in charge, and who should be adjutant but Captain Gowney! And the first time I saw him, he was on a horse learning to ride. He was an absolute scream and the best turn I've seen on a horse.

Chapter Eleven

14 March 1916 – Macedonia

All 1 Brigade was at Stavros, near Salonika, doing outposts and on the 14th all the Malta party embarked on the *Snaefell*, an armed patrol boat and set off to join our battalions. It was a glorious voyage, and I don't think anybody who had a trip on this Isle of Man boat before the war saw such strange and beautiful scenery as we saw. We headed first of all for the headland at the mouth of the Gulf of Salonika. This was a huge mountain rising sheer out of the water and visible for miles. The top was hidden in cloud and what we could see of it from a distance appeared quite barren. As we approached it, though, we could see a tiny village nestling at the foot of the cliffs and several small fishing boats lying close inshore. High up in the cliffs were stuck quaint-looking houses, but how on earth people got up and down from them and how they were built was a mystery.

After leaving that, we steamed for a short way up the Gulf of Salonika, then back, in and out of two more large inlets, passing on the way some of the most gorgeous scenery. Great snowcapped mountains, some close to the shore, others far inland, and in two places we could see rivers of ice gradually working their way down to the sea.

On one mountain and about halfway up was a great castle. Just below it was a shadowy wisp of cloud and again above it was more cloud. The effect of it was to take one back to the fairy-tale days and fancies of giants and their castles in the clouds.

It was a perfect day and a perfect sea. Just enough swell on to make one feel lazy and content to lie on deck dreaming and fancying. We finished up about six o'clock near the village of Stavros in Greek Macedonia and only a few miles from the Bulgarian frontier. It was dusk when we landed at a temporary store pier on which a crowd of Greek labourers was working.

A guide from Brigade HQ met us at the ship and conducted us about two miles over a wet swampy plain to HQ where guides from our respective battalions met us. We were at the end of the plain and right ahead of us were mountains up which, our guide informed us, we were to climb. All this after a month of absolute idleness. We had on our full marching order, two blankets, three days' rations and the usual rifle and 220 rounds of the best. What a journey!

It was pitch dark when we left BHQ and our path was a goat track, now fairly well worn with the passage of troops and mules. Still, it was a difficult passage with our load and the darkness. From around us in the shrub came strange noises and cries and our guide informed us that the country was overrun with jackals. Nobody knew exactly what a jackal was like; we knew it was a wild animal and, judging by its cries, extra wild. Our guide, a most cheerful chap, regaled us with blood-chilling stories of attacks on the troops by these things and how they crept into bivouacs at night and stole all the food. He wasn't carrying a pack, etc.; we were and consequently hadn't breath to spare to tell him our views. Jackals weren't the only things that overran this place. We could hear thousands of frogs croaking from the marshes and pools around us.

We arrived at Battalion HQ about 11.30 but even then we hadn't done. After waiting an hour there for another guide, from the company this time, we trudged on again. Of course A Company was 'right of the line' and camped a mile from Battalion HQ. We reached them at last, 1,090 feet above sea level and the sea only about three miles away. All the chaps were living in bivouacs and, after Charlie and I had wandered about for another half hour, we found Billy and Bob Bayliss and turned in with them. We were in the clouds most of next day but when they did clear managed to get a good view of the surrounding country. We were on top of one of the highest points about here and could get a magnificent view. Behind us lay the sea, a deep blue, except where it broke on the beaches where it was like rolls of snow.

To our front and flanks were high chains of mountains with plains, valleys and a few villages dotted about. The hills around us were covered in a dense scrub of lovely greens. About 3,000 yards away to our right front was the village of Vrusta, and a few miles beyond and along the coast was a great snowcapped mountain, marking the border of Greece and Bulgaria. This mountain was the legendary home of one of the Greek gods. Looking due west and about six miles away was Lake Beshik, and beyond that and seemingly only separated by a narrow strip of land was Lake Langaza. Beyond the lakes – forty miles away – was the town of Salonika. Visible to the left of Salonika was the great Mount Rouzag.

A rough line of trenches had been dug around the forward slope of our hill about fifty feet below the summit and our job was to complete them and clear a space in front of about 150 yards for wiring and field of fire. It was no light task, but one that everybody enjoyed. It was impossible not to enjoy life in such air and surroundings. The scrub was so dense on the hillside that it was almost impossible to get through it, other than by the paths or along the streams. All the cut-down trees and shrubs were dragged to a clearing and burnt. We had some enormous fires.

At first it was almost impossible to sleep at night, for the croaking of the frogs and howling of those wild dogs. I woke up with a start the second night and clutched my stick. One of those jackals was just outside my bivvie but, by the time I was outside, it had faded away into the night. Just below us in the valley ran a small stream which created little ponds in which thousands of frogs lived and thrived. And the row they made was almost unbelievable. Two or three of us made excursions along that stream and slew thousands of the tiny things.

Discipline was pretty slack in the company. Our new OC, Captain Edwards, was far too slack for the crowd of roughs and 'birds' that had got into the company. In fact, there wasn't much stiffness in any of the company officers, Mitchell, Saunders and our own special platoon officer, Surman, who had about as much ambition and backbone as a snake. Sergeant Jeffries was acting CSM and Sergeant Owen was CQMS

The rations were brought up from brigade every day by mules, but were far from satisfying. Our appetites were simply enormous and we couldn't get enough bully and biscuits even to make up. We saw some lovely sunsets from our hilltop. The sun set exactly behind the lakes and the effect on the water was grand.

Billy, Bob and I took it in turns for orderly corporal. Our work on that day consisted of reporting dinner to the sub of the day and accompanying him on his round of the trenches at night. A guard was mounted in the trenches at night with two sentry posts. Mr Saunders was best to get on with but, of course, I always clicked with Mitchell. I'm certain that chap was mad. I used to go down for him about 10.00pm, but usually he'd be playing cards with the other three. If he was winning he'd knock off and go the rounds then, but if he was losing he'd keep on playing and tell me to give him a shake about 1.30 or 2.00am. Poor thing! He used to tremble the whole way and would jump and start at the slightest sound or rustle from the bushes. 'What's that?' he whispered once, 'have you got your rifle, Corporal?' I hadn't. I always carried a stick. He told me in future I must always carry my rifle. His revolver was always out, shaking about in a most alarming manner. He arranged to go over the top one night and drop silently into the trench by the right snipers' pit. His idea was to try and catch the sentries napping. I let the corporal of the guard know and told him to wait for us behind a certain traverse, then challenge. He did challenge and poor Mitchell was speechless. He couldn't answer the challenge and the corporal repeated it. 'Who are you?' he snapped, "Answer quick or I'll put a bullet through you.' Mitchell was still speechless so I had to answer for him. Even that didn't cure him and he tried a few more stunts after that. Surman was just as bad, but got in a worse state of funk than Mitchell.

The place all around was lovely and the ground was covered in a carpet of the most lovely flowers, violets being very common. There were snakes too, rock and grass varieties about three to four feet long, tortoises, little water turtles and endless other creeping things.

On Sunday the 19th a Taube came over and after that we had them pretty often, some dropping bombs on the beach and shipping in the bay. There was a base for sea-planes on the right of the bay but they weren't much use for chasing Taubes, taking too long to climb and being too slow when up.

On the 22nd and 23rd we heard heavy gunfire from the direction of Salonika. The Bulgars were reported at least twenty miles away but one night we got a fright. Captain Edwards came round, white and excited. 'Get numbers Three and Four Platoons in the trenches, Sergeant Major,' he said, 'and get One or Two standing to in support, and send a patrol on the Vrasta Road.' He said the Bulgars were only five miles away and had broken through the Greek troops on the frontier. Of course, it was all a buzz and they were just as far away as ever by morning, and most of us had lost a night's sleep.

On 31 March names were taken for English leave, preference being given to men who had been out longest and who had been wounded. I was nearly at the top of the list of fifty. England appeared a long way off though, even after that. A strong rumour was flying round that all 1 Brigade were leaving this place and a special fatigue carrying out SAA down to Brigade HQ helped strengthen the rumour. The rest of the ammunition went the following day and we expected to move on the Sunday. We moved on Monday 3 April, but only to a spot on the plain where we made fresh bivouacs.

The country all around was beautiful and we were within easy reach of the sea where we bathed every other day. I went out with Charlie one morning up a dry riverbed and the first thing alive I spotted was a huge snake, coiled up on a rock, sleeping in the sun. He wasn't sleeping very deeply, however, for before we could get up, it had slid off the rock into a bush. We hunted about a bit and finally hit it on the head with a heavy stick. I spoilt a razor afterwards in cutting the skin off it. It was three feet long and, after I'd dried it, I put it on a stick. The next thing we saw were four tiny tortoises, not more than an inch big and their shells were quite soft. They couldn't have been alive long. We kept two each and when we got back to camp cleaned all the inside out. I intended taking lots of souvenirs home on leave with me. The job with the big tortoises was how to kill them. Some of the chaps boiled one for about six hours, but it was long enough before it died. We tried letting them walk, then catching their head in a string noose and cutting it off. However, we managed to kill several and cleaned them out. In some we found strings of about six eggs.

We started drill in the forenoons. Platoon and company drill and, heavens, wasn't it sad! Nobody knew anything about it except Sergeant Jeffries, and he knew far too much for us. We had a decent chap for Platoon Sergeant, Jim Hearne he was called, more Jim than Hearne. He was a chap who had spent most of his fifteen years or so in the marines at sea and had finished up in the Heligoland battle. He was badly shaken up there and had been sent to us for a change and a rest.

Orders came round early on Saturday the 8th for the leave party to stand by and we fell in at 5.00pm and, after a pathetic leave-taking with the boys and 'birds', marched off to the beach. Dick Rogers, our battalion sergeant major, was in charge of the party. We embarked on the *Rowan* about 7.30 and left Stavros shortly after.

Arrived in Mudros again at dawn and marched to the RND detail camp where we were shoved in tents, one between fourteen. All our kitbags that had been left at Port Said before Gallipoli had been brought to Mudros and I found mine with most of my private belongings still in it. We were all fitted out with new clothes and uniforms next day. I had a good scrounge round and filled my bag with clothing and souvenirs, two live shells being amongst them. We hung on there without anything happening until the 14th when General Sir Archibald Paris, our GOC, inspected all details going to England. There were some, too. Besides leave parties from all the battalions, two whole battalions, Nelson and Howe, were going home to be disbanded.

On the 15th the whole of 1 RM came back from Stavros and on Sunday we had the most delightful news that the RND had been taken over by the War Office and, in consequence, all English leave had been cancelled.

I didn't say a word !!!?

Our party was busy all day Monday putting up a camp for the battalion ready for its return from Stavros. They came back on the 19th and I went down to the beach to greet them and give them all the latest news from England. The whole division was standing by to move at short notice. We passed the next few days drilling, road-making and trench digging.

Easter Sunday we went into Portiano and watched the fun between the Greeks who were all dressed up in their best – if they had a best – and playing various games. 'Ring a ring of roses' went best. One chap was fiddling away like mad, only stopping to drink wine. Perspiration was pouring from him. Some of the girls looked nice, but they don't keep nice very long out here.

Heard news on the 29th of General Townsend's capture in Mesopotamia and of the Irish rebellion. A 3rd Battalion of Marines had been sent over there. News also came in that HMS *Russell* and a hospital ship had been torpedoed in the Mediterranean near Malta. Things were getting pretty warm out here. Had a whizz–bang on Sunday 7 May.

Order came round at 2.00pm, 'Pack everything and stand by to fall in at 2.45pm.' Not much time, but no one was late. Everybody was ready with full kit, packs full and kitbags full, mostly with souvenirs. I hoped no one messed about with those two shells or they might go off. We were all aboard the *Briton* by 5.00pm and making guesses as to our destination. England was favourite, but not with me.

Underway at 4.00 next morning and we left Mudros for the last time, with the airship *Silver Queen* as escort for some distance. We had a lovely ship with plenty of room to knock about and quite enjoyed the trip. We had fine weather for two days and saw several French troopships going towards Salonika, all escorted by destroyers. The sea got up on the 10th but the ship was very steady. Still rough on the 11th and, about noon passed two rocky islands, probably Corsica and Sardinia.

At 7.00am on 12 May we steamed into the harbour of Marseilles and took up our berth alongside the quay. At least 1,500 miles nearer dear old England. The place fit for heroes to live in? Orders round at 9.00am to get all gear and kitbags off the ship. We disembarked at 1.00pm.

It was certain that we had done with the MEF.

Summary Statement of Royal Naval Division Casualties
Mediterranean Expeditionary Force

KILLED		DIED OF WOUNDS		DIED	
Offrs	ORs	Offrs	ORs	Offrs	ORs
102	1,551	26	574	5	233

WOUNDED		PRISONERS		TOTAL	
Offrs	ORs	Offrs	ORs	Offrs	ORs
199	4,838	–	2	332	7,198

Chapter Twelve

Gleanings from Gallipoli

The British force employed a total of 468,987 men with never more than 100,000 available at one time. Our losses were: killed 33,522; wounded 78,420; missing 7,636 and over 100,000 invalided.

The French force was about 80,000 with proportionate casualties

Turkish losses, according to General Liman Von Sanders, were 66,000 killed and 152,000 wounded.

Up to 5 May the British loss at Cape Helles was 13,979 and the ANZAC casualties in the first two days amounted to 5,000.

In the hot months, dysentery and jaundice claimed 1,000 victims a day and was only ended by the blizzard of November which claimed as victims 200 dead, 10,000 unfit for further service and 30,000 other sick.

The 29th Division, while holding the Suvla position, lost two thirds of its strength.

Chapter Thirteen

What the Turks Can Say of Us

They did not win, but they came across three thousand miles of sea, a little army without reserves and short of munitions, a band of brothers, not half of them half trained and nearly all of them new to war.

They came to what we said was an impregnable fort, on which our veterans of war and massacre had laboured for two months, and by sheer naked manhood they beat us, and drove us out of it.

Then rallying, but without reserves, they beat us again and drove us farther.

Then rallying once more, but still without reserves, they beat us again, this time to our knees.

Then, had they had reserves, they would have conquered, but by the pity of Allah they had none.

Then after a lapse of time when we were men again, they had reserves, and they hit us a staggering blow, which needed but a push to send us, but Allah again had pity.

After that Allah was indeed gracious, for England made no further thrust, and they went away.

These words, I believe, are by John Masefield, the poet.

Chapter Fourteen

More Hopes of Blighty

12 May 1916 SS *Briton* Marseilles

Disembarked at 1.00pm and, after stowing all our kitbags safely in some sheds, marched out of the dockyard, full marching order, two blankets and 220 rounds of ammunition each. The colonel set off with the adjutant, Captain Farquason, in a motor-car and left us to the tender mercies of Captain Tetley, a great big chap with long legs and carrying about as much kit as I had in my tunic pockets.

The first part of the march was a treat. As we went through the main streets of the city, all the people stopped work and came out of the shops to cheer us and some threw fruit and flowers. Some of the flowers hit me but none of the fruit. The streets were set with pavé stones and, as we hadn't marched on roads for months, we soon felt the effects on our feet. They were slippery too, and Bob Bayliss was soon on his back in the gutter. Mr Surman dashed up and wanted to know 'What the deuce' he meant by slipping about like that, playing the fool? He'd no sooner got the words out than down he went with a clatter. We laughed at Bayliss, but there was an absolute roar when our worthy lieutenant went down.

Everybody stuck the march fine until we had done about four miles and the excitement and novelty began to wear a bit thin. Then the men began to drop out, first by ones, then by threes and fours, and after about six miles whole bunches dropped by the roadside. It was a let-down for the battalion, but it was painful marching. A lot of the blame fell on Captain Tetley who was setting the pace like a racehorse. By the time we had done eight miles there were only three left in our platoon and then I dropped out. My feet felt like pieces of raw meat, my shoulders were about raw, and I was wet through with perspiration. It was the first time I had ever given up and I could have kicked myself after; the camp wasn't another 100 yards up the road.

La Valentina was the camp and we were pushed in tents for the night. I bathed my feet in a stream running through it and, after a scratch feed of bully and biscuits, turned in for the night and went to sleep with the pleasing thoughts that I was at least 1,500 miles nearer home. Thank God for that !

The first rumour around in the morning was that we were going straight overland to England. The Navy had no further use for the division, the War Office wouldn't have it as a gift, so the naval battalions would be disbanded and the marines absorbed by their respective depots and sent on ships etc. Very nice, but I had lost all faith in rumours since the Stavros leave affair when I swore never to believe another buzz. We heaved out of bed about 8.00am and I shaved in the remains of a mug of tea, had a wash, cleaned buttons and badges and spruced up generally.

Order round at 9.30am: 'Anybody wanting leave to put in a chit, but only ten per cent allowed out.' Of course, I wasn't one of the lucky ones. However, Billy Hurrell and I soon found a way out of the back of the camp and strolled down towards the city after tea. As we found nothing of very great interest and had no money to spend, we soon got fed up and made our way back. We knew it was no use trying to get in through the front gates of the camp as all passes had to be given up to the sergeant of the guard and then there was the medical tent to be gone through and questions asked by Jimmy Ross, the Medical Officer. If one needed preventative treatment at his hands one received it.

Neither Billy nor I had any use for either the sergeant of the guard or the well-meant attentions of Jimmy Ross, so we made our way round to the back of the camp. On reaching the gate at the top of the lane, we found to our discomfort and consternation that a big Indian lancer was on guard with drawn sword. As we both made a move to get over the gate he made a threatening move at us with his sword, so we got off again. It was policy. 'It's all right chum, we are Royal Marines and want to get into camp,' we told him. 'You go in front way then,' he said. We stuck to him though and, after explaining how things were, he let us go past. He was laughing all over his face and had only been pulling our legs a bit.

Heard when we got in that the adjutant and Transport Officer had gone to le Havre fixing billets and making arrangements for us to cross to England. Of course, spirits went up with a jump. I picked out a leave ticket on the

Sunday morning and half an hour later the order came along 'All leave cancelled; stand by to move.' Just my luck!

Marched from camp at 5.00pm and went right through the centre of the city passing, through the Place Bernex, past the beautiful entrance to the Palais Longchamps with four great lions guarding the miniature lake. The Rue de la Republique and several other main thoroughfares were crowded with people all in their Sunday best, flirting away as though the war was a million miles away. We went through with a swing, singing, cheering and shouting the whole way. Not a man dropped out, owing chiefly to the fact that we were supposed to be going to England and because the excitement came at the end instead of the beginning of the march.

We reached the station at 9.30pm and entrained, eight in a carriage. Billy and I got in a second-class which was very comfy, but others, and in fact most of the battalion, only got the toast-rack affairs. In our carriage was Sid Ward, a deep-sea marine with about ten years' service, a man of varying moods and very uncertain temper, but one of the best when he was all right. Young Turner was with us too, deaf as a post but as game as anyone in the company. Our noble company officers occupied the next carriage to us.

We left Marseilles about 11.30pm and soon after tried to get some sleep, but rest even in a second-class carriage was almost an impossibility when eight men were all intent on the same game. I kept waking up as stiff and grumpy as it was possible to be.

Our first halt was at 6.00am for breakfast when fires were made on the track and tea made. We certainly felt better for the refreshment. Some of us managed a wash and, after getting under way again, I shaved, then settled down to enjoy the scenery which was lovely. We passed right up the beautiful valley of the Rhône, past Valence, Vienne and on to the great city of Lyon, where we were served out with hot coffee and tea by charming ladies (of varying ages) of the French Red Cross.

Before entering the station the train was pulled up on a big bridge or embankment overlooking a busy part of the city and we were able to buy wine, bread and fruit etc. from the crowd below. The method was for the French to throw up a cord with a basket attached to the end. Money had to go down with the demand though. An officer who had only lately joined us soon put a stop to matters by throwing back two bottles of wine into the street below, thereby nearly causing a mutiny among the troops and bringing upon himself the curses and jeers of the French crowd below.

One astounding thing about the French railway stations was the great number of Frenchmen, all with yards of gold and silver braid and stars stuck on their uniforms, who were apparently necessary in the process of letting our train go by. They appeared to be mostly older men though, and most were very fat and, I should think, quite unfit for more strenuous work in action. One could hardly imagine them leading a charge of infantry at Vimy or Souchez.

The pace of the train wasn't exactly swift and we had no fear of jumping the metals, the average speed being about 12mph. Sometimes it would reach 20mph, then the whole battalion would send out a rousing cheer, which usually had the effect of reducing it to about 5mph. The country through which we passed was really lovely though, and our reception while going through the towns and villages was tremendous.

The demand for souvenirs being more than we could supply, most men were soon without buttons or badges. French girls seemed to be both lovely and lively and quite came up to our preconceived ideas of them. Whole crowds of them would stand and wave the train out of sight, blowing kisses in a most sweet manner which, however, left me very dissatisfied.

The nights were the worst to get over when, after vainly trying to drop off to sleep, we should have to get up for a rest and a stretch. Even that was difficult as two of the men were laid out on the deck.

We had dinner on the 16th at Juvisy, then made a detour of Paris, passing through the lovely suburb of Versailles. We stopped for a considerable time in the great gloomy station of Amiens then went on to Criel, where the order was passed along to 'Stand by to detrain at 1.00am on the 17th'. However, it was 1.00pm instead when we detrained at Pont-Remy. Our welcome had worn very thin and it was very evident that a British Tommy was no novelty but something to be endured and used whenever possible as a means to cheap living. Buttons and badges were not so much in demand as bully beef or Maconochie's.

After getting sorted out we set off for the village of Longpré les Corps-Saints, about six miles away. It was a rotten march; most of the men being asleep the whole way, it was more of a drunken stagger. On arrival at the village, which appeared of decent size, we were put into barns and sheds according to company and platoon. Both our platoon (No. 1 A Company) and No. 2 were put into a huge barn very near the centre of the village. These, I presumed, would be our billets at le Havre and the boat would turn out to be a trench-board forging its way up some water-logged trench near here.

After a wash and clean-up, Billy and I had a stroll in the village and weighed things up a bit. Rum could be got, quietly, and plenty of the red and white kinds of wine. The bread shops were soon doing a roaring trade, and an hour after the battalion's arrival there wasn't a loaf to be bought. Some loaves were about a yard long, others had the appearance of grinding stones, both varieties eating more like a sponge than bread. However, it was a change from the eternal biscuit.[1] There were two fair-sized spinning mills in the village and just outside was a huge modern basket factory, making carriers for great French shells. Billy and I decided to learn the language as we realized the possibility of staying in this country for the duration and a little knowledge of the language would be very useful.

It appeared that our pleasant stay in Longpré, which extended until 28 May, was for the purpose of getting us acclimatised and fitting the division out according to the ideas of the General Staff. We changed our rifles for the high velocity kind, Mark VI, and received the latest thing in gas-bags. We did very little drill and only about three short route marches, so that discipline was a bit slack. The men behaved extremely well though and the standard of health was good throughout the division.

The War Office had decided to take us under their wing but, the Navy having need of certain classes of reservists, the division was soon cleared of a lot of its real fighting strength. Reinforcements came out from England to bring up the total but still, although the numbers were there, fighting efficiency was reduced greatly. We heard that all sorts of changes were to take place. Senior officers of the Brigade of Guards and other crack regiments were to be drafted to the various Naval battalions to shake them up and

---

1. Army biscuit was not a confection. The original French, *bis cuit*, means baked twice and thus Army ration bread, or biscuit, was bread that had been baked twice and, as a result, was hard.

discipline was to be very severe. The Naval manner of saluting was to be done away with and the brass were not at all satisfied with the naval slang. None of these reforms applied to the Royal Marines as, of course, we were equal in all respects to any crack regiment in the Army.[2] The War Office might have saved itself a lot of trouble. None of the reforms ever took root and the Army officers from the crack regiments soon had gone. Those who escaped the shells and bullets of the Bosch went sick or drifted back to their own regiments, leaving management of the Naval Division in such hands as Freyberg, Asquith and several other equally fine leaders.

It's very amusing when you come to think how those rough, pig-headed Tynesiders came to take on the traditions and customs of the Navy. Some had never seen a ship before joining the Royal Naval Division (RND); then it was only a matter of one transport after another. However, stick to the traditions they did and even after the Armistice they were saluting in the approved Naval manner.

Up at 5.00am on 28 May, with everything ready for moving. Moved off to Pont-Remy after saying farewell to all the friends we had made in Longpré. There were some wet eyes behind when we marched at 7.30am, but none in the ranks: we were all pretty eager to see how France compared with Gallipoli.

We only had a train of cattle trucks this time and about thirty-five men were pushed in each truck which, considering the gear each man carried and the bundles of blankets, was quite enough. Moving off at noon, we had a fairly decent journey considering the discomforts, with several long stops on the way. Once the train stopped in the middle of a large orchard and, of course, half the battalion got off to pick apples and pears, but the train started straightaway without even giving the warning whistle. About fifty men were left behind. Only Joe Woods and young Nicholson were adrift out of my truck. Of course, if anybody was adrift at all it would be Joe Woods.

We passed a large German prisoners' camp at Acheux and all the prisoners were at work on the line. As the train passed through they all dashed up to us

---

2. The Royal Marines held precedence in the Army List after the Royal Berkshire Regiment, formerly the 49th Regiment of Foot.

yelling for bully and biscuits and we threw out what we could spare. It was a sight to see the Jerries as they fought and fell over one another for the stuff. They must have been hungry to fight for muck like that.

Some of our chaps started throwing biscuits out of spite and one hit a starved-looking young German on the cheek, cutting it open and making a horrible gash. It made my blood boil to see it and I could have shot the chap who did it without any compunction. I don't believe in hitting a chap when he's down and certainly these poor devils were down and, hang it all, they were only fighting job for the same reason that we are: it's a question of the politicians laying down our lives for their country.

In my opinion one German who fights for his country is worth a dozen Englishmen who refuse to fight for theirs. In fact, some of the devils won't even work for their country.

Chapter Fifteen

28 May 1916 – Action in France – With Pick and Shovel

We detrained at Barlin, the railhead, during daylight at about 8.00pm and, as we got out of the train, stiff and cramped, the sound of gunfire very near at hand and the sight of Very lights going up from the line ahead, helped to cheer our tired spirits and ease our aching bones.

Having marched about three miles to a mining village called Hersin, the whole battalion was shown into a convent and school where we turned in for the night after drawing our blankets. There were signs of the convent having been occupied by troops before. Every available inch of plaster on the walls was covered with rough and sometimes good drawings, nude, rude and otherwise, beside copies of regimental badges, mottoes, names of posterity-desiring Tommies and some very unflattering remarks about the Kaiser.

King's Royal Rifle Corps (KRRs), London Irish, King's Own Yorkshire Light Infantry (KOYLIs), East and West Yorkshires, and numerous other regiments were represented artistically, and it wasn't long before our artists and would-be artists were busy. It wasn't long after satisfying the inner man before I turned in and was soon lulled off to sleep by the sound of gunfire.

The Turks must have sent on a recommend about our prowess with the pick and shovel. We were up at 7.00 next morning and on the way by half-past with pick and shovel for digging just behind the support trenches. We dug our way on Gallipoli, we dug all the time we were there and we dug our way off. Then we dug the tops off several mountains in Macedonia and now we were to start and till the soil in France. I expected that we'd finish by digging a fresh channel for the Rhine. However, we had to learn the Army method of doing things and they may have had another way of digging to what we had been used to.

We marched to the outskirts of Aix-Noulette, once I suppose a lovely little village with a fine château, but reduced to a heap of skeleton houses and piles of brick dust. What was once a pretty church was nothing but a battered heap of white stone. Lying near to the remains of the main porch was the broken crucifix with the shattered image of Christ still hanging to it. Our job consisted of widening the road but we had instructions from the engineers in charge to stop work immediately the Bosch put up an observation balloon. He had several balloons up but apparently not one watching our sector.

The engineers told us that this was a road the Bosch had no idea about and it was a big help to our chaps at night for getting rations and ammunition up to the line. Knowledge of the road or not, it wasn't long before Jerry started searching the sector with 5.9s, great black things that burst like the crack of doom, some of them dropping very near the road. Two or three of our party were hit with splinters of shrapnel and had to be dressed.

Our platoon officer, Mr Surman, was soon a pitiable object, dashing about from group to group, just like a two-bob horse, and all of a sweat. Granted it was his first time under fire, but there was no need to show off in that manner, especially to chaps like us who weren't even bothering to duck for cover. It only proved our opinion of him though, an absolute funk who would never weather it.

Back again in Hersin by 4.00pm, pretty well fagged out, but after tea and a spruce up I went with Billy and Charlie Hamilton on a voyage of discovery down the village. The people appeared to be carrying on pretty much as pre-war, although there was plenty of evidence to show how the place had been shelled badly. Just on the right of our billet, only a matter of fifty yards away was a colliery with a huge chimney stack that the Bosch had cut in two with a shell. The mine was still worked at night and the railhead was moved up to there at night from Barlin.

I watched one of our aeroplanes over the German lines doing thrilling stunts to avoid the anti-aircraft shells which were bursting round him by dozens, nasty wicked-looking red flashes of fire turning afterwards into a puffy ball of very white smoke. The effect of all these scores of fluffy white balls was certainly pretty against such a background of lovely blue sky, but what about the feelings of the poor devil up there amongst them, and those of the German gunners as time after time they missed. During the whole course of the war, in which I saw millions of shells fired at aeroplanes, I only saw one plane hit: that was a direct hit on one of our planes which came fluttering down in several parts.

The last day of May and 1 and 2 June were very quiet days for me with nothing to do but march the sick up to Jimmy Ross in the morning and write letters in the afternoon. The evenings I spent scrounging down the village with Charlie. Whenever we went down the village, which was full of troops, we were always the object of much comment, especially Charlie, who still wore his shorts from Stavros. Charlie had a fine well-made figure and his bare knees were a picture. We always took a pride in our appearance and whenever possible had everything cleaned and bright that would clean. I expect other troops were thinking we had just come out of the box.

On 3 June names were taken for English leave, but I got a miss. They were obviously working leave on the system that the first shall be last, etc. After tea, Charlie and I had a stroll for about two miles beyond Hersin, through Coupigny (where the houses had suffered badly from shells and bombs) then to the top of the Lorrette ridge, where we had a splendid view of the whole front from Loos to Vimy. It was a beautiful evening, the air was clear and one could almost feel the quietness. Objects stood out clear and distinct. We could see plainly the twin towers of Loos, the Fosse at Caloune, and the great town of Lens along the nearside of which ran both the German and our own trenches. Lens itself looked almost untouched by the war: the number of church towers and steeples was astonishing.

We had heard that our artillery only sent shrapnel over the place occasionally. The trenches were easily discernible owing to the white state of the ground where the chalk had been thrown out. There appeared to be little activity apart from trench mortar strafes: every few minutes we could observe a great upheaval of earth amongst the trenches, followed by a huge column of smoke rising in a dense mass to about thirty or fifty feet. Of course, we were guessing whose trenches were going up and how many poor devils had gone to Glory with such explosion. Very likely there would be no one hit. It took a lot of bullets, bombs and shells to kill a man, such was this war. We stayed on the ridge until it was nearly dark, then called and cheered our spirits up with a few *vin blancs* and *rouges*. Eggs and chips at a quiet little establishment; after that and we were both ready for bed.

'Forget Me Not': a souvenir photograph of Harry Askin in the full-dress uniform of the Corps of Royal Marines.

Harry, front left, with three friends in 1916. Seated beside Harry is Bill Hurrell; standing are Jack Senior and Charlie Hamilton. All except Charlie Hamilton are lance corporals. The two inverted chevrons on Marine Hamilton's left forearm are good conduct badges indicating eight years' service.

Harry pictured in Malta in 1916.

Second Lieutenant Harry Askin shortly after being commissioned in 1918. The three vertical strips above his left cuff are wound badges.

A French battleship bombards Turkish positions along the Gallipoli peninsula.

A view of the scene at V Beach at Helles, with landing barges in the foreground and the build-up of supplies evident on and beyond the beach.

In a trench on the peninsula with Royal Marines and Australian 'diggers'. Both Australians are observing the Turkish lines through trench periscopes.

Another trench periscope in use. Watching the enemy through these instruments reduced the risk to front-line soldiers of being shot by snipers. These soldiers are wearing tropical pith helmets, or sola topees. Steel helmets had not yet been issued.

Two Royal Marine officers enjoy a cup of tea in the beachhead while a third, standing, has lit up a cigarette.

BROWN HOUSE
CAPE HELLAS
GALLIPOLI · 1915

H. Askin

MUDROS BAY
AND SARPI 1915

H. ASKIN

Harry Askin was a talented artist as shown by these sketches of the 'Brown House' at Gallipoli, above, and Mudros Bay, below.

Royal Naval Division troops go over the top in a training exercise on the Gallipoli peninsula.

Harry Askin's Officer Cadet Training Unit in 1918.

Harry Askin after receiving his commission.

Too old for active service in the Second World War, Harry volunteered to serve in the Local Defence Volunteers (LDV), later renamed the Home Guard by Winston Churchill.

Mary and Harry Askin with their daughter Nancy Richmond and granddaughter Jean Mary.

Harry and Mary with their friends Reginald and Dorothy Stenton and, in front, Nancy and William Askin.

His soldierly bearing still evident,
Harry Askin takes a stroll by the sea.

The Gallipoli Monument,
commemorating all those who
lost their lives in the ill-fated
campaign, including so many of
Harry's friends in the Royals.
This photograph was taken by
his granddaughter Jean Baker in
2014.

A party went up the line at night in motor lorries for digging and we heard the next morning that they had dropped in for it nicely; a shrapnel burst over one of the lorries killing and wounding eight. The doctor at the Field Ambulance went off alarming about it and said that had they had steel helmets most of the casualties would have been avoided.

Set off to go digging at 7.00am on the 5th. We had to move up in artillery formation, that is, sections in file at fifty paces interval. As we approached a small village between Hersin and Aix-Noulette the Bosch started shelling it and the road with 5.9s and one dropped in the centre of the village. As we passed through we could see where the shell had dropped. It had blown the front of a house down and we could see the old couple who lived there busy clearing away the debris from the table where they had evidently been at breakfast.

Our job was deepening the communication trench just off the Arras- Lens road to lay an artillery cable. All the time we were there the Germans were sending over trench mortar bombs (*Minenwerfer*) weighing something like a hundredweight (112lb/50kg). The sound of the explosions was frightful, just as though some mighty giant had ripped open the earth and thrown a row of houses into the crack. Some burst unpleasantly close to us too, bits of casing whizzing down amongst us with a wicked zip. We were up there till 5.00pm. Not bad for a day's work: three to four miles walk, ten hours digging in a shelled trench and then the march back. Nothing to eat but a half tin of bully and a couple of biscuits, and only water to drink. This life would soon sicken a pig!

Every day up to the 12th (Whit Monday) was a repetition of the 5th. The weather was simply terrible, nothing but torrents of rain and we were caked in mud. We finished digging on the Monday night; our job was a six-foot cable trench just on the left of Aix-Noulette and we were told when that was done we could go home. Easy! We were in a cornfield and after getting about two feet of muck out we struck solid chalk. It poured with rain the whole time. We finished the job about 2.00 in the morning and got back to the convent where we had two hours' undisturbed rest.

Chapter Sixteen

13 June 1916 – Instruction in Trench Warfare

Fell in at 7.45am with everything we possessed and marched to the trenches, everybody looking more or less like Christmas trees. We arrived in the firing line at 12.30pm and found everything thick with mud. There were some decent dugouts, some going down as much as twenty feet, but most were occupied by officers, sergeant majors and sergeants of the London Irish who were doing a turn in the line. It transpired that we were only up for a few days for instructional purposes and our tutors were the 18th Battalion London Irish, part of 47th Division.

We found very little to do once we were allotted to our respective companies and platoons, except dodging rifle grenades which the Bosch were sending over with far too much accuracy to suit us. Our tutors were doing pretty much as they liked, one man being on watch in about every third fire-bay. I was warned off to go with the ration party at night so that on future occasions I could act as guide. The ration party set off in pouring rain for the dump somewhere on the Arras road, where we had to wait for about two hours. The road had been shelled and somebody's rations had gone west. As our rations came up each man was given full sandbags, some of meat, bully, bread, jam, biscuits etc., all the bags being tied in pairs so that each man could sling two bags over each shoulder

We set off back, a lance corporal of the Londons acting as guide with two jars of rum, me following with the company mail. It struck me after a time that our guide was more or less at sea. By the time we had reached the reserves he was hopelessly lost. We were all drenched to the skin, the rations were soaked and the men were in a frightful mood. They were cursing and swearing the whole way and time after time would come along 'so and so' has dropped behind, his strings broken. Then we'd halt until 'so and so' had tied his 'so-and-so' bags together again. We were wandering about for hours, more often than not up to the knees in water and mud. The men got so fed up that they dumped the rations in a battered dugout and made their own way back to the firing line.

I got back myself after a time and found the London Irish even more minus than during the day. I am afraid it was very little these chaps could teach us about trench warfare. The only things they were likely to teach us were: how to make 'meself' scarce and how to dodge the issue. I believe some big general said that 'The first duty of a soldier is to sleep' and these chaps were carrying it out to the letter. No working parties were about, no one wiring and even the ration party failed to deliver the goods.

The London lance corporal managed to stick to his rum and an officer and sergeant major of the regiment came round as we 'stood to' on the fire-step and served every man out with a good 'tot'. It was like new life to me after the wretched night I had had and, after stand down, Billy and I set off in search of some of our rations. After about an hour we found a few bags that were marked No. 1 Platoon A Company. So we lugged them back. Just as we got by company HQ in the support line we met Mr Surman, who was trying to find his way to the front line to do his turn on watch. He was quite at sea as to his direction so we suggested that he should go with us. We were in a good piece of trench quite six feet deep and Surman was in front. All at once we were surprised to see our worthy officer fall flat in the bottom of the trench. 'That's the worst of being so damned tall,' he said, 'I'm sure their snipers can see me.' Somebody had fired a rifle away up by Vimy and the idiot thought they were firing at him. He postponed his visit to the line. The rations weren't much use when we got them opened, all the bread and biscuits being nothing but pulp. However, as most of the men had brought parcels and food up the line in their packs, we managed for the day.

The London Irish had an idea that we were just out from England and were trying to stuff us up with all manner of tales, what they had done at Loos, Hulluch, tales of la Bassée Road, etc., but keeping very quiet about Vimy Ridge and how they lost it after the French had taken it and handed it over. We listened to all their tales of war, then told them quietly that most of our chaps had been wounded, a lot of them twice, before they ever saw a trench.

That old soldiers' song fitted very well in their case:

Who are the lads that fighting's for?
Who are the lads to win the war?
It's good old Kitchener's Army
And every man of them's tres bon,
They never lost a trench since Mons,
Because they never saw one.

I had a walk down the trench to see Charlie after dinner. I got to where a listening sap went out towards the Bosch trench when I heard the pop of a rifle from across the way and knew that a rifle grenade was coming over. I ducked of course when I heard the whizz and the thing dropped in the next bay. No sooner the explosion than the cry for 'Stretcher-bearers'.

I dashed round the traverse and found two men dead, one of the London Irish, a big jovial Irishman, and the other a young lad from my own company. The grenade hit our chap on his steel helmet, because it was ripped and torn like brown paper and the poor kid's head was completely blown to bits. The Irishman's head and face had suffered terribly too, besides having his body riddled. There was another chap in the bay and he said they were all three on the fire-step talking. He wasn't even scratched. Our bombing section under Grindy and Pilgrim, both Conspicuous Gallantry Medal (CGM) men from Gallipoli, got busy after that and sent over about fifty grenades in quick time, piping down the Bosch for the day.

I was guide for the ration party at night and we set off at 'stand down' and were back again by 11.00pm without getting lost. A party of Londons went out about 3.30am on the 15th and we 'stood to arms', but nothing happened. The sector was very quiet and I don't think there was one shell over on our part. There was a certain liveliness up at Vimy on the right and at Loos on the left.

I had to go down to the battalion HQ at 7.30am on the 16th to act as guide to C and D Companies who were to relieve us and got them up by 1.00pm without anything going wrong. When they were bedded down we made our way back to Hersin and the convent again. Everybody was in a shocking state of filth and our clothes and gear were thick with mud and chalk. The English leave party was curtailed to three per battalion, so my hopes of Blighty were very obscure, without I stop something, and there was always a risk about that.

We spent three uneventful days at Hersin, our time being occupied chiefly in getting clean and doing various drills by numbers. The battalion dwindled down again to its usual Active List, all the square number men dropping in for further cushy jobs. Officers and NCOs were sent away on courses. Those who went were the ones who had never seen any fighting with the battalion, and were never likely to do.

The War Office had officially taken us over and we were to be known as 63rd (Royal Navy) Division. General Sir A. Paris was still in charge and the division consisted of three 188, 189 and 190 brigades, the last-named, including 1st Battalion Honourable Artillery Company; 4th Bedfords; 7th Royal Fusiliers; 10th Dublins, under Brigadier General Trotman CB was not immediately but would probably join us when the divisional artillery came on the scene. We were still waiting for the Divisional Train and First-line Transport. All the transport we had in Gallipoli was three field kitchens per battalion. I believe most of those were left there.

Our brigade (188) was under command of Brigadier General Prentice DSO and included 1st Battalion Royal Marines (Deal and Chatham); 2nd Battalion Royal Marines (Plymouth and Portsmouth); Anson Battalion, and Howe Battalion.

Under Brigadier General Philips 189 Brigade was a Naval brigade and consisted of the Hood, Drake, Hawke and Nelson Battalions.

Our conduct during the period of probation up the line must have pleased the brass because we received orders on the 19th to get ready for the line on the morrow. We were to take over a small sector just on the left of the Souchez river and a lot of us were in great hopes that things would be a bit livelier than before.

Set off about 9.30am on the 20th and went up the Arras–Lens road as far as we dared, then dropped into a communication trench that ran along the roadside. When we first struck the road the trees which ran along either side were lovely, full of green thick foliage; as we neared the line the foliage got thinner and here and there the trunk of one would be splintered by a shell. By the time we took to the communication trench the trees were practically barren of leaves and even branches and on all was the green tinge of poison gas. It was easy to distinguish where the front-line trenches were because there were no trees at all. Alongside the road were the remains of some of the night ration strafes: dead horses and mules, broken limbers and GS wagons and lots of other implements of war.

Our company was to be in reserve and our trench was really the bed of the Souchez river, very near to what had been the village of Souchez. Just to the right were the lower slopes of Vimy ridge, looking from here one mass of shell holes. Somebody from the orderly room was saying that Colonel Hutchinson had decided to liven things up a bit in this sector. He was a great believer in the slogan 'Get on with the War'.

General Paris is another such believer and there was betting in the ranks as to how long he would be before he offered to capture Vimy ridge or Lens. They say that the success of a general is measured by the amount of men he has killed and wounded. Surely General Paris should not be far off the top of the tree: the division had already been practically wiped out two or three times.

We had some of the new Stokes trench mortars, both light and heavy. The lights fire a shell weighing about 10lb and an efficient operator could get as many as eight or ten shells in the air at once. The other kind fired a 60lb 'toffee apple', a great ball of iron about the size of a football, full of high explosive, stuck on the end of a steel rod. They meant trouble for someone.

The first afternoon was very quiet and the night passed without incident. Next day Bob Bayliss and I were sent down to Aix Noulette with ten men to make and bring back forty gallons of anti-gas solution to fill up the sprayers. Bob and I had a good scrounge round the orchards in the village but found nothing except a few strawberries and gooseberries that tasted too much like explosives and dead men to eat.

We were back again for dinner (bully beef and biscuits) and soon after 1.00pm our chaps opened up with the 'toffee apples'. We could follow them as they went through the air, turning over and over until they got about fifty feet from the ground before plunging down, ball first, to the earth, exploding with a most terrible crash.

The Bosch stuck it for an hour and then started slinging over his *Minenwerfers* and 'Rum Jars' by way of retaliation. Those things made our 'toffee apples' sound like Chinese crackers. They were simply stupendous and shook us up pretty well, even in reserve. The game was kept up until 4.00pm, our chaps sending over about two to his one. C and D Companies, who were holding the line, had seventeen casualties, three killed. The firing line was battered in in several parts and Captain Morford of C Company was blown from one end of a fire-bay to the other, but was alright.

Our old Roman Catholic Padre, Father Davy, turned up trumps. Not supposed to be up the line at all, he pleaded so hard with the colonel who let him go up and during the strafing he was in the firing line helping to dig out the poor devils who had been buried.

The next day was very quiet in the forenoon. Billy and I took a party digging a new communication trench across the Souchez valley on ground literally covered with dead French soldiers; as we dug we kept coming across more. One body lay right across where we were digging, about two feet from the surface. 'What shall we do with this mouldy old b——?' Jack Spencer shouted to me. There was only one thing to do – carry on digging, so we got him out in pieces and threw him over the top. It was a sickening job and the stench from all those dead bodies was frightful. The fighting around there must have been awful. I remember reading about the French retaking this part of the front and how heavily they lost. No wonder. All the bodies had bright red breeches on; the German machine gunners could hit them a mile off.

The strafing started again at 2.00pm, both sides going at it for all they were worth. Word was soon passed down for stretcher-bearers and the old Padre was up again right in the thick of things. One stretcher-bearer did some brave and fearless work too, and was afterwards awarded the Military Medal (MM). The Bosch smashed our line in again in several places and C Company had four more casualties, Lieutenant Steel killed and three men badly wounded, none expected to live. Our artillery opened up about 3.30pm and Jerry packed up. Just after four o'clock about twenty German aeroplanes came over our lines but were soon driven back again by our men who were up in force.

Some German planes dropped some wicked-looking darts, things weighing about a pound and a half. I shouldn't like to be hit with one of them! Bob Hacking picked one up. I'd like to gamble that he had more souvenirs than anyone in the battalion. I only knew one chap to equal him: Houlet who hadn't been seen or heard of since he developed fits on Mudros.

We had a little spasm at night. The Bosch sent up a small mine on our right and both sides opened up with the guns. It didn't last long, but we had to stand to until the spasm had died down. German aeroplanes over again all the next morning; ours, of course, being absent. Expect our chaps were having a cosing or a lecture. Things were pretty quiet again until 2.30pm when the trench mortar stunt started again. After about ten minutes word came down that Sergeant Owen of C Company was dead. He saw a big 'Rum Jar' coming over and got all his men into the dugout. He had just got inside the entrance when the thing burst just outside and blew the entrance in. The Padre and Captain Morford helped to dig him out, but he was blown to bits. Two more chaps were buried with him and weren't much use when they got out. Poor old Sal Owen, one of the best, who looked after us on Gallipoli like a father, got jaundice and dysentery there and was sent to C Company on rejoining.

C Company always was unlucky and Captain Morford wasn't a chap to avoid things for the sake of a peaceful life. He was an officer on the *Majestic* when she was sunk off Gallipoli and he swam ashore with the ship's books and attached himself to the marines on shore. He showed himself a daredevil while out there.

The strafing came to rather a sudden end about 3.00pm. A severe thunderstorm came on suddenly and with it a cloudburst, which in less than half an hour absolutely flooded the trenches. Trench-boards were floating about on top of two and in some places three feet of water. We got to work right away letting out the water where it was possible and I spotted what appeared to be a disused dugout with the floor about three feet below the level of the trench. Joe Woods and I immediately set to work to knock a hole in the front of it and a lot of the water from the trench ran into the dugout. With the first rush, an officer, dripping water, dashed out of the dugout. 'What the hell are you doing to my dug-out?' he yelled. 'Sorry Sir,' I said, 'we didn't know it was a dugout, we thought it was an old latrine.' He was battalion Trench Mortar Officer and had turned in for a sleep. It was hard lines but we didn't feel very upset about it because he was the chap who threw the bottles of wine overboard at Lyons. And the wine belonged to Joe Woods so that straightened that out. We helped to salve some of his gear but none of it was much use.

I was warned off as guide for the relief which was supposed to arrive by about 10.00pm. I had to go down the CT to where it joined the Arras road and get particulars from the Battalion Sergeant Major as to which company of the Howes I was to meet. What a journey! In the lower levels of the trench the water was practically up to my neck and in no part was there less than a foot of water. When I'd got the particulars I had to make the journey back and wait until 9.00pm before I went down again for the relief party.

I was at the rendezvous by 10.00pm again and the Howes arrived at 1.30 the next morning, which happened to be mid-summer's day. There was a bitter, cold wind blowing and a steady downpour of rain, but I didn't mind the rain so much; it would have been impossible for me to get any wetter. A young idiot of an officer of the Howes was leading the men and had lost them about three times before he had reached the trenches. 'I've been trying to keep the men dry,' he said. 'Then you've been wasting your time,' I replied. I could have said a lot more but thought I'd better not. I warned him to leave trench-boards alone if he saw any as they had a nasty habit of moving when you got one foot on them and that meant a dive, besides delaying the company behind. It was after 3.00am before our company was relieved and Captain Edwards told each platoon officer to get his platoon down to the crossroads in Aix Noulette when they were relieved. Dear old Surman turned up from somewhere, the first time we'd seen him since we came up the line, and led us down the trench.

After two or three wrong turns, and after we had nearly arrived in the front line, Jim Hearne, our sergeant, suggested that I should be guide. 'Why should Askin know his way better than I do?' said Surman. 'Because he's been there and back six times since stand-down last night,' said Jim. Surman said I'd better get on with it then. Just beyond Company HQ I got out of the trench and set off down the Arras road. Surman didn't like the idea. 'Hadn't we better keep to the trench a bit, the Bosch might shell the road or open up with a machine gun?' he said. Nobody took the trouble to answer him.

We were down at Aix Noulette in less than an hour of being relieved and most of the men were comparatively dry.

We all turned into some battered houses to wait for the rest of the battalion. In our particular house a few of the 'birds' had gathered. Besides myself, Billy and Bob Bayliss, there were Spencer, Joe Woods, Sid Ward and Bob Hacking. 'Kelly' Clayton tried hard to get in but was too lousy and festered for even our company so we kicked him out. We had a huge fire in about five minutes, then some hot tea and a sleep. The smoke from the fire just about gassed us. After about an hour Surman came dashing in. 'Get a move on you lazy swine and put that fire out,' he yelled. There was a chorus of 'Go to Hell' and 'Get to Hell out of it' with a few more choice expressions and someone let fly with a loose brick just as Surman beat a hasty retreat. Unfortunately, it missed its mark.

Chapman, our company sergeant major, (sober for once) came along soon after and told us to fall in outside. He told us Surman had said there was a mutiny in his platoon with the men refusing to obey him.

We found the whole battalion ready to move off when we fell in.

Chapter Seventeen

Midsummer 1916 – A Cruel Experience

The battalion moved off and it was soon apparent that we weren't going back to Hersin. We turned left through Aix Noulette and climbed up through Bouvigny where we had our first, welcome, halt. We were all more or less asleep, chilled through and through with the rain and biting wind, and sore with four days' filth of the trenches. Apart from that none of us had had a decent meal since we left Hersin. We were half an hour in Bouvigny, during which time most of the men went to sleep by the roadside and the battalion took some getting on the move again.

We had a great ridge to climb and cross and before long the battalion looked for all the world like Napoleon's retreat from Moscow. Several men collapsed in the road; others managed to get to the banks on either side and lay there absolutely beaten. The officers couldn't do anything and they realised that it wasn't a time for the application of discipline: the men just couldn't go on. The CO kept taking turns with packs and now and then would relieve a man of his rifle. I saw Captain Tetley at one time carrying two packs and four rifles. Very few finished the march to Fresnicourt, which was about ten miles from Aix Noulette. Some men were crying out of sheer misery and helplessness. Not even the hardiest spirit in the battalion could raise a song or a whistle. It was a terrible march and one of the roughest times I had experienced up to then. However, I stuck it and arrived at our destination with the few. We were put in some Army huts belonging to the French troops on arrival, and the cooks were all ready for us with hot tea and rum and a good hot stew after that.

Hot shower baths had been rigged up for us and I took advantage of them, then turned in and after two hours' sleep felt like a new man. The rest of the battalion were all day getting up here and as soon as they arrived they went to sleep, in all their filth.

Chapter Eighteen

Monotony Sets In

The day following was Sunday 25 June, a lovely summer day. After getting the mud off and sprucing up a bit I went for a stroll with Billy and Charlie. The country round about was lovely, all pretty villages and thick woods. Fresnicourt was a pretty place and so was Ohlain, another small village nearby; Fresnicourt contained the church that does for both places. However, as Ohlain contained the estaminets and cafés we made our way there. We were just trying to decide a very important point; should we go in that estaminet for a vin rouge or should we go into that café for a *tasse* du fresh?

We had almost decided on the vin rouge when a vision of loveliness all in the black of France swept past us with a swish of silk and a very demure 'Bonjour Messieurs'. We watched her with our mouths wide open. We couldn't imagine the war had left things like that hanging round there. We watched her as she turned into a farmyard and, as she glanced round once, we decided to ask for a glass of milk. 'Oh yes,' they had milk, but perhaps we would sooner have bière, or wine or champagne at 15 francs a bottle?

We had vin rouge and grenadine several times. Jeanne was a charming girl and made us feel quite at home, even before she had taken her hat off. She had been to church at Fresnicourt and was in black for one of her brothers who had been killed in the fighting at Souchez. He may have been the poor devil we chopped up while making that communication trench. We decided to make that our café special for as long as we stopped at Fresnicourt.

We had five very uneventful days until 1 July. Monday the 26th saw a start with proper routine. Up at 6.00am for PT, then breakfast, then, from 9.15am to 11.30am, turnings and saluting by numbers, section and platoon drill, and company drill from 2.30pm to 4.30pm. The troops were absolutely fed up to the teeth. We didn't know very much about drilling sections and platoons, but we did know our job up the line, and that's more than our company officers did.

Captain Edwards was a dream. He knew very little about drill and up the line was about as lively as a dead horse. Lieutenant Torrens was a bit better down the line and up the trench he would come and mix with the men a bit. Surman, of course, was a washout both up and down the line. The remaining officer was Second Lieutenant Mitchell, 'Wanky Mitchell' we called him. He was as loony as anything I've seen in a Sam Browne, with perhaps the exception of Compton Domville of Gallipoli fame. None of our officers had seen active service before and now they'd had a taste they didn't seem enamoured. Time would tell with them. Perhaps we wouldn't have long to wait for a fresh lot of officers.

Billy and I shared sick corporal's job, so that wasn't so bad for us. The rain came down in plenty which didn't help to cheer the men up much. The rats in the huts caused a little diversion at night as the whole camp was overrun by them; one night I was awakened by a brute as big as a rabbit sitting on my face. I knocked it off with my hand and it scampered off with a cry of rage, leaving three claw marks down one side of my face. It put the wind up me for the rest of the night and, in the morning, I organised a rat hunt in which we caught and killed eight. Great big brutes they were, quite capable almost of killing and eating a man. We had always plenty of dogs hanging around for a job of that description. Almost every time we went out for a march two or three mongrels would attach themselves to us and either follow us to camp or up the line, whichever way we were going. A dog never stayed up the trenches long, though. It would cringe and cower with every explosion until, its fear getting the better of it, it would set off for the nearest village again. Cats were just the opposite and so were birds, the latter not fluttering a wing even when a shell burst nearby.

The monotony of life was broken a bit on 1 July. Taubes came over in the morning and dropped several bombs on the countryside, but did no great damage. Then we could hear heavy gunfire from the south practically all day. Towards five o'clock orders were issued with news of the 'Big Push' on the Somme. III and IV Army Corps., in conjunction with the French, had advanced and had made good progress at practically all points. Another item of interest; we were paid, so Billy, Charlie and I went down to Jeanne's and had a bottle of champagne to celebrate the victory. Heavy firing in the Vimy sector continued all night, but died down towards dawn. Good news continued to come through the next day: our troops had gained considerable ground and had captured more than 6,000 prisoners and over 100 guns.

I was strolling up from Ohlain about 6.00pm with Charlie, when we came across a queer-looking chap wandering aimlessly about on the road. He was dressed in a filthy suit of khaki with neither cap nor belt. All his buttons were tarnished through being exposed to poison gas, and he was muttering away to himself. I spoke to him but he took not the slightest notice of me, and then I could tell by the expression on his face and in his eyes that he was daft. I asked him a few questions. Where had he come from? What was his name and regiment? Had he a paybook on him? He just shook his head as though he didn't understand my language.

I made for his pocket to see if he had a paybook but he fired up at once. 'Don't touch that,' he said, 'That's my wife.' He pulled a photograph from his pocket then and started kissing it and crying. He had a letter, too, and said someone had sent it to tell him that his wife had gone off with a black man. 'I'll kill 'em!' he started shouting. Then he called his wife all the things that applied to a woman of that description and a few that didn't apply but which added a bit of colour to it and then kissed the photo again and said he loved her. I induced him to go with me as far as the sick bay where I turned him over to Jimmy Ross. He wasn't long before he turned him over to field ambulance.

Sergeant Jeffries found a site suitable for a rifle range, so on the 3rd we had to start firing a short musketry course. That man was rifle mad.

Ohlain was placed out of bounds. Joe Woods and a few more 'birds' caused a rough-house in the Army Service Corps canteen down there one night and half a dozen men had to receive medical attention. They spoil everything with their rotten old soldier moods.

The battalion was inoculated against typhoid on the 5th. That makes about the umpteenth time since joining up. We reckoned to have forty–eight hours stand–off after an affair like that, but we carried on with drill. A touch of typhoid more or less was nothing compared to acquiring a knowledge of the *Drill Book*. Joe Woods always said he could quote anything from either the Bible or infantry drill. That's all he had to read when he did 'cells' in the Army before the war. He must have done some cells in his time to swallow that lot.

Chief item of interest during the next few days was the departure to England on leave of an officer who came out last October. Both Captains Eagle and Tetley were granted their majorities and Tetley was to leave to take over the command of Drake Battalion.

We gave in our blankets on 12 July. It was very evident that our stay in these parts was drawing to a close. Everybody was fed up and a change, wherever it might be for, would be welcome. Marched to Hersin on the 13th at 2.00pm and were billeted in the convent again overnight. Moved to the Bully Grenay sector next morning, our company being in general reserve for the start. Our trenches were about 500 yards in front of the little village of Corons d'Aix and, though the Bosch was always dropping shells in it, the French people were living there pretty much as usual. To our right rear was the white village of Aix Noulette.

We had some decent dry dugouts constructed in a valley behind the reserve trenches, so that we had plenty of freedom of movement, being quite unobserved by the Bosch, but liable to get plenty of shells as our artillery had a field-gun battery just behind us in the valley. We passed a lot of time watching the efforts of the Bosch to hit this battery, but he was never successful. When the Bosch, with the aid of his aeroplanes, thought he had got the range nicely, the gunners would move in the night to an alternative position, and the next morning Jerry would waste a lot of ammunition on the deserted gunpits.

We lost our Mr Surman who volunteered to go to a mining company where he need never go up the line. I tried my hardest to persuade Kelly Clayton to go with him, but he wouldn't. That man used to get more lousy every day. I think that when lice crawl out of a man's lace holes, he must be lousy indeed. It was a sight to watch Kelly doing two hours on the fire-step. His body would keep undergoing various contortions. First one shoulder would go up, then the other, then his body would slew round, then he would shake first one leg and then the other. His hands were nearly always pushed through his tunic front and shirt and his thumbnails were always thick with the blood of murdered lice. 'What the Hell are you wriggling about for Kelly?' we would say to him at times. 'Just turning t'owd b******s on the back to gie' young uns a chance' was usually the response.

We had another in the platoon almost as bad, George Hedley, who went out to Gallipoli with us on the *Gloucester Castle*. He was even lousy before we had been at sea seven days and was the cause of the whole battalion having our first 'Scabie' exam and a sulphur bath. He deserted from the trenches at Gaba Tepe and was found a week later wandering about on the beach. He was court martialled, did part of his sentence, and was sent back to us to try and make good but we could make nothing of him: the man was too damned lazy to scratch himself. There was only one thing he got enthusiastic about: jam. He'd thieve and scrounge jam from anybody and at all times. I'd seen on Gallipoli, when we couldn't bear the sight of jam, the whole section would pass him the jam ration, and he would open and eat tin after tin. It's a peculiar thing but neither Kelly nor Hedley would 'pig' in with the other. Hedley said Kelly was too lousy to live with and Kelly, who had a sense of humour, said he'd got a decent breed and wasn't going to let them mix with Hedley's. So much for the present about the lousy ones. I should say the extra lousy ones, because everybody was more or less lousy. The Colonel even kept having a quiet fake.

A Mr Wrangham took Surman's place as platoon officer to No.1 and had every appearance of being a decent chap. He had seen service before, having been a corporal in the King's Royal Rifles (KRRs).

Chapter Nineteen

July 1916 – We Relieve 47th Division

T he 1st Royal Marines (1 RM) were holding the line and things were very quiet. A patrol of an officer, a sergeant and six men went out the first night. The sergeant, badly wounded, crawled in about dawn with the information that the others were all lying dead in a shell hole near the German wire. They had been spotted from the Bosch trench and a couple of stick bombs had been shared amongst them.

All the front line was prepared for a cloud-gas attack. In every fire-bay the special section of gas engineers had fixed huge cylinders of poison gas with pipes and nozzles extending over our parapet and pointing towards the German lines. The engineers were only waiting for suitable weather conditions to turn on the gas, the artillery would turn on the guns and a raid by the infantry would follow to ascertain the effects of the gas. Conditions were thought favourable on the night of the 16th and we manned the reserve trenches. The bombardment started at 1.00am on the 17th and carried on for twenty minutes, but the rain came pouring down and the gas attack was a washout. All excitement died away with the bombardment and we returned to our shelters.

Later in the day we were paid 15 francs, but what use it was I'm hanged if I could see. Some of the chaps managed to get back to Corons d'Aix and brought back some bottles of beer. Soon after that a brag and pontoon school started. They finished up with Jock Baird possessing most of the 15 francs paid out to each man.

Things were very quiet up the line all day and at 8.00pm we all went up the line, digging and improving the trenches until midnight. The most interesting event next day was the tossing up for the platoon dinner. The four section leaders tossed up and Bob Bayliss won the lot for his section. We did without dinner, and had to manage on biscuits. There was another, and more violent, bombardment at night, the gas was let off and a raid was carried out, but by the battalion on our right. We stood by in our dugouts to reinforce the line if necessary, but were not called upon.

Our division had now taken over the sector from 47th Division. Our ground lay between Lens and Vimy, through Calonne and Angres and across the Souchez river. We relieved 1 RM in the front line about midday on the 19th and found both the firing line and supports in a shocking state. The trenches had been battered in all along the front by the German shells during the night and 1 RM had left us to repair them. Burst sandbags were strewn all over the place, and over everything was the smell of decay and poison gas. I had a good look over the top when I got up the line and could see the German front line about 120 yards away with a belt of wire in front about twenty-five feet thick. It was a solid mass of thick barbed wire about two and a half feet high, sufficient to stop an express train.

Our platoon had one dugout allotted to it, a filthy affair about twenty feet down and simply overrun with great rats. One of the entrances had been battered in and the place stank of everything vile and rotten. I decided that, come over what may, I would live on the fire-step and set about at once making a grenade-proof shelter. I scrounged a sheet of corrugated iron and, with about twenty sandbags and a waterproof sheet, made myself a fairly decent weather and splinter-proof abode.

Jim Hearne was sent away to field ambulance with something or other while we were at Ohlain and a Sergeant Doran took charge of the platoon. He was quite new out and not used to any of us and our little ways. We told him not to expect the same routine here as he was used to on Pompey parade or on a big ship, but he was determined to have his way with the platoon.

The first night, as soon as it was fairly dark, Corporal Tolly took a party out to repair the wire, which was in a poor state. The Germans could have walked through it naked and blindfold without discomfort. Tolly took with him Rendall, Spencer and a new chap just to show him what it was like. Sergeant Doran said he would go with them just to get his hand in. They had been out about ten minutes when the new chap dashed in for stretcher-bearers. Doran had been hit. I knew it would be a long job if word was passed down the trench so I dashed along for them. I met Mr Wrangham on the way down and told him what was doing and he dashed straight over the top to help them. When I got back with the SBs they had just managed to get Doran out of the wire. A German bullet had got him through the thigh and he was losing a lot of blood. By the time we had got him in the trench and on the stretcher he was very weak and said he didn't think he'd live long. They got him away after a bit more fuss and we carried on with our respective jobs, either repairing the trench or keeping watch. I kept throwing a Very light up and then having a shot into the Bosch wire. It's all a matter of luck, though: you might hit something, even a mile off, and yet you might miss.

Writing of night firing reminds me of Gallipoli, when we were about four miles behind the line lying in holes in the ground. One night we had three men wounded with stray Turkish bullets from the line. It's all luck, and so was Doran's wound. When the stretcher-bearers got back they said he died half an hour after they got him to Jimmy Ross. That meant another good opening for a platoon sergeant. They buried Doran behind Brigade HQ next day, 21 July: Tolly and two men went to see him put away.

The Bosch sent over some 5.9s during the morning and smashed the trench up a bit. Things got so unpleasant I had to take shelter in the big dugout. Even while we were down there the rats were running about and half the men had had their rations eaten by the brutes. I didn't stop down there long, but it's a good job I went down, for when I went back to my shelter on the fire-step I found it smashed in. A trench mortar bomb had dropped on it. A bit of luck for me, but it meant more work getting it up again.

Our trench mortar squad got to work in the afternoon of the 22nd and we had a good view of the effects of our toffee apples. They were dropping in the Bosch wire and in his front line, and great sections of wire and sandbags were flying up in the air every few minutes. Most of us had our heads stuck over the parapet during the strafe and we must have looked like a lot of Aunt Sallies to the Bosch, had he been looking, but I expect he was twenty feet below the ground waiting for the spasm to pass. They stuck it quietly until teatime then he started with his Rum Jars and *Minenwerfers* but I stuck in the trench. It was fairly easy to dodge one as you could follow the flight in the air and judge nicely the spot where it would drop.

The gas engineers were preparing for another discharge of gas from our front and a bombardment by Jerry made things distinctly dangerous from our point of view. The trenches were full of gas cylinders and we stood the double risk of being both blown up and gassed. However, nothing very exciting happened and the two days following were the same: the usual strafe and counter-strafe in the afternoon, ration and working parties during the turn off watch and the eternal 'stand to' at dawn and dusk when nothing ever happened.

I never used to sleep at night when up in the front line. If possible I got down to it just after 'stand down' in the morning and tried to get two hours' sleep. That would satisfy me for the day, except if things were slack in the afternoon: if they were I would snatch another hour. I could keep on all night providing I found myself something to do, such as sniping, wiring or lying out in front of the wire in no man's land acting as covering party for the wire menders.

We had a chap called Hobson in our platoon, only lately joined, and one of Lord Derby's men. He didn't like warfare and didn't want to fight and if he had anything to do with it he wouldn't fight. He swore he would give himself up at the first opportunity. And I swore I'd shoot him if I saw him attempt it. Billy and I used to get some fun out of him at night. We would wrangle it so that he was missed out of the ration parties etc. and get him on watch. I asked him once, when he was supposed to be on watch, why he kept his head below the parapet. 'Well there's a moon, Corporal,' he replied, 'and the Germans might see me.' Then I asked him what he was afraid of. 'It's not me I'm frightened for, it's my wife and two kiddies at home,' he would wail. He used to make me sick with his cowardice, but no matter what we said or did to him he never got any better and we never turned him into a soldier.

Billy used to get on top of a traverse and heave a lump of chalk at him while he was skulking and the poor devil would fall off the step with fright. I took him out wiring for half an hour one night and had to fetch him back out of the trench three times. Every time the Bosch sent up a light, instead of standing still, or dropping flat, he would scamper off to the trench, usually making a horrible clatter. He stood far more chance of stopping something by doing that than he did in stopping by me. Just before we had finished the Bosch sent over a rifle grenade which burst between the firing line and supports, but it was enough for Hobson. I lost my assistant and he sort of 'went to the latrine before he got there'. He stuck with us through the Beaumont Hamel job and the further struggles on the Ancre early in 1917 and then walked into a group of Germans at Gavrelle in April. That must have wanted a lot of pluck of a sort. He went straight from the tape with his hands up so that he knew where he was going.

Chapter Twenty

July 1916 – In Bully Grenay

We were relieved by 1 RM at 2.00pm on the 25th and we made our way down to the village of Bully Grenay, which was just beyond the bottom of the Bully Alley CT. The village was really a double one, Bully where we were billeted, and Grenay, farther to the left, which contained a mine that was worked at night, and the railway station, very badly battered and to which no trains now came. Grenay was more thickly populated by the French, owing I suppose to the coalmine, and there were several fairly decent shops in the main street. There were very few people in Bully though, and the French there all ran estaminets to make a living out of the British Tommy. They didn't always come off best though; we had some sharp lads in the Naval Division. It was a sight how much wine and bière these chaps could drink when they got it for nothing.

Just try to imagine the following scene: a fair-sized estaminet in Bully, the big room set with small tables and chairs. In one corner a counter behind which is the proprietor's stock of drink, bottles of vin rouge and vin blanc, Champagne, cans of bière, and the syrup grenadine and citron. All the tables and chairs are occupied with soldiers of various regiments. In one corner a group is playing at House or Lotto at a penny a card. Other groups are talking quietly together, perhaps discussing old battles and making plans of the trenches on the table top with a finger dipped in the bière. There at one table is a Mons hero belonging to the Army Ordnance Corps (AOC) who spent 1914 most likely at le Havre, and round him, listening spellbound with mouths wide open, is a group of soldiers, obviously out for the first time, and swallowing everything he tells them. Every few seconds his fist will thump on the table, which I suppose means another Bosch he has killed. And the listeners are paying every time. All of a sudden the scene of peace is shattered. Six Bosch shells burst with a crash amongst the fallen houses around; Madame immediately seizes the cash drawer and disappears down the cellar, quickly followed by the waiting Jeanette or whatever they call the pretty girl with short skirts and skimpy blouse. The new soldiers jump to their feet with scared expressions on their faces, but sink down in their chairs again when they see the others sitting still. The Mons hero has gone though, probably to his depot to draw a new pair of trousers. The quickest to move though are the 'birds' and the back of the counter is thronged with them, pushing bottles of bière, wine or anything else that is handy up their tunics. Then they disappear into the street before Madame comes back to find her loss. They always made sure of their money though. I never knew one to forget her till in her flight.

We were down in Bully for nearly four days during which time we had a bath, clean underclothes, socks etc., and managed to get a few fatigues in, such as digging new reserve trenches, mending old ones, and carrying gas cylinders, weighing 90lb, up the line at night. A party went up one night at 10.00pm carrying the things and the engineer acting as guide lost himself. The men were lugging the things about until 4 o clock next morning in pouring rain. The sense of direction some of these men possessed was simply appalling. God knows what would happen in open warfare. Half the blighters would be in Jerry's trenches.

We spent our time in Bully very pleasantly on the whole, though, and had a fairly decent billet. That isn't to say we had a featherbed and clean sheets, but we were in a fairly whole house with a wooden floor to sleep on, which was far preferable to the ground floor of a French house. They were all covered with tiles and it was like sleeping on blocks of ice.

Moved up in reserve again on the 29th and found some very decent trenches. Most had been constructed by the French who certainly believed in safety and comfort up the line. The trench, which was wide and deep, was covered for a good part of its length with shrapnel-proof protection, well supported with strong poles. The worst of a covered trench though is that they got so lousy. An open trench was bad enough, but with a trench of that description it was impossible to keep the lice in check.

Our divisional artillery had joined us and for a few days had been getting into position. They woke things up a bit in the sector and I don't know what the London Irish would have thought had they come back. We could get a very good view of a considerable part of the front trenches and spent most of the four days we were there watching the various strafes by the trench mortar sections. Nothing of very great interest happened to us, though; after spending five monotonous days in the reserve trenches we went back to Bully.

The first day down I had to see Jimmy Ross. I had been bitten badly by mosquitoes and one eye was completely closed. Hot formulations soon fetched the swelling down.

August passed along pretty much the same as July. As our division still only consisted of two brigades, and it was a two-brigade front, our spells in the trenches were longer and more frequent than they should have been. Things were very quiet, however, and life up the line got very monotonous.

The next time up in the front line, the Bosch exploded a small mine, between our front line and his, but we were prepared for it. Not knowing exactly which part of the front it would go up on, each of the two companies holding the front line had a crater jumping party always standing by.

I was in charge of A Company's rifle party and, as soon as the mine went up, had to dash to the far lip of the crater and take possession before the Bosch got there. Each man was told off for a special job, such as bomber, bayonet man, or digging party. It's a queer sensation, to be sitting over a mine expecting it to explode at any minute. Our company was spared the agony, however, and D Company on our left dropped in for the job. Nothing very serious happened; the mine, which was only small, exploded in no man's land and, after a bit of scrapping, (in which Lieutenant Wing of D Company distinguished himself) our party got possession of the crater and our front line was later on carried round it. It made things pretty lively all night and we lost a few men wounded. The trenches were in a poor state of repair by the time Jerry had finished strafing.

A very interesting piece of news that came through from General Paris was that all English leave was cancelled, but anybody bringing in a German prisoner would get ten days' special leave. That was after being out from England for about twenty months and being wounded twice. All sorts of special stunts were suggested and thought out, but only one came off.

One dark night two officers and twelve men of the Ansons on our right went across to the German front line and captured a sentry. He was proving awkward so he was hit on the head with the butt of a rifle, then they dragged him back across no man's land and through both lots of wire with a rope tied round him. Coming back both officers were shot, one very dangerously, and one man was killed. The poor devil of a German was dead when the rest of the party got back to our own line and leave was granted to none of them because old Paris wanted a live prisoner. However, they got identification of the regiment opposite, which was the 103rd Saxon.

About the middle of the month, 190 Brigade made its appearance and we had various lots of them up the line with us for instruction. The Dublin Fusiliers were the first to come and they were proper Irish. One day in the front line about eight of them, a section in fact, were arguing the point about rations and had nearly got to blows. The row they made was simply awful and the Bosch must have thought we were massing for an attack. Anyhow, he sent over a Rum Jar that dropped amongst the lot and put an end to the argument. Five Dublins were killed and three got Blighties.

General Paris was often round the trenches and would come strolling round at any time of the day, so that we had to have things spick and span, rifles clean, faces shaved and trenches swept and dusted. He came round one very quiet afternoon when the war appeared to be hundreds of miles away. Everybody was intent on his own job, which, with the majority of the men, consisted of sleeping; others were sketching, carving figures out of chalk or burning clusters of lice eggs out of the seams of their shirts. The general asked the sentry if he could see any movement and then passed on and went down Bully Alley. Bill Burn, our platoon sanitary man, followed him down after a few minutes as he had to fetch some chloride of lime from the FA at Bully. The French, while holding this sector, used to have an artillery observation post near the bottom of Bully Alley but a spy gave the position away since when the Bosch had strafed it every few days with 8-inch shells. He happened to strafe it then, just as General Paris got to it. One 8-inch shell dropped in the trench about ten yards from the general and when Bill Burn arrived there he found poor old Paris on his knees unable to move. He asked him to help him up and keep with him till he got to Bully. We could quite understand how it would shake the old man up: he must have been about seventy years old.[1]

One day, early in September, we were holding the front line again and I was talking to Corporal Pilgrim of the bombers. All at once I heard the whizz of a rifle grenade and the next second the thing burst on the back of the trench, a piece of it hitting Pilgrim on the thumb, nearly smashing it

---

1. Paris was born in 1861 and was fifty-five at this time. He was wounded severely in October 1916 and lost a leg.

off. I was untouched and put a field dressing on Pilgrim straightaway, then hurried him away to Jimmy Ross. He got home with it and the next time I saw him was in Aldershot. He had passed through the Cadet School and had got his commission a week or two before me.

On 5 September we were sent down in reserve and the same night were on a fatigue: pushing wagons full of rations, bombs and ammunition on the light railway from Bully to the support trenches of 189 Brigade. It was all uphill going and the quartermaster of the Ansons who set us off warned us not to ride back on the wagons. One man had been killed only the other night through doing it. A chief petty officer (CPO) of the Ansons went up with us and when we had discharged our cargo he told us to jump on, which we did. All went well until we came to an extra steep bit with a sharp turn at the bottom. Downhill we went at about 50mph and the wagon jumped the rails at the turn, finishing its flight through the air ten yards away, upside down. We went in all directions. I turned about two somersaults and landed on one knee on the bank, putting my kneecap out of place. I could only get back by hopping and holding on to one of the men. The CPO had his leg broken and had to be carried down on a stretcher. All the others came off with a shaking. I didn't report sick, but could only hobble about for days.

I was warned off for a course on 7 September and the 8th saw my departure from the Bully sector. Having drawn a decent bit of pay, I joined the rest of the party from the division for the course. I was the only NCO in the company who hadn't been away for a course of some description, so I think it was my turn.

We went by motor lorry to Pernes where a divisional school of instruction had just been started. Pernes was a lovely little town surrounded by beautiful country. Our school was a canvas camp, nothing very elaborate, and the exam and lecture room was a big barn. Work was hard and hours long, but we had every night after tea on our own. These were spent in various ways, either a ramble round the country, a night in one of the cafes, or else at the pictures, the first cinema show I had seen since leaving Port Said. The course should have lasted a fortnight but after a week orders came through to break up the school and for all men to rejoin their battalions.

Sudden orders from Army HQ had been received for the division to hand over the Bully sector to 37th Division on 16 September and to move back to villages lying between St Pol and Arras.

Chapter Twenty-One

September 1916 – Training for a Big Push

When I found the battalion on 16 September it was in the village of Monchy Breton, billeted in barns, cowsheds and pigsties. My section was in a pigsty but with plenty of cleanish straw on the floor to sleep on. The battalion was once more greatly augmented by the square number men and NCOs and the division was up to full strength. It was wonderful how the same old faces reappeared as the battalion came away from action. I don't suppose many of these chaps ever fired an angry shot all through the war.

I soon had a chance to show off some of the knowledge I had gained at the school, as the battalion started drilling next day. Section and platoon drill, company drill and, in the afternoons the everlasting battalion attacks. Later on, we did attacks by brigades over rough lines of trenches that we dug and which were supposed to represent the trenches over which we should do our actual push.

A good report must have come through from the divisional school because, on 26 September, I was made full corporal, which was very pleasing from more than one point of view.

Time passed very pleasantly at Monchy Breton in spite of the drill and marches and the weather was fairly good. The battalion was in good health and fairly good spirits and I think everybody was looking forward to the next turn of action, when we could show the Army what sort of division we were.

We now had the three brigades, divisional artillery, divisional train and transport, and the officers of each battalion from company commanders upwards had horses. Some of them looked proper cuts on them, too. I think there had been some talk of Naval Division cavalry, but the sight of some of our officers mounted must have knocked that idea out of the heads of the proposers. All the NCOs of our company had their photo taken before we left Monchy Breton. A rare lot we were too, but very few were left after six months.

On 2 October we received orders to pack up and stand by to move but the order was cancelled until next day. When word came round to fall in next day we found about twenty of A Company adrift. A hunt round found some in their billets and others in estaminets, all helplessly drunk. Of course, Joe Woods was one and I think the worst was Jack Spencer, who was unconscious through the effects of some rum they had bought from a Frenchwoman. The company was nearly half an hour late on battalion parade and the CO was just about frantic. All the drunken ones were placed under arrest and had to march off the effects of the drink as best they could.

We entrained at Tuigues in cattle trucks and after a long weary ride arrived at Acheaux. Once more we detrained to the pleasant sound of guns booming, shells bursting and the cheerful sight of shell holes and all the bustle of a busy sector.

Chapter Twenty-Two

October 1916 – The Battle of the Ancre

We arrived at a poor specimen of a village called Hedanville on 5 October after a ten-kilometre march along roads thick with mud and almost impassable owing to the continual streams of motor lorries passing both ways. On arrival, we were shoved in some filthy huts at the lower end of the village. We hadn't been there two hours before fatigues started and a party was told off to carry 'Toffee Apples' up the line. I missed it for once and, after a stroll round the village, turned in for the night.

Our 190 Brigade had gone straight up to take over the line from Serre to Beaumont Hamel, and rumours were strong that the division would attack either one or other of the villages. We had attacked both, along with Beaucourt and St Pierre Divion on 1 July with all the advantages of surprise, good weather and fresh troops and suffered a costly defeat.

The Germans still occupied their original trenches which had been considerably strengthened. Apart from that, the weather had broken up and the ground was in a terrible state. To make matters more pleasant for us, we kept hearing tales of the various divisions that had been practically wiped out attempting to take the ground. The unlucky 31st, the glorious 29th and the Newfoundland and South African contingents had all gone under there. I should imagine the Army had Headquarters think it a good plan for getting rid once and for all of the Naval Division. We'd always been a bugbear.

The fatigues we were called upon to do certainly had plenty of variety about them. We laid tracks for railways, constructed new roads, repaired old ones, made and repaired trenches and acted as carrying parties for 190 Brigade up the line. 'Toffee Apples', Stokes shells, bombs, SAA, rations and scores of other things had to be formed into dumps up the line in readiness for the attack. And through it all we were always under heavy shellfire and the Bosch was drenching the ground with gas shells. Almost every time a fatigue party went out it suffered casualties. The continual work, lack of sleep, poor food and wretched weather conditions soon found work for Jimmy Ross and men were going sick every day.

On 12 October we were moved to Englebelmer, a battered village much nearer the line, where at first we were billeted in the houses, such as they were. We had less distance to walk on fatigues up the line for which, of course, we were very thankful. Our band from Deal Battalion had been sent out to cheer up our spirits a bit, but it was little of the band we used to hear. Most of their music was played at Divisional HQ, miles and miles from our place of abode.

One night a small party went out carrying trench-boards up the line to Jacob's Ladder just by Hamel. An 8-inch shell dropped amongst them as they were coming back by the cemetery gates and killed ten men. They, or rather the remains of them, were buried in one blanket next day. Men were continually fainting through lack of food and rest.

We had a new captain in our company besides Captain Edwards, a chap called Captain Bissett and when down at Hedanville and not engaged on fatigues, he would have us out for company drill at which he fancied himself. One afternoon, after most of us had been out all night, he had us doing drill. Marching up and down, up and down for an hour without a stop, and all the time with fixed bayonets at the slope. Two or three of the men dropped out of sheer exhaustion. We only hoped that the swine would take part in the attack when it came off.

On 14 October we learnt the news that General Paris had been dangerously wounded and that Major Sketchly, the GSO 2, had been killed by a 5.9 hitting their motor-car while they were on a visit to 190 Brigade. General Paris had been warned against going any farther in his car, but he went on.[1] We weren't long before we had another divisional general and he soon made his presence felt. Shute was his name and was considered a most successful general. We knew what that meant.

Changes were soon apparent. Officers from the brigadier and colonels downwards wore a worried and harassed look. Their tempers got shorter

---

1. Paris was wounded in the shoulder and the back and lost his left leg. He died in 1937 at the age of seventy-six.

and our lives grew less and less bearable. Buttons, badges and boots had to be cleaned every day. Men had to shave and wash; eating and sleeping were only very minor matters.

New Army officers kept making their appearance and disappearance. It was surprising how small a time they stayed with us. There must have been something about the Naval Division that didn't agree with them. Discipline was stricter all round. Guards on various headquarters had to be mounted and dismounted in proper Guards' fashion and not as before, in ragtime Navy style. The change in generals meant a change in the plans for the attack and General Shute impressed upon Army Headquarters that, if they were desirous of wiping out the RND, we should stand a better chance of that happening if we took Beaucourt and St Pierre Divion.

On one occasion he expressed the opinion to some of our officers that we weren't capable of taking a set of trenches on Salisbury Plain. Of course, that comment got round the various battalions and made old Shute one of the worst hated men in the Army. We'd show the old Chute and prove him one, a Maltese one at that.

We moved to the 1 RM bivouacs, just in front and to the right of Englebelmer, on 28 October. The ground was knee-deep in thick mud and the bivouacs consisted of tarpaulin sheets slung about three feet from the ground in the middle, the sides being held into the mud by sandbags. Into these six men had to crawl like dogs into a kennel, if they got the chance to sleep. Our bedding consisted of a bed of juicy mud, a blanket, a cake of mud and then a blanket over the top of us. To make matters better we had three days' sharp frost which just about froze us stiff. For myself I was in excellent health and no matter what hardship I went through, or how bad food was, I did nothing but thrive.

Billy and I set to work on our bivouac and built the sides up with sandbags which gave us sufficient room inside to sit up. The rest of the battalion soon followed suit, and then we started with huge campfires made with wood from the broken houses of Englebelmer. Then we would sit or stand round them, telling tales or singing. We wouldn't have cared a damn about anything so long as they would get on with the stunt and let us go over and fight, instead of so much juggling about with bombs and flares, iron rations and 'toffee apples'.

Another little job we had was making bridges for the tanks. There were three or four of them in a valley just below our camp, all covered over with camouflage, and they were supposed to take part in the stunt with us.

Our last fatigue up the line for a few days was on 4 November. Mr Wrangham took a fairly large party, of which Billy, Corporal Grindy and myself were members. We had to go to Knightsbridge Dump, pick up an assortment of things such as trench-boards, barbed wire, picks and shovels etc., and make a dump behind the support line. Just before we reached the dump Jerry started slinging over 8-inch, 5.9s and shrapnel around the dump and the entrance to the CT.

Instead of waiting a bit until the spasm had died down, Wrangham took us straight into it. We had a dozen killed and badly hit in the first two minutes. Then he told us to get what cover we could. It was proper hell for about ten minutes. I heard two men of the Royal Field Artillery talking. 'You can't get past there,' one of them was saying. 'Half a dozen marines are going mouldy.' So they stopped in their funk holes.

I missed Billy and Grindy and didn't see them again for two hours when we were ready for coming back. Wrangham asked me to look for them, so I scrounged round the bottom of Gabion Avenue (the CT) and found them at last, sitting in a small funk hole. Each had his arm round the other's neck and both were as drunk as could be. They had found a water bottle of rum and had drunk the lot. Of course, being drunk, they offered me a drink and I could have done with one, too; the shelling had shaken me up a bit. The 8-inch shell that caused most of the casualties dropped only five yards from me and knocked me back into a trench out of which I was climbing. However, there was no rum left and before the night was out I was cursing rum and all its effects. Wrangham saw the state they were in and told me to see that they got back safely to Hedanville. We had six or seven kilometres to go and, soon after I got them started (which was a job), the heavens opened and it poured and blew and thundered and lightninged. What a night!

Those two idiots kept falling full length in the road, which, in a few minutes, was like a river. Then they would kiss one another, shed a few tears for the ones who had departed this life during the evening and stagger on for a few yards. It was 4.00am when I got them back to camp and the last thing

Billy did before reaching the hut was to dive headfirst into a heap of sludge that had been cleared off the road.

We had to be on the march at 8.30 the same morning. The brigade was marching back to Ruchvilliers, about twelve kilometres, for an inspection by General Shute. Billy stuck it for about four kilometres, during which time he was continually running to the side of the road to part with the rum. They found room for him in the ambulance at the finish. We were all pretty well fagged out by the time we reached our destination and we were billeted as usual in barns etc., but we had a rest and got cleaned up and had our inspection the next day.

Next day we were on the move again, back to Englebelmer where we were again shoved in the bivouacs. I think the state of the ground was even worse than before. We were visited one day by Sir Douglas Haig who rode up with his escort of lancers, stopped long enough to remark 'A filthy lot', and rode away again.

We moved down to Hedanville again on the 9th where we expected to receive definite orders for the attack which was now imminent. They came the next day when the strength of every battalion in the division had dwindled down from about 800 men to an average of less than 500. And tired, weary and fed up men they were too, but determined to do their damnedest and to make old Shute apologise for his words about the trenches on Salisbury Plain.

The attack would be carried out on Serre, Beaumont Hamel, Beaucourt and St Pierre Divion, by 2nd Division (XIII Corps); 3rd, 51st and 63rd Divisions (V Corps); and 31st Division: (II Corps). Our sector had a front of 1,200 yards and our objective was Beaucourt. Definite orders to move came on the 11th. Orderlies (brigade, battalion and company) were dashing about with numerous chits to various HQs and we were soon away to Brigade HQ to stow our packs with all the gear that we shouldn't need. From dawn to about 9.30am our guns had been thundering out their messages to the German lines. For weeks it had been the same. Just before dawn broke all our guns would open up on the Bosch positions and play hell for about four hours, but the first half hour was always the most intense. The country would shake and tremble with the concussion.

After masticating our share of bully stew, Billy and I had a dash round the village to try and buy a bottle of vin blanc, but it was a hopeless quest. The Deal Band, who were billeted there, had run the place dry. There were only two estaminets in the place, which I think was the most miserable place in France that was supposed to be inhabited by the French. I only saw two girls in the village and even Billy fought shy of them. Their faces had as much expression as turnips.

Orders to move came at 2.00pm and we wended our weary way up to Englebelmer in battle order – haversack on the back in place of our usual pack. Once more we were stowed away in the bivvies, only this time without blankets. However, we had a generous issue of rum to make up for them and when darkness came on we lit campfires and gathered round them singing songs and telling yarns. Sergeant Jock Berry and Corporal Tolly were vying with each other as to who could tell the filthiest tale. We were all in pretty high spirits, most likely because we knew that at last we had our job to do. I slept like a top that night with my greatcoat and waterproof sheet wrapped round me. Even the frantic efforts of the lice failed to disturb me.

It took a battery of our 60-pounders to wake me at dawn next morning. They were in the corner of the next field only about fifty yards away and with the first shot every gun for miles around opened up. It was pandemonium. From around us came the terrific crash of the 60-pounders, from ahead came the sharp bark of the 18-pounders, hundreds and hundreds of them, and from behind came the deep boom of the howitzers – 4.5-, 6-, 8-, 9- and 12-inch – and occasionally the RMA[2] would send over a 15-inch for luck. Not only at dawn but several times a day would this happen. The batteries would get the word to stand by, then 'rapid fire', and they would blaze away sometimes for a few minutes, sometimes for an hour or two. The Germans must have been having an absolute hell of a time.

About 10.00am several strange cases made their appearance outside Battalion HQ and soon afterwards we were marched up by platoons and served out with the contents. Bombs, red flares, Very pistols, lights, rockets,

---

2. Royal Marine Artillery. At this time there were two major elements of the Corps of Royal Marines, the RMA and the Royal Marine Light Infantry, of which the author was a member.

wire-cutters, and picks and shovels. Each man carried two bombs in his haversack with either one or two red flares, the latter for giving our position to the aeroplanes.

Our company and platoon officers were closeted with the colonel for about an hour getting the plans and time details. Mr Wrangham came along as soon as he could and gathered the platoon round him, all seated in the mud of a huge shell hole. There he expounded to us all that he had gathered from the colonel's lecture. It wasn't much. Sometime on the morrow (he couldn't tell us the exact time yet) we were to go over the top. During the darkness we should be lined up on tapes in various waves.

The 1st Royal Marines, who were holding the line, would form the first four waves and take the first German position, which consisted of three lines of trenches. A Company 2 RM would make the fifth wave. When the barrage started we should wait three minutes, then move forward at a steady walk, taking care to keep five paces apart and in line. We should go straight over the position taken by 1 RM and advance to the next German position just behind the sunken Station Road which was about 700 yards away. We should wait for the barrage and 1 RM, who would advance about another 1,000 yards, then we should go through them and dig in about 100 yards in front. The band would not be in attendance.

The whole operation would take about three hours. Zero hour would be told us later; and never was! We were all ready for marching off by 1.00pm, everybody looking like Christmas trees, but hardly so cheerful looking. Everybody looked fed up and felt it. Why the hell couldn't somebody devise some method of rushing fighting troops up the line in a fresh, clean and light condition. By the time a soldier reached his position for battle, he was half dead.

Three officers would go over with our company, Captains Edwards and Bissett, and Second Lieutenant Wrangham. Company Sergeant Major Jeffries was to meet us as we came back and regale us with hot tea and rum before we got in the motor-buses that were to take us back to the coast for a rest. What a dream!

Just as we were passing through the lines of field guns, some idiot passed the word along 'Rapid fire'. If there is one thing I hate worse than anything else it's to be passing a battery in action, but it wasn't a battery, it was every gun in the corps sector. Thousands of 'em! As the firing died down a bit the gunners came along to talk to us. 'Were we going over in the morning?' because they had orders to put up the heaviest barrage that had been put up in this war.

Just before we reached Knightsbridge Dump I got what I had been waiting for since setting off. Just a 'Good luck mate,' from one of the men who were watching us go up the line. Not much perhaps, but it was my return ticket for me. German shells had been dropping thick and fast round Knightsbridge Dump and several chaps were lying about in various attitudes just by the dump, nobody taking the slightest notice of them. There they lay, some on their backs, others doubled up all with glassy, staring eyes, and their hands clutching the muck in which they lay. Why bother about one or two, there would be thousands presently.

I was marching in the front of the company with Captain Edwards, Mr Wrangham and Sergeant Osgood, our platoon sergeant, and one of the nicest chaps in the battalion. He had taken over the care and transport of a big bottle of rum, all for our platoon, which would do during the night in lieu of blankets. We were making our way up Gabion Avenue trying to reach our trench for the night, which went by the rather imposing name of Buckingham Palace Road. The chap who named it must have had a keen sense of humour. The CT was full to overflowing; when we got in it the Ansons were already there trying to get up, working and carrying parties were trying to get both ways and parties of 1 RM were trying to get down. Some were wounded, some had shellshock, and others had just been buried. Our howitzers were busy cutting the Bosch wire, or thought they were. As a matter of fact, they were filling our trenches up and cutting our own wire.

We got orders to move on past the Ansons, who should have been away on our right. We managed to struggle on for 200 yards in two hours and then got stuck and could neither move one way nor the other. There we were, two battalions trying to get up, one trying to get down, besides the carrying parties and wounded. To help matters the trench was practically knee deep in thick mud. Just in the thick of everything and just as two idiots got out on top with a stretcher, the Bosch started throwing them over. We could hear them coming and they burst one, two, three, straight up and down the trench, 8-inch shells, 5.9s and shrapnel. The nearest dropped over the top ten yards away. We were covered with dirt and the lumps of casing kept buzzing amongst us.

There was a chorus of 'Get on in front', and 'Ease away to the rear', but nobody made a move. They just couldn't and a man hates to be held up in a crowd when the Bosch shells. They came over thick and fast and all we could do was to get down into the smallest possible space and trust to luck or the Chief Delivering Angel.

It wasn't long before the cry for 'Stretcher-bearers' came along. 'Stretcher-bearers at the double.' Who the hell could double up a trench like that? full as it was with filthy, cursing, grovelling humanity. 'Make way for the wounded,' was the next cry. And for another hour they kept coming steadily down. They were all walking cases as it was impossible to get the stretchers down. Most of the poor devils had been buried and those that weren't wounded were suffering from shellshock. We had to laugh at some of them. First of all amongst the shellshocks was the great and glorious Paddy Logan of Antwerp fame, and it was obvious to all of us that he hadn't got shellshock. What he had was what we were all suffering from: a very bad attack of 'funk', but he had let his get beyond control. I think the sight of Paddy and the good laugh we had at him helped to steady most of us.

The next was a corporal of B Company and he had got it. We knew him for a steady chap and he had been with us from June on Gallipoli. Two men were helping him down and we could hear his screams even above the burst of the shells. 'My God! My God!' he kept yelling and his face was horrible to see. Every nerve and muscle in his body was twitching violently. 'My God! My God!' We could hear his cry from far down the trench as they led him away.

Word came along that Colonel Saunders, the fine commander of the Ansons, had been killed by a shell and then later came word that Colonel Tetley of the Drakes had suffered a like fate. The Bosch kept the strafe up for nearly two hours and the nearest we had was a dud 5.9 in our parapet. All of us in that piece of trench gave thanks in our own way.

Through all the strafe Sergeant Osgood had nursed our bottle of rum like a mother looking after her young and there wasn't even a scratch on it. Nearly all other fancy gadgets such as rockets, flares and Very pistols had gone west in the crush. As the shelling got spasmodic we got a move on and soon after we turned into Buckingham Palace Road. Just as Osgood and I turned into the first bay an 8-inch shell dropped into the second one, filling it completely and burying five or six men. Some of the fellows who were in started digging away like mad to get them out and we had to get out over the back of the trench. It was just as Osgood was dropping in again that the dreaded thing happened. Just a stroke with a pick, just a little hole and all of the precious fluid was wasted. As the spirits dropped through the bottom of the jar, so our spirits dropped and we felt cold, cheerless and friendless. No one blamed Osgood. Poor chap, he was almost heartbroken, although I knew it was very little of the rum he would have had. However, it was gone and perhaps we should accomplish more without it.

We found all the shafts and dugouts occupied by all sorts of vaguely attached units. Royal Engineers (REs), Royal Army Medical Corps (RAMC) advance HQ, etc. We had about four hours to wait before going over to the tape and nowhere to get down for a sleep, except in the mud of the trench. Most of the fire-steps were taken up by dead men, some on stretchers, and a lot of them must have been there a day or two by the condition they were in.

After a lot of aimless wandering about, I managed to squeeze on the top step of a shaft. On each of the twelve or fourteen steps to the bottom were two or three drowsy recumbent figures. In the well at the bottom somebody had a fire and was endeavouring to make some tea or cocoa and in the attempt was almost gassing the occupants of the steps.

Corporal Tolly wandered along after a time with the cheerful news that Billy had been buried by a shell and had gone down with shellshock. Nobody was eager for conversation and the doings for the dawn were never mentioned.

Everybody was eager to get as much sleep as possible before going over. I'm hanged if I could sleep a wink, the smoke and fumes from the shaft bottom almost choking me. My thoughts were on those at home. I knew they would be worrying as I hadn't been able to write for some time and if our scrap was big enough for a mention in the papers they would imagine things straight away. My thoughts weren't very lively and as I sat there I was shivering through and through, seated in two or three inches of sloppy mud with a cold, wet wind blowing. The smelly warmth from the fire and from the bodies of the men was just enough to keep my bones from breaking

through my skin. My God! And they call this war. We had as much chance
of getting out as a celluloid cat has out of Hell.

Things were very quiet except for an occasional rifle shot or a pineapple
from Jerry. Every few minutes the reflection from a star-shell would light
up the trench, showing everything in its state of filth and rottenness. It was
a relief to me when Captain Edwards came along. 'Get your sections and
platoons out on top' was his order. It was just 5.00am on the 13th when
we scrambled out on top of the trench. A thick white fog had settled over
everything, blotting out even near objects. The few lights that were being
sent up by some tired fed-up German reflected dully through the mist.
There wasn't a sound to be heard as we followed miserably behind Captain
Edwards. The men were too fed-up to grouse and that's saying a lot. We
had another trench to cross and about twenty yards in front of that came to
our tape where we were spaced out five paces apart with strict instructions
to keep at that: there was to be no bunching when we moved forward. My
particular spot was a hole made by a 5.9 and I lay down in it and dropped
into a half daze, shivering with the damp and cold as though I had ague.
Perhaps the feeling of expectancy had something to do with it, although I
felt no fear, and I'd little or no doubt as to the ultimate issue as far as I was
concerned.

At 5.40am, when the mist was thicker than ever and lay like a wet blanket
over the earth, everybody woke up. The earth underneath us shook, just
as though a huge mine had been exploded underneath us; the violence of
it shook us to our feet. Simultaneously, a deluge of shells poured down in
front of us. An idea of the end of the world couldn't be more awful or swift.
It came upon us in a flash, one stupendous soul-splitting crash, then the
thousands of shells and we knew that the time had come to walk on.

To the front, showing up through the fog, was a vision of Hell, all fire
and brimstone, and our way lay in the very midst of it. We groped our way
blindly forward, at the start alone, but by and by through loss of direction
and the desire for companionship, in bunches of threes and fours, falling
into shell holes, over wire and over the dead bodies of the men of the earlier
waves.

Something dropped with a dull thud just by me, exploded but left me
untouched. I muttered 'that's a b--- pineapple'. About six yards away on my

right I could see Tolly stumbling forward. All at once there was a tremendous flash at his feet and he disappeared. I was conscious of fellows going down all round me. We got over our front line and scrambled through our wire in front, on which scores of our men were hanging in all attitudes, and made across no man's land. The barrage had now lifted and was playing some 250 yards ahead on the German support trench. It had been obvious all through that a German had stuck to his machine gun. As soon as the barrage lifted others joined him and bullets were zipping amongst us with effect.

It was suicide to go on, so, as we came up to the Bosch wire, we took cover in the shell holes until 1 RM should finish their work. We could see the flashes of fire as the bullets struck the wire in front of us. There was one chap already in the hole when I dropped in it, a Lewis-gun ammunition carrier of 1 RM and he was loaded up with about a dozen drums of ammunition. I asked him if he was wounded and he mumbled something and pointed to his ribs. 'Why don't you chuck those ruddy things off?' I said. No, he was alright and he'd stick to his ammunition. I'd an idea he was foxing, but had no more time to bother with him.

Sergeant Osgood fell forward into the shell hole, his face ghastly and the lower part of him covered with blood. 'Do what you can for me, Harry,' he gasped. He had got a bullet through his wrist and his hand was hanging on by just a bit of skin and flesh. The main artery was severed and blood was pouring out of him. I hardly knew what to do, but took off my lanyard and tied it tightly round the upper part of his arm, then I put his round, making a slip knot, and pulling it tight. It appeared to stop the flow of blood and I then put a bandage loosely round his wrist. Poor chap, he cried out with the pain and the broken bones rubbed against one another. I settled him as comfortably as possible and turned my attention to matters just around me. I asked the 1 RM chap if I could wrap him up but he said no, he was alright. 'What the devil are you doing here then?' I asked. He only mumbled something about being hit, so I left him alone.

I'd no sooner turned away from him when something hit me a terrific blow on the back of my head, knocking me silly for about five minutes. There was no wound though, just a huge bump and I had to shift my steel helmet several degrees to the front to get it to fit. The helmet had a nasty sharp dent in it, so I gave it a few silent thanks for saving my life and looked about me. There was Willett in the next hole with Holt, both of my section. 'Come on, Corporal,' Willet yelled, 'let's get on!' 'Get down you big-headed idiot,' I yelled back. I could see it was sheer murder to move yet. Being hot-headed on Gallipoli, and getting wounded twice under practically the same circumstances, had taught me a lesson in caution. I realised too that two or three live men would be worth a whole company of dead ones in this scrap.

I saw Sergeant Jock Berry of No.2 Platoon dash forward (full of rum he was), get in the wire and fall dead. Then someone dashed past me from the rear, reached the same spot and got shot down. The bullet must have gone through his chest and out through his haversack, firing one of his red flares. I knew the chap most have at least two Mills bombs there too, and that it wouldn't be long before they were off. I dashed forward, opened his haversack and threw out the bombs and flare, then turned the chap over. He was past aid though. I got back to Osgood and told him I would try and get the men forward. 'Good luck, Harry,' he said, 'I'll be alright now.' We could see the Red Cross men making their way up from the rear. 'Are you ready, A Company?' I yelled, and Willet bawled out 'Come on the Royals!' and we got on, through the thick belt of wire, over the first German trench and stopped for a breath in his second trench. The first and only live man I saw there was Captain Bissett. He was facing our way and, judging by the expression on his face, he must have thought we were Germans. 'Where are we, Corporal, and which is our front?' he asked me when he had gathered himself together. 'We're in the second German trench,' I said, and pointed to our front, which was thick with fog and the smoke of battle. In fact, the fog was thicker and it was impossible to see more than a few yards. I looked round amongst the men and felt thankful for the presence of some of them.

About twenty-five of my company had followed me, amongst whom was Willett, bigheaded and pigheaded, but game, Holt, steady and slow, young Nicholson and Bob Hackett from Wigan, not one of the bravest but willing to face the unknown terror of a German dugout for souvenirs. 'Let's clear the dugouts first,' I said. Thereupon Bob Hackett slung a gas bomb down one of the shafts nearby, following it up with a Mills. About six yards away to the left was the other shaft and in about two minutes we heard a 'Kamerad', then a Jerry appeared, followed immediately by a dozen others, all of them half-blinded and choking with the fumes from the gas bomb. Then Hackett made his way cautiously down the first step, a bomb in one hand and his rifle in the other. All the way down the steps we could hear his voice, 'Come up, you square-headed b******s.' In about five minutes time he reappeared, with, however, no more Germans, but in the possession of an Iron Cross that he had found on one of the tables below. I sent the German prisoners back with Nicholson with orders to come back as soon as he had turned them over.

I went to Captain Bissett who was still sitting on the back of the trench, just then having a drop of something out of a flask. 'Hadn't we better be getting on, Sir?' I asked. I reminded him that our first objective was beyond the Sunken Road, but he said we had better wait there a bit and see what turned up. Then he said that, as he didn't feel very well, he would sit on the dugout steps for a bit. And that was the swine who drilled us in thick mud for an hour with fixed bayonets at the slope. I shouldn't be a bit surprised if he had been granted the MC or the Distinguished Service Order (DSO) for his bit.

I started scouting round then with Willett. First I went left trying to get in touch with some of our lot. The first chap we saw was the 1 RM who was supposed to be wounded. There he was stuck up to the armpits in mud. 'Get me out of this,' he moaned. He did look a miserable object. I called two of the other men up and we tried to get him out but couldn't budge him an inch. 'I'm sorry mate, but you look like being there for the winter,' I said. However, I gave him an entrenching tool and told him to dig himself out.

Then I went farther left alone. I had got about twenty-five yards on and had just rounded a traverse when I came face to face with a German standing at the top of a dugout shaft. He had his rifle and bayonet in his hands and I don't know who was the more surprised. He opened his mouth to shout but too late because just then I pulled my trigger and he went backwards down the steps, and I knew he was dead. I gave a shout for Willett, but he was already on his way. The shot had attracted him, so we proceeded to clear the dugout. Down went a couple of Mills bombs and out came nine Germans headed by an officer. He looked a fierce devil and when he saw only two of us there I thought he was going to turn awkward. However, a threat with my bayonet against his stomach and he was all for peace. Two of our chaps now came up. Hackett was one and I told him to take them on to where the other chaps were. He told me some more of our troops had now turned up.

I went farther left but this time I told Willett to stick to me. The first thing we found was a German *Minenwerfer* emplacement with two ugly squat guns in it, one already loaded with a 10-inch bomb. Several extra bombs were stacked up in one corner. We left there and twenty yards on came to another huge dugout, which went down forty or fifty steps and down each shaft ran a smoke chute and a ventilation shaft. Scores of German rifles and bayonets were stacked down the shafts and rows of equipment were hung neatly from pegs. We threw a smoke bomb down one shaft and waited at the top of the other but no Germans made their appearance, so we made our way back.

We had seen only dead men belonging to our lot, all from 1 RM who must have got cut up in our barrage. There were scores of them lying about and at the top of the shaft, where I shot the German, one of our men was lying all over the place. His trunk was acting as a doormat for the dugout, one leg and an arm were on the fire-step and the other two limbs were on top of the parapet. God knows where his head was. There wasn't one wounded man about. All dead.

The fog had lifted a little by now and I could see the German third trench about 200 yards ahead, but who was in it I couldn't say. Between the two trenches was a stretch of shell-swept mud. I enquired for Captain Bissett when I got back to the first dugout, but was told that the worthy gentleman had gone away suffering from gas. Lieutenant Commander Fairfax had now joined us with remnants of his Howe Battalion and with him was the adjutant, Captain Ellis. I made known to him what I had done and how far I had been and he sent one of his petty officers along with six men and a Lewis gun to act as left-flank post. He said I had better attach myself and my men to his battalion for a time at least. I asked if he knew who was on our right and he said, as far as he knew, only the Germans. They were holding out in a strongpoint, but he would like me to work my way as far to the right as possible and he would then place a strong post there. I set off with Willett and half a dozen more of my chaps. About thirty yards along the trench I could get a good view of the trenches on the right, as the fog had thinned out considerably.

About a hundred yards away, and running as if for dear life, was one of our troops. Two German stick bombs were thrown at him, but even then I thought he would manage to get away. Fate was against him, though, in the shape of a piece of barbed wire over which he fell and the two bombs burst practically on top of him. Bullets zipping into the trench just by me induced me to get down, and we pushed farther along, working our way cautiously round traverse and fire-bay, I with rifle and bayonet ready for immediate action, Willett pressing close behind with a bag of bombs slung over his shoulder, one ready in his hand with the pin out. We got about seventy-five yards on and nothing happened except that Willett and I found ourselves quite alone. The other chaps hadn't acquired that roaming spirit. We went on for about another thirty yards and came to where a CT led back to the third German trench, and the trench we were in was filled in for about ten yards.

We decided to go back then and report. When we got back I found Jock Saunders (one of our sergeants) had turned up. A cool, steady stick although it was his first time fighting. I reported to the commander and he sent Jock along with six men to form a post at the top of the CT. They took a Lewis gun with them, and Jock was awarded the Military Medal for his little bit.

A lot more of our people had come forward now, amongst them the Stokes trench mortar squad. I went straight to the commander and asked if he could get one or two Stokes guns playing on the redoubt while some of us went forward. He said I could go and ask the Stokes gunner if the guns were alright. I found the sergeant in charge, but he dashed my hopes. Not one gun was fit to fire and no ammunition had got up.

Jerry started slinging 'Pineapples' over very soon after and our men were soon getting killed and wounded. Their snipers were busy, too, and were continually getting home on some of our men who were unlucky enough to keep their heads up too long in the same spot.

That redoubt and the third German trench had a fascination for me. Twice I pushed my way past Jock Saunders, over the filled-in trench, where I had to dash for my life and pushed ahead for about fifty yards but came back when I felt how useless it was and how much alone I was. If only the commander had sent a strong bombing party along that trench with me we could have cleared the redoubt. Three times I went down the CT and the last time got to where the trench lost itself in a maze of mud- and water-filled shell holes in which were bodies of Germans, our men and some Scotties, belonging to 51st (Highland) Division who went over on our left, and had evidently lost their direction. One poor devil was stuck straight up in the mud of a shell hole, upside down with only his legs showing from the knees. Fifty yards on my right I could see the German redoubt spitting death and destruction out of numerous loop holes.

On reaching the top of the CT for the last time I saw Captain Gowney of the Ansons nosing round with his field-glasses handy. 'Hello Corporal Askin,' he lisped, 'You still here?' 'Yes Sir, but not very still,' I answered. 'Get your rifle and find a spot for shooting.' Then I sniped at the redoubt while he spotted. It was surprising how much movement I could see in the German trench and how many heads were bobbing about. 'Good! Good!' Gowney kept exclaiming, 'I'm sure you got him that time.'

Commander Fairfax sent for Gowney after a time and I got down and went for a chat with Sergeant Saunders. Another chap got up in my place and when I came back ten minutes time he was still there but with a bullet through his brain. Fairfax sent for me then. He said he would have a walk as far right and left as I had been and would pick out suitable places for posts, for the night. Just as we were leaving the first dugout, where he had made his headquarters, we saw two engineers walking over the top, reeling out a telephone wire. One was a Royal Marine captain and the other a sergeant. We yelled to them to get down, but just then the captain got a bullet through his thigh and, instead of dropping straightaway, he stood looking round him with a look of pained surprise on his face. Then we yelled again and he dropped in the shell hole. Meanwhile the sergeant made a dash for our trench, reached the edge and got a bullet through the pit of his stomach. He pitched headlong into the trench just where I was standing. He was dead, killed instantly, and the look of horror and fear on his face was awful to see. He stuck there all that day, pushed into a sitting position in the mud, his mouth wide open, as though he had opened it to yell and had died before he could close it again. His face had turned a horrible green and his eyes remained open and glaring. I'd never seen such a horrible expression on a dead face before.

The commander and I resumed our walk after that episode but he was soon tired, too tired to drag himself to the left where walking was a terrible fatigue. It was simply madness to put one foot down and give it time to settle. It needed the utmost strength to pull it out again and by then the other foot was stuck. One had to sort of run on it and not in it. It was more like the miracle of walking on the water. One had to have faith, otherwise you floundered in a sea of stinking mud.

I was feeling pretty well done up by about 2.00pm. Not a bite or drink since the previous morning and not a wink of sleep. When the commander had finished with me I went along to the dugout where the chap in bits was. It was well lighted with candles and partly furnished. There were two chambers, one evidently for the men and the other for the officers. Each was fitted with wire-netting bunks, stoves and tables. In the officers' place I found a camera and a whole selection of photographic materials, negatives by the thousand and several printed on postcards, a selection of which I took away with me. I drank a bottle of Bosch mineral water, ate a few of his biscuits and a tin of bully and turned into one of the bunks. Half an hour later came the call 'Corporal Askin.' I reckoned to be deaf but it got so damned insistent that I had to roll out. 'Commander Fairfax wants you at his headquarters,' somebody told me. I wandered on and he told me to get all the marines together and 'stand by' for the redoubt. An artillery liaison officer was there and he was trying to get in touch with the guns. They were to bombard for ten minutes, then we should go over and rush the place. I had a rare job hunting up my marines. Willett had gone back with a piece of Pineapple in his leg. Hackett had gone back with some Germans and I could only find Holt and about half a dozen more. God knows where the others were. I noticed that no one was trying to rouse out the Howes. All the devils were asleep, even the men who were supposed to be on watch. I only wished I could find a place where I could 'die' nicely for two or three hours.

All at once the shells came over but, instead of playing on the redoubt, they were bursting on our trench. I thought we should all be wiped out. Shrapnel was bursting amongst us and we hadn't a scrap of cover. I was crouched near the artillery officer and heard him as he frantically tried to get in touch with the batteries. 'For God's sake stop the guns,' he yelled, 'you're wiping us all out.' The fire died down but there was no attack. Nearly all our men had fled to safer regions. Two or three more wounded wanted attention and a dead man or two required carting away after that spasm.

Some of the Howes and Ansons who had been in the first German line came dashing up the CT to take part in the attack on the redoubt. The first party I saw were headed by Sergeant Major Sands (a marine but attached to the Drakes). He came back again in three minutes with a piece of shrapnel in his leg; and for that, his first touch of fighting, he was awarded the Distinguished Conduct Medal (DCM). He stopped for a chat with me and then went down to have his leg dressed. He said he wasn't sorry to get away from it. He had only got as far on the trench as Jock Saunders' post.

Then along the trench dashed 'Dickie Downs', the battalion sergeant major of the Ansons, and after three minutes he was back again; and for that, he was awarded the DCM. It was damned little gallantry those two could show in the time. They never even got out of our trench.

The redoubt still held out and continued to dole out casualties amongst us, mostly now with trench mortar bombs and grenades. Things got very monotonous and I asked the commander if I could take the marines forward to join our own battalion. He didn't know where they were, though, so we had to stick it. Part of the Bedford battalion came to reinforce just before dusk, but why? The Lord only knows. The trench was full of scroungers enough.

Darkness came on and with it a bit of peace from the redoubt. No peace for me, however. Commander Fairfax wanted some Very lights and light pistols. Could I find some? I said I would try, but I remembered the strafe we had coming up and didn't think I should touch. I hunted round and found some German lights and a couple of pistols, but the commander wouldn't use them. He said the artillery might think the Germans were sending them up and shell us. The Germans in the redoubt were soon sending up lights in vast numbers, evidently under the impression that we should attack under cover of night. I don't think anybody thought about that, however.

I turned in again for about half an hour, but again came the cry 'Corporal Askin' and there was no turning a deaf ear to it, so I went along again. Just as I reached Battalion HQ a 5.9 burst in the trench amongst a group of us, killing three outright and wounding four. One poor Irish kid was cut to pieces terribly. I was the only one unhurt, although I was badly shaken and the cries of the Irish boy and the moans of the others got on my nerves. 'Jesus! Mother! Oh Jesus! Don't let me die.' The cries of the Irish boy shook one up as much as the shell. I sent for stretcher-bearers and with them came the Roman Catholic padre who tried to comfort Irish but the poor kid was soon dead.

Commander Fairfax was down the dugout and he asked me to get four good men together and patrol the front of the trench for two hours when he would send out a relief. He said Captain Ellis was taking one of his men and would try to get in touch with the party in front, either on the Green Line or wherever they had got to. No messages had been received from them, and of the many runners who had been sent forward none had returned.

I was out 'til 4.00am with Holt and Nicholson, the only men of mine who I could find and a terrible job we had, prowling about in the dark fifty yards in front of our trench, stumbling in and out of shell holes full of water up to the knees in sticky mud the whole time, and always with the risk of falling into a trench full of Germans, or stumbling on a strong patrol of them. Then if we worked too far to the right we ran the double risk of being shot by our own men behind and by the Germans in the redoubt. Sniping was being carried on by both sides. After being nearly shot up from back and front we decided on the safest part of the front to stick to and stuck to it. We waited in vain for the relief to come out to us and with all three feeling about all in, tired, hungry and caked from head to foot with mud, I decided to go in and report. The commander said we might turn in until it was light, when we could rejoin our own battalion. Captain Ellis had located them dug in just beyond the Sunken Road.

I turned in in a different dugout, and there, fast asleep in one of the bunks, was one of our company sergeants, Dick Howarth. Some of our lads said he had been there all the time and had never even put his nose outside the dugout. There is one good thing to be said about Dick Howarth though: he never brags about his bravery.

I turned in without anything to eat and was soon well away, but by doing so I missed a smart bit of work by two tanks. One of the marine officers, Captain Campbell, guided one tank over to the redoubt at dawn and the garrison numbering 776 surrendered right away.

About 7.00am on the 14th Commander Fairfax sent along for me and gave me orders to get all the marines together and take them along to his headquarters. After a lot of trouble, and with the help of Dick Howarth, who had managed to get a move on, we gathered all the visible ones together. Commander Fairfax and Captain Ellis were at Battalion Headquarters and they showed me which way to take. In fact, I could see our chaps lying out under the lip of the Sunken Road, evidently taking cover from a German strafe with heavy black stuff. They were about 800 yards away and Captain Ellis told me to take them straight over the top and report to Colonel Hutchinson who was in charge of our battalion.

It struck me as peculiar that these orders should be given to me, a corporal, when both Jock Saunders and Dick Howarth were there, both of whom were regular sergeants with years of pre-war service in. However, it was so. Commander Fairfax practically ignored both of them, and the funny part about it was that neither Saunders nor Howarth appeared to mind it.

You can imagine it didn't take me long to get my lot over the top and away to the Sunken Road. The ground was cut up in a terrible state by our artillery strafes and the weather had made it into a stinking quagmire.

The German shelling had died down to just a stray 8-inch shell trying to get the Sunken Road, and I was able to join up with the battalion and report to the colonel without loss. I found the battalion down to about eighty men with three officers, the CO, the Medical Officer Jimmy Ross, and Lieutenant Abrahams, and I think the latter's lack of spirit and inability to get a wriggle on got him through. He was a perfect dream.

On our left, towards the remains of the village of Beaumont Hamel, were the remnants of 1 RM, about sixty men with Colonel Cartwright and one other officer, and on the right were the Ansons with two officers, one of whom was my old friend Dave Gowney. They had evidently suffered some casualties during the last strafe. They had been holding and working in the trenches just beyond the top of the bank when Jerry started sending over 5.9s and 8-inch shells and one big shell dropped amongst about a dozen men, killing several and badly wounding the others. Even while I reported to the CO I could see Jimmy Ross giving morphia to one of the chaps who, I found out afterwards, was one of my own platoon. He was dead though when I found that out. Most of the men who were left were loaded up with souvenirs, German helmets, revolvers, field-glasses and boxes of cigars and gold-tipped cigarettes. I knew where the majority of that stuff would land if the men managed to get it back. As soon as the francs got scarce they would sell them to the Army Service Corps people, and booze away the proceeds. I think the ASC and Army Ordnance Corps are the only people who will have anything to show after the war. They have money to burn, getting five times the amount of pay the infantry gets and their risk of getting put out of action is about the same as the people at home.

An infantryman has little chance to get home with souvenirs unless, of course, he gets away on leave straightaway. I think that even if a chap found a bag of gold he would part with it after he had carried it in his pack round the front and trenches of France.

We carried on consolidating in the trenches throughout the day and nothing very exciting happened. Jerry tried occasionally to hit us with 8-inch shells, but most of them dropped across the Sunken Road, making a nasty mess of some of his dugouts. I noticed three shells drop exactly on the entrance to one dugout, so that did away with the theory that shells never hit the same place. Word came along later on that Lieutenant Colonel Freyberg had taken Beaucourt and had been wounded three times at the head of his men. A brigade of a rifle division had been lent to us and had gone forward to occupy our last objective, and to fill up gaps in the line occasioned by the holding on of the Germans in the redoubt.

As dusk approached we manned the trenches for the night and patrols were told off for the front, but luckily I missed that. I turned in in the trench and tried to sleep but found it too cold, so tried digging with an entrenching tool. What with that and a feed of German bully and biscuits I managed to keep fairly warm, but I felt just about at the end of my endurance, and I was longing for dawn and a chance to turn into some hole for a sleep.

Dawn did come, a cold foggy dawn again, but no chance to turn in. Jerry had been waiting, too, and sent us a few 8-inch and 5.9s to try to dispel the fog. Word was passed along to keep on the alert as the Germans were preparing for a strong counter-attack; very soon after shells were falling about the trenches in a most unpleasant manner. After about half an hour the CO told us to get back to the Sunken Road and take cover there. We were very thankful too as it gave us a chance to make some tea. Tommy cookers were knocking about in plenty, mostly German and they were better than ours. They actually boiled a canteen of water, provided you kept the draft away. Very near to me was the CO's servant, vainly endeavouring to make some tea for the colonel. He was struggling with a wood fire and the old man kept stamping up expecting his tea to be ready. We were all drinking ours and the sight made the CO mad. He stormed at his man and put him in such a flurry that, just as the water was ready, he upset the whole lot on the fire. Colonel Hutchinson got no tea that morning for just then the Bosch opened up on us with a terrific hail of heavy stuff. There was a mad dash for the shelter of the bank and there we stuck for two hours while Jerry kept it up.

It was obvious to us that the strafe was due to a trick of the Germans. Just after dawn, when we had left the trenches, an aeroplane came over from our front, flying very low and dropping red lights. It had on it the red, white and blue circles of the British planes so we thought it wanted our position. The CO passed word along for any men with red flares to burn them, so of course we did. Very soon the edge of the Sunken Road for as far as one could see was one line of red flares. Then the aeroplane, with a burst of machine-gun fire, disappeared in the direction of the German lines. Hence the strafe. The devils had sent over one of our own planes that he had captured at some time.

Some of the shells dropped very near and we were peppered badly with lumps of casing and covered time and again with dirt. Not one man was hurt though and we all kept fairly cheerful, smoking his cigars and cigarettes and eating his rations each time he sent over his kind regards.

Word came along that we were to be relieved at 1.30pm, for which our grateful thanks were very audible. Everybody from the CO down had had quite enough. We were all anxious to get back to the promised hot tea and rum, more particularly perhaps the rum and the ride back in the motor-buses. The time for relief came, but no relief, but we moved away and left the Sunken Road to anybody who wanted it.

We struck off right, almost to the front of what was once Beaumont Hamel, now a churned up heap of sticks and stone and stumps of trees. Then we entered a wide tunnel that had served the Germans as a communication trench. It was a splendid piece of work, the roof, floor and sides lined with heavy planks. Along one side, and strapped to the woodwork, was a set of light rails that could be let down and used with a light truck set for rations and ammunition. At intervals, large rooms for different staffs were let off on either side and access could be had to his three lines of trenches with large dugouts in each line. Large basket-covered bottles were strewn about the place, which had contained cognac not long before the Scotties of 51st Division had taken the place.

Some of the chaps said that the place was found full of drunken men with kilts on, and all the Germans that were found were dead. Progress up the tunnel was slow for various reasons. Our battalion was, of course, last to leave the road and some of the other battalions had got hung up at the entrance to no man's land where the Germans were dropping 8-inch shells near to the tunnel outlet. Then, of course, we were all on lookout for anything we could pick up, but nothing useful had been left by the gangs of souvenir hunters. Had they carted some of the dead bodies away instead of leaving them to stink and rot in the tunnel, our progress would have been quicker. We got to no man's land eventually, only to be strafed with 8-inch shells on our emergence into daylight; and it was a case of dashing for cover as soon as a shell had burst.

We got to Knightsbridge Dump about 5.30pm and once there felt safe and, of course, not a little bucked with ourselves at accomplishing so much. We knew that we had done practically all that had been asked of us, and in some cases more, but no details were yet to hand.

We struggled our way down to Hedanville as best we could, and it was a struggle; some poor devils could hardly keep going. It was a pitiable sight, a thin staggering, reeling line of mud-caked men, about eighty strong or rather weak, all that was left out of nearly 500 or 600 men three days before.

Colonel Hutchinson was marching slowly along at our head with Jimmy Ross and looking as proud as punch. Lieutenant Abrahams was dreamily bringing up the rear. Damn it, I thought, we ought to be marching back with a swing as though the band was at our head. Where was the discipline of the marines? Discipline was there alright though. The colonel hadn't forgotten who we were. A man belonging to some regiment ran across the road with a Dixie of tea, broke through our straggling ranks and made for a group of his kind who were standing watching us pass. Before he could reach them, however, the colonel had hold of his tunic collar and was shaking him like a terrier shakes a rat. 'What the devil do you mean by breaking through my ranks?' he roared. He said a lot more, then made the chap walk back across the road, but away round the rear of the battalion. Our men woke up after that, they seemed to realise that we were Royal Marines and tried their best to live up to it.

It was a weary lot of men who lurched into the huts at Hedanville about 7.30pm, absolutely beaten. The first chap I clapped eyes on was Billy Hurrell, who, it appears, had not been badly hurt and was by then quite fit again. Several other fellows were also in the hut who we all thought had got Blighties and they had nothing to show apart from bruises or scratches from the barbed wire.

I looked a sorry mess when I got into the light of the hut, caked from head to foot in thick mud and my tunic and trousers caked with dried blood from poor old Osgood and others. Jeffries had been true to his word and, as soon as I had dropped my gear, he was waiting with a mug of hot, steaming tea with plenty of rum in it, which was very acceptable. When it was finished I felt as though I could do it all over again, but as there was no need for that I set to and shaved the three days' growth of beard off my face with the remains of the tea and rum.

My pack had been brought up from Brigade HQ, so I stripped, had a good rub down in lieu of a bath and put clean pants and vest on and I needed them. I don't think I have ever been more lousy. All the chaps were congratulating me and I was certain for a medal, so they said. I said very little to that, but all the same I knew that no one had worked harder than I had.

I turned in with Billy and slept like a log until 3.00am when we were all roused out. The motors had come for us and we tumbled sleepily into the lorries and continued our sleep after the grumbling had died down. Why the b***** hell couldn't they leave us till daylight.

We were soon bumped and jolted as far as Puchevilliers, where we were shoved in billets, or rather barns and cowsheds, and told to clean ourselves up for the colonel's parade.

The colonel made a speech to us, not much, just said how he appreciated the spirit in which we had done our job, in spite of the hardships we had had to endure beforehand, gave us a few details as to what we and the division as a whole had accomplished, then touched on the losses we had suffered, which he said were heavy, but not in comparison with the gains of the battle.

We had been engaged, he said, in an action bigger than the Battle of Waterloo and no one could say yet what far reaching results would accrue from it. He asked us to give particulars of the known casualties, but unless we had actually seen a man dead we were to state that he was missing. Then he thanked us for what we had done and for the way we had carried on the glorious traditions of the Royal Marines.

There were tears in the old man's eyes at the finish and his voice broke. Some greasy sergeant from D Company called for three cheers for the colonel which, however, were given right heartily. Then we were dismissed with the exception of platoon sergeants and officers. One or two officers had remained behind on the 12th so we weren't quite destitute. I might say, though, that the best were gone. Major Eagles, our second in command, was left behind at Englebelmer to superintend the traffic and for that little job was awarded the DSO.

It transpired that the sergeants had stopped behind to discuss with the colonel any case for a distinction and very soon Dick Howarth came for me. He told me he had strongly recommended me to the CO who wanted to see me about Willett and Saunders. I told the Colonel about the fearless way in which Willett had gone ahead into the redoubt time after time and that he had been a big help to me in taking several prisoners, but I didn't mention that on each occasion he was behind me. I gave him an account of the post of danger that Jock Saunders took up on the right, and how he had stuck it. I didn't mention, though, that it was probably because he was comfortable. I didn't mention either that Willett and I, several times myself alone, had gone ahead past Jock for over fifty yards into the trenches occupied by the Germans. He kept me about ten minutes and then dismissed me.

Orders came round a little later to get ready to move in the morning. We were going back to the coast for a rest. And we needed it, too.

Chapter Twenty-Three

17 November 1916 – We Recuperate at the Seaside

We were away on the march at 10 o'clock on 12 November and joined up with the whole of our division on the road. General Shute was stationed at one spot on the road watching us all march by and the remark we heard from him was 'filthy'. Quite true, we were filthy, but the conditions were hardly conducive to cleanliness. We went about ten kilometres to Gezaincourt where we stayed the night, with strict orders to get cleaned up for the morning, every man to shave, every button and badge to be bright and every vestige of Ancre mud to be brushed off. Shute would again inspect us on the march. The old devil! Curses were levelled at him from all angles and from all ranks. I think even the brigadiers cursed him; because he strafed them; they in turn strafed their colonels; they passed it onto company commanders and so on down to section leaders whose job it was to make life for the men miserable, until old Shute was satisfied with his rag-time Navy.

Our next move was to Bernaville, where we stayed until the Monday morning. Our brigade was formed up in the village square and General Shute made us a short moving speech. We must have done wonderfully well to fetch such words of praise from such a man. He told us we had created two fresh divisional records: first, we had advanced further than any other division during the war and the other, that we had taken more prisoners than any one division had taken before. It had been an absolute triumph and messages of congratulation had been received from the King, Sir Douglas Haig and both Army and Corps Commanders. Certainly it was a triumph but at what a cost. From 1 to 16 November our division had lost, in killed, 100 officers and 1,600 men, and, in wounded, 160 officers and 2,377 men. And more than three quarters of those casualties were sustained by the two naval brigades.

We were marched back to our billets after a time and dismissed. About ten minutes later somebody dashed in, 'Corporal Askin, Major Eagles wants you outside.' Now what the devil have I done? I thought. I went out and found Major Eagles and Lieutenant Commander Fairfax of the Howe Battalion. 'The Commander wishes to speak to you for a few minutes, Corporal,' Major Eagles said. The old lieutenant commander was very nice and thanked me for all I had done for him on the 13th. He then shook hands with me and told me to get along to his adjutant, Lieutenant Ellis, and give him my name and other particulars, also the name of my Bomber Willett, who was away in hospital. After I got back, all the chaps crowded round. 'Lucky devil,' they said, 'It's a VC at least.' I began to think myself that I was in for a medal of some sort, but evidently it miscarried. One came through for Willett and one for Jock Saunders and one sergeant in the battalion got one – he had been in a dugout for the three days writing despatches to the CO.

We had a stand easy for the remainder of that day but 10.00am on the Tuesday saw us on the road again, this time for Cramont where we were paid and so drank to our victory and soon had the village as dry as a stick. Marched to Brailly next day and on the Thursday to Forest l'Abbaye, all the marches being about fifteen to eighteen kilometres.

We carried practically everything we possessed excepting our blankets, which went on battalion transport, so that you can imagine, after about fourteen miles of slogging with about 90lb deadweight hanging on to us, we were pretty well on our knees by the time we were finished. However, we were no sooner in our billets before Billy and I, and sometimes Bayliss, would drop our gear, see our own men settled, clean our buttons, have a wash and be off down the village to pick out the best estaminet before the crowd woke up. The best estaminet, of course, being the one in which the belle of the village dispensed the 'doings'.

The last march of this series took us to Romain, a dead and alive hole about which I have only the haziest recollections. I know we marched nearly thirty kilometres to get there, were pushed in a barn and as soon as the old lady of the farm had had even a glimpse of us she had taken the bucket out of the well, locked up her fowls and ducks and buried her money. What gratitude! Here we were, fighting up to the neck in blood and mud to get them their rotten country back from the Germans and they begrudged us a drink of water. Besides, what did it matter about an odd bucket or two missing or lost down the well, or a few odd fowl and ducks absent from parade. They could always get compensation. We were a fairly decent crowd, but things like that would fetch the devil out of anybody, so we smashed the windlass, scrounged a few eggs and hadn't been there long before we had thinned the poultry ranks down a bit. I had only been there a day or two before Sergeant Major Jeffries told me to get ready for leave. And not before time either. My last leave was Christmas 1914. It was then nearly Christmas 1916, and I'd been through a hell of a lot.

I arrived home in the early hours of Wednesday 23 November 1916 and spent a glorious ten days there, one day of which was taken up entirely in getting married.

I'm surprised at the War Office granting leave at all to soldiers on active service. There's nothing that takes the fighting spirit out of a man more or unsettles him than a visit home. No wonder men desert. All good things come to an end and I set off for London from home about 9.00am on 8 December and arrived too late to catch the boat train from Waterloo. I spent a terrible day in London wandering aimlessly about, writing letters in the YMCA, and finished up with an evening at the Victoria Palace.

Left in the morning at 6.15am for Folkestone. Arrived there and found my boat was an old, old French paddle-steamer, sister ship to the 'Ark', judging by her antiquated condition. To make the trip more interesting, there was a nasty sea running, and pouring rain, and I felt as sick as a pig before I even stepped on board. Got on board, went below and found a fairly dry corner as near midships as possible and went to sleep. And that's as much as I remember about the crossing.

The usual fuss and confusion on landing at Boulogne, then a climb to the camp at the top of a great hill. Spent the night there and took train to Noyelles on the 10th where I joined up with my own mates again in the same billet at Romain. Billy Hurrell, Bob Bayliss and one or two more were just ready to sit down to a feed of roast fowl, baked potatoes and mashed turnips. After a good feed and a good old chat with my chums I turned in, and stayed turned in all the next day as I felt ill.

On 12 December the battalion moved to Rue, a small town near the sea, but I was too ill to walk. Went on the motor lorry that took the blankets etc., then helped unload it, no light task with a bad attack of lumbago, but I turned in in the new billet and stayed there for two days, unable to stand or even to turn over.

Saw the doctor on the 15th and he excused me duty. While in the Sick Bay, waiting my turn for the doctor, who had just come up on his horse, he turned to number one on his list. 'What's wrong with you, my lad?" he said. 'Pains in the head and back, Sir.' 'Take these two number nines and go outside and hold my horse,' said the kind-hearted Medical Officer. Our own doc, Jimmy Ross, had gone to England ill and this chap had been sent to us temporarily from some horse lines I should imagine. The next chap had a temp of 102-point-something, and pains in the back. 'Sit over there for ten minutes,' he said to the sufferer and to the sick bay corporal, 'Take his temp again in ten minutes, it looks like a case of cordite chewing.' True enough the man's temperature was normal in ten minutes and he was sent back to duty and a report sent to the CO. No end of men had got away with that dodge but the MOs had just about got the topside of the mysterious disease. I've seen men, just before reporting sick, empty two or three .303s, miss breakfast and chew the cordite on the way to the sick bay. Result: a high temp, which, however, only lasted about ten minutes. I was excused duty for about a week and was really ill the whole time, and had no occasion whatever to chew cordite.

I returned to full duty on 22 December and took part in whatever training was going on. We never seemed to get away from the old infernal squad and section drill, and the men were in a terrible mood, ready for anything, and longing for the freedom of the trenches.

Christmas Day came along again; that made three away-from-home three Christmases and the rotten war was only going to last six months. However, no one thought very much about that, we just hoped in an off-hand way that the thing would be over in another year or so. What we were more concerned about was keeping the spirit of Christmas 1916 up.

About six of us clubbed together for two fowl and these with a good supply of potatoes and turnips (scrounged) and a few bottles of wine made us a good dinner. We invited the cooks to dinner on condition that they made us a good meal, and real well they did it.

Boxing Day came and with it a great outcry from a Frenchwoman for two white geese. Huge quantities of white feathers were found but nothing more.

We settled down to strict training, both company and battalion, and with an irresponsible like Wanky Mitchell in charge of the company we cut some queer capers. There is no doubt the man was mad. There he was perched on a great horse like a monkey yapping out orders that no body of troops on this earth could have carried out. The CO came along one morning and chewed him up in front of the whole company. He had managed to get us into a most hopeless tangle.

New Year's Day 1917 came and with it another good feed on poultry (paid for), and more drill. We practised brigade attacks along with 1 RM, the Ansons and the Howes over newly-dug sets of trenches, representing, I suppose, some enemy position. That kind of routine carried on with unvarying monotony until the 12th when orders came along to stand by to move. Our period of rest was at an end, and now for more business.

Where? No one knew and not many cared. Whatever part of the front we went to, we didn't expect to miss many of the horrors of the horrible war. Once more must we go through that nerve-shattering ordeal of the first few crashing, crunching shells; not so bad perhaps for some of us veterans as for the new reinforcements, many out from England for the first time and a lot of them with very little heart for the fight.

Two months of rest in which the division had been built up to its proper fighting strength. Two more months in the line and how many of these chaps would be there with us? Winter and every appearance of being a real old fashioned one with plenty of snow and with it acres and acres of mud. Mud! I hardly know which was the worst thing we had to face – shells, bullets or mud. It wasn't mud as we knew it in England, the kind of stuff that splashed your clean boots, and then came off with a little brushing. This was horrible stuff, clinging, cloying and an incredibly tenacious mass of filth and rottenness. Stuff that dragged the very soul out of a man and often left him floundering up to the neck. There was no getting away from it, it was our home, and even with the luck of a deep dugout it was still there, a slippery, sucking surface to everything.

Saturday 13 January saw us on the move, a march of seventeen kilometres to a place called le Titre. We were moving back in the direction of the Ancre, but the journey was too young to forecast with any certainty and, of course, being in the Navy, we never knew where we were bound for until we arrived. Sixteen kilometres the next day to Fontaine-sur-Maye where Billy Hurrell had the good luck to touch for leave. Sixteen to eighteen kilometres is just a nice march, and we had the heart left when we got in billets to get cleaned up a bit and make a dash to the best estaminet in the village. On the 15th we marched thirty kilometres, or rather we marched twenty and crawled the last ten. A terrible journey! From 8.30 in the morning to 6.30 at night and from 3.00pm we marched through a blinding snowstorm.

We stopped that night and rested next day in a fairly decent village called Autheaux. We needed that rest too. Why on earth couldn't they provide us with motor buses or lorries if they were in such a hurry to get us back to the front?

Moved at 11.00am on the 17th and for two hours before we moved off our company had a terrible snow fight with B Company, officers, NCOs and all the men taking part. On top of that, a day's work in itself, we slogged it for nineteen kilometres to a Godforsaken hole called Raincheval. We weren't very far from the Ancre then; the desolate aspect of the countryside told us that. Everything was frozen hard and the cold was intense.

Chapter Twenty-Four

January 1917 – Back to the Ancre

A short march on 18 January brought us to the all too familiar desolation of Englebelmer, looking, if anything, worse than when we left it. It was more battered, more empty, the roads were ploughed a foot deeper, and the mud was everywhere and more plastic. It had defied even the efforts of the frost.

There we stopped for the night and after a sleep in whatever shelter we could find we stowed our packs at Brigade HQ and marched by way of Mesnil and Hamel to Thiepval Wood where the whole of our company and B Company were shoved in a long German tunnel in the hillside to act as general reserves. That meant work, plenty of it too, with very little time to sleep.

The tunnel was in a shocking state. Whoever had used it before us must have been filthy pigs. Some had used it instead of the latrine and bully beef and Maconochie's were strewn about in various stages of decomposition. The stench was horrible and the whole place alive with lice. Thank God our period in General Reserve was only for forty-eight hours, then for a spell up the line. In the valley below us was the river or swamp of the Ancre and across the other side the battered and barely visible remains of the station at St Pierre Divion, taken by the Hoods under Freyberg on 13 and 14 November. All the water in the valley was frozen and the ground all round was frozen hard, too.

I had a scrounge round in the morning among the German trenches and dugouts and came across one of our tanks that had been put out of action and left derelict. From the top of the hill I could see half a dozen such tanks. I crawled inside that one for a look round but couldn't make much out of it, except to feel sympathy for the poor devils who had to fight in them. Certainly they were secure from such things as rifle and machine-gun bullets, but a 5.9 would make a hell of a mess of one and its occupants. I got out rather hurriedly because Jerry had started slinging a few shells over. The tunnel gave one a sense of security but the stench in it almost drove one out again to risk the shells. It is an open question, whether it is better to be shot or poisoned.

There was a huge quantity of German implements of war knocking about on the hillside, rifles, trench mortars, ammunition, bombs, and rifle grenades. We soon had fatigue parties out clearing up and one new fool, just out, mistook a German bomb for a cricket ball and kicked it. It detonated. Result: one reinforcement, minus one leg, not expected to recover. Some of the new men needed nursing like babies. They were in for a good breaking in in this sector, though, as far as I could judge.

I was put in charge of a ration party at night and sent up to the front line with huge metal flasks of hot soup. They were made on the Thermos principle, held about two gallons of liquid and were strapped on the backs of the men. I went in front with the guide, and our way lay over a frozen expanse of mud and snow, part of the way along a duckboard track. At times the duckboards ended suddenly in a shell hole made by a 5.9 or an 8-inch and, as the night was black as ink, some of the men had nasty falls. However, I got my party up without any serious hurt and with all my soup intact. I reached one trench which I took to be the firing line as the men were on watch on the fire-step in good strength. 'Where do you want this soup?' I asked the first sergeant I saw. 'We could do with it here,' he said, 'but they want it in the front line.' The front line was another 300 yards ahead and consisted of a series of shell holes, not connected in any way. The men were doing forty-eight hours in front and no movement at all was possible during daylight as the Germans could spot their every movement and were continually shelling them.

The poor devils were about frozen stiff and some of them were running and stamping about on top of their holes when we got up to them. 'Where's Headquarters dug-out?' I asked one chap. 'The next hole on the left,' he replied. I made him take me to it because my men were fed up with wandering about in the dark and things seemed so damned uncertain. I had been used to a continuous trench with a belt of wire of sorts in front, something definite separating us from the German. Here everything was different and one got a distinct sense of insecurity and lost the sense of direction that comes from a proper trench.

I found a better constructed hole at the next with an officer and a sergeant in a little dugout. I'd just reported 'Rations for your party, Sir' when Jerry sent over a couple of whizz-bangs, wicked devils of things that burst twice, once in the air and again on concussion. They were right amongst us but no one was hurt. It was a wonderful thing because my party were all bunched together and we could feel the lumps whizzing past us and smell the fumes from the explosion. 'For God's sake get down,' yelled the officer, 'he'll shell for ten minutes now.' He didn't, however, and we carried on serving soup. Back again to the tunnel about 3.00am without further incident.

Our turn on outpost at night and we moved up about 5.00pm. Just as we reached the support line we got shelled pretty badly. Jerry opened up with a few 8-inch, 5.9s and we had several casualties. We took what cover we could until he had piped down and then made our way out to the shell holes. I was in charge of one shell hole, with six of my section, and some attempt had been made to consolidate it. We carried on the good work with our entrenching tools and made it deeper and also made a fire-step in it. It kept us warm and it was absolutely necessary to work to keep ourselves alive. I had never experienced anything so bitterly cold. The next hole to us on the right, about fifty yards away, was manned by the Ansons and one of their men froze to death during the night.

My recollections of getting through the day that followed are very hazy. Most of my men were in a sort of coma and it was only by continually keeping on the move that I kept alive. I dug away with my entrenching tool until my hands were raw and my back almost breaking but I kept my blood circulating. We could get nothing hot to drink and had nothing to eat but biscuits and frozen bully beef. I kept having a look out to the front during the day and to the left front some distance away could see the remains of a village which I made out to be Grandcourt. Just to our front was a dip and the Germans were down there. Nothing much to fear from them except at night when they might make a sudden raid on one of our outposts. Nothing to see to have a shot at, but in any case it was a question whether the rifles would work. The bolts were frozen in.

Relieved at 6.00pm. Thank God. Another twelve hours of that would have killed some of us off. Only moved back to the support trench where things were very little better, except that one could move about a bit more freely and make a fire to brew some tea.

We were practically all on watch at night as Jerry was supposed to be on the prowl. He was expected to be moving back from there any time but was putting up a feint of aggression in the form of sudden raids. Spasms of shelling all night and everybody was about frozen stiff. I was sent back to the tunnel at 1.00pm on the 23rd with a party of eight men. 'Get a rest, a feed and get back to the line by 8.00pm with picks and shovels for dugout work.' Six hour shifts. What a life! Horses were dropping dead in hundreds but the RN Division carried on.

Back to the tunnel after my six hours. I had no need to dig but I did it to keep myself awake and alive. I turned in when I got back, in the filth and muck and lice of the stinking tunnel, and had a sleep, the first sleep since leaving Englebelmer on the 18th; it was now the 23rd. There was a spasm on 190 Brigade's front during the night: a strong party of Germans made their way down the frozen river and cleared one of the Hood outposts. After a pretty severe hand-to-hand scrap the Germans were driven back, having sustained several casualties. They left a few dead to be buried, but a few of the Hoods too, the officer, Sub-Lieutenant McCormick, and seven men killed and a score wounded. Little things like that never found their way into the papers at home, but it was an everyday happening on the front and part of our routine.

Jerry shelled the valley and the road to the tunnel during the night and most of the next day (24th) but it would have taken a pretty hefty shell to reach us in the tunnel.

Our battalion had arranged a raid for the night, one officer, Lieutenant Spinney, and two bombers from C Company. They went over without any fuss and took possession of a German outpost, killing the garrison and smashing up the place pretty badly with bombs. The same officer, with Lieutenant Wren and four men, went over again the next night but failed to pull things off quite so easily. Spinney was wounded and died shortly after they got him back to our lines. It wasn't wise to tempt fate too often. She is a fickle jade, one day all for you, and throwing an invulnerable curtain around you so that you can face the horrors of the war with impunity, but the next day she is for somebody else and you get what you have been asking for.

Saw a splendid fight in the air during the afternoon. Three Taubes ventured over our lines and managed to get through the curtain of anti-aircraft shells that was thrown at them. Two of our fighting planes dropped down out of the blue and one Taube came crashing down to earth. That evened up the party and we watched some very pretty stunt-flying for five minutes before Jerry turned tail and made for home, one of them obviously in trouble, for he made for the ground as fast as he could with safety.

News around on the morning of the 25th that 1 RM would relieve us at 1.00pm. The relief came off to time and we made our weary way back to Englebelmer. Shoved into tumbledown billets, which we set about making as habitable and comfy as possible. It was a queer thing this taking over of billets: whenever we left any we had a proper cleaning-up time; in our battalion platoon NCOs were responsible for their billets being spotless, with no litter, empty tins or chunks of bully lying about. Floors had to be swept, usually with old sandbags, then the company OC came along and they had to satisfy him. But when we took any over, even from our 1st Battalion – which, by the way, was always second to ours, except in number – we always had the same process to go through. We would find everything in a state of filth.

Twenty-five degrees of frost failed to curb the frantic efforts of the lice. The extreme cold was killing off horses and men but had no effect whatever on lice, except to make them dig in more. Kelly Clayton and George Hedley were in one continual squirm.

The postbag kept us all more or less busy until time to turn in: parcels and letters galore.

Morning came and with it a keener frost than ever. Some bright engineers had rigged up hot shower baths in the village and we marched down by platoons for the unexpected luxury. What a disillusion. Our platoon of course, being No. 1 A Company was first, and we found the floor of the baths a sheet of ice on which we had to stand shivering in our nakedness until the hot water gradually thawed its way through the blocks of ice in the few watering can knobs above us. We must have been hard as nails to stand that lot. I really think that the worse conditions seem to get the more we thrived.

The Marine Band from Deal played in the YMCA hut at night and cheered us up a bit. It's wonderful what a bit of decent music can do to a chap.

I got a shock on the following morning, the 27th. Company Sergeant Major Dick Howarth asked me if I would like a square number. 'What is it, Dick?' I asked him. 'Anything to do with the line?' I was a bit dubious. 'No, it's alright,' he laughed, 'it's a good number, and I've to pick a good corporal and nine men to be attached to the REs at Aveluy.' I accepted. REs usually knew how to do themselves well and it meant a few trips to Albert, only twenty minutes' walk from Aveluy.

Set off about 3.00pm with my nine good men and true and reported to the REs' sergeant major. It was a mining company and about every other man from the major downwards had a decoration of some sort or other: VCs, DSOs, DCMs and MMs were as common with them as hard tack was with us. 'How did you get all those?' I asked one sergeant. 'Rations,' he said with a grin, 'one comes up every week whether we want it or not.'

We were stowed away in a palatial dugout with spring mattresses on the bunks. Found various other fatigue parties there from the Howes and Ansons, about sixty of us all told. Rations were fine and work not very strenuous. We went up to Thiepval a few times; the REs were constructing new, up-to-date dugouts in the remains of the village and our job was digging and carrying out the earth and rock while the REs got busy with tape measures and two-foot rules, and a few instructions.

Not one trip up to the first trench system did we do, our nearest being a general reserve trench where we constructed a new dugout. I think it only fair to say that, during the time I was attached to that company of engineers, none of them received any additional medals.

Why we should have been constructing brand new dugouts with steel girders and walls lined with one-inch planks I am at a loss to understand. The Bosch was expected to flit from these quarters at any time, and signs were fairly obvious that our people were making preparations to help him away with a push.

Our 189 Brigade attacked on 3 February, just a trench-to-trench attack timed to take about ten minutes but which actually took fifty hours of terrible fighting in which the brigade lost twenty-four officers and 647 ORs, a big proportion of them killed. They succeeded, however, and took two lines of trenches commanding Grandcourt. Captures amounted to two officers and 225 men, about forty of whom were wounded, and a few machine guns.

The success of the attack was soon apparent, for on the night of the 5th, when our Brigade had taken over from 189, a patrol of the Howes pushed into Grandcourt and came back with rifles left by the Bosch. Upon receiving this information, Colonel Hutchinson took our battalion forward and took possession of the whole place without a casualty.

Thus started the first move in the great German retreat. Well done the Navy!

Chapter Twenty-Five

The RN Division persuade Jerry to Retreat

L ife was very uneventful for me, not much work being done by the REs and no excitement except a few bombs at night from Jerry's planes. Some of his bombs made holes big enough to drop a house in, but none reached us in the dugout, and very little damage was done by them with the exception of a few horses killed.

I made several trips to Albert, a decent-sized town, but it had very little of interest in it, with the exception of an Expeditionary Forces Institute (EFI) canteen, and a battered cathedral. A very remarkable thing about the cathedral was the figure of the Virgin Mary hanging in a horizontal position from the top of the main and only remaining spire. The whole place was a wreck and it seemed wonderful that the figure should be hanging on as it were by the toenails. I believe the French engineers had been up and secured the figure and the French people said the war would end when the Virgin fell. It's surprising some of our credulous men hadn't tried a Mills bomb on her before then. (The Virgin, with the remains of the Cathedral at Albert, was battered flat by the Germans in March 1918, just before they re-took the place.)

The 2nd Royal Marines should have been relieved by 1 RM on 8 February, but for some reason or other they couldn't bring off the relief till the 9th. I went over to Englebelmer to see the boys on the Saturday morning and got to know all the latest news and rumours. The chief buzz was to the effect that the RND was to be relieved and sent home to Blighty. The relief came off alright; 1 RM was only up the line a day before turning over to the Army and going back to Englebelmer.

My company had a decent few casualties during their last spell up the line. German planes came over Aveluy again at dusk on Saturday and dropped more than twenty huge bombs in the valley where our dugout was situated. Very little damage was done, however, beyond a few more horses killed and maimed. I fail to see what attracted the silly blighter over that valley.

Heard news that 190 Brigade, who took over from our brigade on the left, had been making things hum. The HAC went forward another 600 yards and took Baillescourt farm with eighty-one prisoners. They lost their commanding officer, Colonel Boyle, who had been in command since the battalion landed in France.

On 14 February 2 RM was once more wending the weary way up the line again, battle orders with two days' extra emergency rations. More business, and I was missing it nicely, although I was sorry in a way not to be with them: it looked like being a decent-sized scrap. Two or three fresh divisions were sending troops up the line and Albert was full of 2nd and 8th Division troops and one had to nearly fight to get anything from the canteen there. Our artillery was busy and was pumping hundreds of tons of high explosive into the Bosch every day. His guns weren't altogether idle and there were times when it was hardly safe to go far from cover.

The attack came off at 5.45am on the 17th, the RN Division on the left of the Ancre, led by our brigade, (1 RM and two companies of our battalion) and 2nd and 18th Divisions on the right of the river. From what news we could get, the attack was a howling success, although both marine battalions suffered badly. The Bosch barrage had caught them in the open before the attack started and they had to stick it in the shell holes until the time came to get a move on. It's bad enough in a trench when Jerry puts a barrage down, but a hundred times worse when one is lying out in the open with hardly a scrap of cover. The marine casualties were over 400 killed and wounded, nearly 40 per cent. The loss for the whole brigade was about 700, but what's 700 casualties when the objective is gained?

I had a casualty in my party on the Saturday night. One of my men, Thompson, who had been with the battalion nearly as long as me, had a walk to Albert after tea and, whether he got drunk or not I can't say, he managed to fall over the low parapet of the railway bridge, and his cold body was found on the lines twenty-five feet below in the morning. Nearly every bone in his body was broken and his neck too, so that he didn't suffer a deal.

The thaw had set in with a vengeance and the ground, which for months had been frozen solid was now a stinking, slimy quagmire, in which one floundered up to the waist.

Orders were issued on the 19th to the effect that all details of 188 Brigade were to re-join their respective battalions on the 20th. Paraded at 8.00am and found I was in charge of fifty-seven men with three NCOs from the Ansons and Howes. One leading seaman of the Ansons went sick straightaway when he heard that our destination was the front line. He got away with it, although there was nothing more wrong with him than a bad attack of funk. For myself, I felt fit for anything and took charge in quite a happy frame of mind. The rest with the REs had done me no end of good and I felt fairly eager to get back to my own chums and a bit more real soldiering.

I was given the position of our Brigade HQ where I had to report and got all my party there by about 1.00pm. There we got rigged out in battle order and were given a good hot feed of bully stew and tea. We set off at 7.00pm from there with a guide who would take us to the Advanced HQ. 'Do you know your way there, Corporal?' asked the officer to our guide. 'Yes, Sir,' the guide replied. 'I've only just come from there.' Yes, he had! My God, what a guide. He had us wandering about for two hours in that godforsaken stretch of mud and shell holes with the rain beating right through us, flashing his electric torch all over the place and remarking every few minutes 'Yes, this is the right way'. The chap was dizzy; there was no doubt about that and he was wandering about aimlessly, lost. The remarks he kept getting from the men in the rear did nothing to help steady him and I kept cursing him. 'Where the hell are you going?' I asked him after about an hour and a half. 'I don't know, I'm B--- if I do,' he said. Soon after a voice called out 'What party are you?' 'RND details, are you the Advance Battalion Headquarters?' I asked. 'What the devil are you doing here? You left this place two hours ago.' That guide got chewed up a treat and he deserved it. We had wandered in a complete circle, and off we had to go again. We were in a murderous mood.

We met a party of officers and men looking for us with flash lamps about half a mile from the place we were trying to find. An officer was waiting there to guide us up the line and I could see as soon as he opened his mouth that he didn't like his job and was all for speed. 'Tell your men to keep closed up, Corporal, and whatever they do they must hurry,' he said. He told me our way was through the Valley of Death or Death Valley and every so often the Bosch opened up with all sizes of guns and nothing could live in the place once he started.

He was a most cheerful officer and went on to say that the whole place was full of dead men and nobody dared out to bury them. A pity he wasn't one of them. 'Quick march,' he shouted as though he were on parade at Crystal Palace and off he toddled, his long legs making light work of the knee-deep mud. After five minutes, 'Ease off in front, we're not bloody racehorses' and off I had to dash to the rear to buck the stragglers up. There was no easing up in front though, and I had to fairly skim along the top of the mud to catch up that brilliant officer. 'We shall have to go steady, Sir,' I told him, but he wouldn't have it. 'If they can't keep up they will get left behind,' he said, 'I'm not hanging about in this place.' He said he was expecting the Germans to open up any minute, and off he went again.

I was on a continual run backwards and forwards along the line, trying to keep the men together. Some of the poor devils were about all in and, after an hour, some of them sat down in the mud and refused to budge. I left one of the leading seamen with them and told him to bring them along as best he could. I never saw that officer again and about a dozen of the leading men had gone with him. Where to go I hadn't the faintest notion, but one thing I was determined on and that was to get out of that stinking 'Valley of Death' and the sight of two GS wagons with horses and drivers smashed to bits lying in the stinking mud just by the side of the so-called track speeded my resolution up.

It bucked the men up too. 'Get out of this bloody place, Corporal,' someone yelled and I made off for the high ground on my left. I struck a trench on top just as Jerry opened up with a battery of 5.9s and we could hear them as they exploded with a sickening squelch in the valley below. The trench was full of water. In places we were wading up to the armpits in the foul stuff.

I had no idea how far the line was ahead, but after struggling on for about 500 yards up the trench, I came across two chaps trying to patch up a telephone wire that the Bosch had smashed, and got to know from them that there was a battalion HQ about half a mile ahead under a bank.

We got there, more dead than alive, and I found the imperturbable Lieutenant Abrahams, our acting adjutant, in a shell hole with a roof on. I reported to him and gave him my opinion of the officer who was supposed to guide us up here. 'All right, Corporal Askin,' he said, 'I know the swine and I'll send a report back to Brigade Headquarters about him.' And I guessed he would too.

One o'clock in the morning, nearly dead with fatigue and with soul cases nearly dragged out of us with the mud. And I reckon I had dragged my way through three times as much mud as the other men. I had been on the double continually, first finding the way and then dashing back to the rear of the line to herd the stragglers together, then on again to the front. I just felt like something that had been left on a plate in the rain all night for the cat. I hadn't finished though, not by any means.

Our adjutant gave me instructions to take the men of 2nd Marines to our Company HQ somewhere in the front line. He said we were to be relieved any time now; in fact some of the relieving troops were already making their way up the line ahead. I set off again, very nearly on my hands and knees and soon struck a communication trench, more like a young canal though than a trench. The going in that trench was worse than anything I had ever experienced before and progress was a terrible struggle. We soon came across parties of the relieving troops, absolutely stuck fast in the mud and many of them making no effort whatever to get out of it. 'What division are you, Mate?' I asked one poor devil. 'Sixty-second,' he said. That was the division that had earned the nickname of John Bull's Division; and this was its first trip out from England. What a breaking in. One of its other members told me they had been three days making their way up the line from Englebelmer. Some were crying out of sheer despair at their inability to move. Others were just sitting in the mud cursing.

Found the company at last in the front line, sadly depleted and nearly dead with exhaustion from the mud and effects of the attack they had made. 'Have you seen anything of a relief, Harry?' Billy asked me when I saw him. 'I've seen it Billy, but don't set hopes on it, they'll want relieving before they get up here.' I set about making a canteen of tea as soon as I settled down with my own platoon. None of the men had had anything hot to drink for four days and had lived on nothing but dried bully and biscuits with water to drink. Fires for cooking were out of the question, wood was practically non-existent, and so were Tommy cookers, but I had taken a few candles up in my haversack and one of those broken in two, wrapped in a piece of 4x2 and put in a cigarette tin was just sufficient to get a canteen of water on the sing. That was good enough to mash tea when one wanted it as badly as I was.

As dawn had broken by the time I had finished, I set to and shaved and washed in the remains of the tea and felt heaps better. Poor old Charlie Hamilton had got his ticket at last. To get through the nine months of hell fire on Gallipoli without a scratch, then all these last months in France. Billy told me how he had died; quite a peaceful end for the old boy. He had laid back on the trench for a sleep, with the mud for a bed and a shell had burst killing him as he lay asleep. Billy was walking round the trenches and came across him and thought him asleep. Charlie had gone though, and with a smile on his fine face. Billy cried like a kid when he told me. It had only happened on the day before I got up, but I couldn't get to see him as Billy had helped to bury him. He had taken his things from his pockets and said that he would write to Charlie's wife when he got down the line. Another of the old boys gone, another real pal, and there's a bonny little chap in Portsmouth will never see his dad again.

And what in Hell's the reason for it all and what good can possibly come from all this rotten sacrifice and bloodshed? The hundreds of splendid men and lads I've seen killed in this war and the hundreds of thousands killed that I haven't seen. What have they gone for? It makes you curse war when you come to think about it and curse the men, too, who made the war and who no doubt get out of it scot free. It's a blessing, really, that we get hardened both in body and mind and that we lose all sentiment and feeling, otherwise we should go stark staring mad. It's not that way, though, it's just a shrug and a brief moment of regret at still another good pal gone west. 'Poor old Charlie,' and then we have to carry on. No time to dwell on it, we might have to go any time. And who cares a damn when the time should come? I am certain that when a man has reached such a state of abject misery and exhaustion as some of the lads around me, death must seem a merciful relief and an easy way out of it all.

Apart from the relief when one is killed, one is placed amongst the immortals amongst the glorious dead heroes, all who died for a cause, while the ones who struggle on through the lot will earn for themselves nothing but the name of fool.

I managed to get through that day, the 21st, safely, although the Bosch strafed us pretty badly in spasms and his snipers had a fair command of sections of the line. The company had a few casualties during the day and several men had to go back suffering from exhaustion. The news that a sufficient number of 62nd Division had managed to crawl up the line to effect a relief was greeted joyfully and a few smiles were seen on the gaunt, haggard faces of some of the men. Nightfall came and with it some very tired mud-caked and fed-up men from Yorkshire who would relieve us. Our 190 Brigade was to go forward and clear the enemy rearguards out of his positions at Miraumont and Gommecourt, while we were recuperating at Englebelmer.

We left the line at 1.00am on 22 February and struggled back to Englebelmer as best we could. When we reached the road at St Pierre Divion we found our cooks and kitchens there and were served with hot tea and a good tot of rum. It helped us well on our way and we hardly troubled about the state of the roads, which in places were nothing but rivers, in places knee deep in water and mud. Just imagine the splash when a lorry loaded with 8-inch shells went lumbering past. Who cared? Were we not being relieved, going back for a rest, where we should have our buttons and badges clean and perhaps start saluting and turning by numbers and once more go through the thrilling exercise of loading by numbers. What a life! From one hell to another. We dribbled back to our billets at Englebelmer just anyhow and in any order, and on being told off to our particular ruin we dropped down like logs.

It was 7.00am when I arrived and by 9.30 I was told off to take charge of a scavenging party to clean up some billets that 62nd Division had left, collect all the refuse and burn it in an incinerator. Some idiot threw a Mills bomb or a dud shell in and the thing went off when we were all stood around. It blew the incinerator to blazes and covered us all with scalding hot jam, Maconochie's etc., but hurt no one.

I thought that after that little episode we had done enough cleaning up for other people and that it was high time we started on ourselves. Personally, I was in a shocking state of filth and some of the men were far worse. Kelly Clayton, for instance, even when sleeping like a log, was one continual move and so was his opposite number George Hedley. I'll bet it's impossible to find two lousier men in the whole of the British Army. I paraded my men in front of Company Sergeant Major Chapman who had just rejoined us from England. 'All right, Corporal,' he said, 'Dismiss your men and tell them to get themselves cleaned up.' We spent all the day on the job but made very little impression on the dirt.

Saturday we spent in a similar manner with the exception of a speech to the officers, NCOs and men of the two marine battalions by the commander of the corps to which we were attached. He didn't say much, but what he did say came right from the bottom of his heart, and I think I am right in saying that every man present felt himself very proud indeed to belong to the Royal Marines and to be a part of the Royal Naval Division. The old man made us feel like real soldiers, veterans in fact, and said that the results of our attack would be far more important than many people would imagine. The Bosch was already going back; how far, nobody knew as yet, but he thought he'd go back a long way.

Sunday came and fairly late in the morning we got news through that 190 Brigade had occupied Miraumont without firing a shot and with no loss of men. Our dear Company Sergeant Major Chapman and Company Quartermaster Sergeant Jerry Dunn celebrated the occasion by drinking most of the company's issue of rum and were caught by Colonel Hutchinson, who happened to be looking for our captain. Both were put under arrest, but didn't care; they were too drunk. Poor old Jerry Dunn was insensible and didn't know he was under arrest; Chapman was only partly aware of it.

Orders round on 26 February to pack up and stand by to move. Which way, up or down? That was what interested us most. The Bosch was getting out of it as quick as the rotten state of the country would permit him and we quite expected the order to chase him.

The next day he was reported to have gone back as far as the line running through le Transloy and Loupart. Our 190 Brigade was relieved then by IV Corps and we joyfully commenced our march back for another rest.

Chapter Twenty-Six

February 1917 – A Change of Scenery

Our last day in the godforsaken village of Englebelmer was 27 February 1917. A sure sign that the Bosch had evacuated: three females were seen poking about in the village looking for a few signs of their homes. Poor devils! What a job.

We made a short march on the Wednesday to the village of Bouzincourt. Only a short march, but the terrible state of the roads made it seem ten times as far as it was. Found it not much better than the place we had left, but there were a few signs of civilisation about: several French people knocking about, and two or three of the inevitable estaminets where we could get rid of our francs. I had drawn forty francs on the Monday and they were burning me. Billy, Bob Bayliss and I made a fairly high night of it. We each stood a bottle of champagne and felt very little worse for it.

I had been acting platoon sergeant for the last week, but Jim Hearne joined us up again that day from hospital and took charge. Once more that extra chevron slides into the background, although Jim Hearne said it wouldn't be long before I got it. We stayed at Bouzincourt until 4 March, just trying to get clean. Baths were rigged up and the division had now its own laundry with fumigator complete. I suggested to Kelly and Hedley that I could very likely get them a good square number on the fumigator staff, but they both declined my offer. We did our best, Billy and I, to get the two dirty dogs clean, but it was an impossible task. They must have been lousy in civil life and I'm certain that Kelly is one of those people who breed lice in their skin.

Our next move was to Acheaux, the old railhead for the Ancre. There we entrained for Candas, thirty-five men with all their gear stowed in a cattle truck. We arrived at our new destination about 11.00am and, after the usual mess up with billets, got stowed away. All our platoon were shoved in a big barn in the centre of the village.

The next day saw us well on our way towards our rest. Up at 6.30am and marched down to the railway sidings where we put in eight hours a day making sandbag walls in some ammunition sheds, all of which were full of shells of all calibres.

Our dear CSM and Jerry Dunn had their court martial but the luck of the Devil seems to stick to Chapman. He got off scot free, and Jerry Dunn was severely reprimanded and lost three years' seniority. That was that. Chapman came back to the company with more arrogance and bombast than ever before.

The fatigues carried on with unbroken monotony every day until the 19th, with just one day off for a bath. There was a gang of German prisoners working on the sidings, too, and I'm certain they were treated with far more consideration than we were. Their hours were less, their work was less strenuous, and I guess their food was better. We had the nights to ourselves, though, and could get into the village for a drink when funds permitted. The Royal Flying Corps (RFC) had a centre at Candas and a fine concert party that gave some jolly good entertainments in the YMCA hut there.

Our work had been monotonous and hard, but we were considerably better off than some units of the division. They had been finding working parties for the Canadian railway engineers who were extending the line up the Ancre valley in readiness for another push at the Bosch when the weather permitted. Others had been making new roads and re-making old ones, all under practically continuous shellfire.

A short march to Gezaincourt on 20 March where we joined up with our battalion. Next day fourteen kilometres to Atainville, a village consisting of about three houses. There we got in line with the rest of the division and were ready for anywhere, or anything. On 22 March we marched sixteen kilometres to Beavois where we stood easy for the next day.

A fresh general had taken over from General Shute. I think the old Shute had changed his opinion about the RND, about its fighting capabilities in any event, and I expect he would get a corps now. Major General Lawrie was now in charge, but we knew nothing about him. Time and circumstances would tell and so long as he didn't try to make the division all 63rd instead of RND I didn't see why he shouldn't get on.

We appeared to do our marches with a lighter step and a lighter heart now that we had left the terrible valley of the Ancre, where everything had the touch of death and desolation on it. The Royal Marine Band from Deal was at our head and a march of twenty-six kilometres to Coucy a la Tour on the 24th was like a pleasant stroll. Boots cleaned, buttons and badges sparkling, we looked like barrack-square soldiers again. Stayed at that place two days and managed to get rid of all our surplus francs and began pestering our company officers for more.

Moved again on the 26th through pleasant country, through the half-battered town of Béthune to a small village three kilometres beyond. The 29th saw the end of our marching, at all events for a time, and we settled in fairly pleasant billets at Sailly Labourse, a decent village amongst the slag heaps of the Lens district.

The trenches are only a short distance ahead and this fact made itself apparent after tea when quite a number of heavy shells went screaming overhead to burst amongst the workings of a pithead lying behind the village.

Chapter Twenty-Seven

March 1917 – Standing by for the Arras Push

It was 30 March and we were hard at it drilling: squad, section, platoon and company varieties just to get a little discipline into the troops. The air was blue with curses. 'Just imagine,' the men say, 'two years of fighting and then they make us slope our so and so arms by so and so numbers. Why the Hell don't they get on with the war?' I expect it's necessary, as necessary as it is to make the troops grouse. A contented lot of soldiers, if such could be found, would accomplish little in a hard scrap. They've got to grouse and, my God, they do. We got news around that we were in reserve for a new big push at Arras and Vimy to come off at any time and we are the flying division – to be ready to reinforce any part of the Army front.

Good Friday, 6 April, I saw my name in Battalion Orders. I was appointed lance sergeant and made bona fide corporal from Portsmouth, so that means no more dipping. On two hours' notice to stand by to move on the 9th.

The new push came off on the 10th with varying success and part of the division went into the line: 1 RM and the Ansons at Angres on the outskirts of Lens, the divisional artillery with the Canadians at Vimy, where they did splendid work. A patrol of 1 RM were first to notice the retirement of the Bosch from the Angres and Lievin sector. Colonel Cartwright took the battalion forward and took possession of the evacuated German positions on the night of the 13th/14th. Both 189 and 190 Brigades went into the line in front of Gavrelle on the night of the 14th/15th and got within striking distance of the Bosch. Here they advanced their line in broad daylight and in full view of the Bosch and paid for their jolly dearly. We moved on the 11th, but only to the village of Ourton through Bruary. The weather was vile – snow, sleet and cold, piercing winds.

We left Ourton on the 14th and marched thirty kilometres along one of the main Arras roads to Ecouvrie, a village just behind Arras. It was a hard march, the pace was fast when we could get along, but the road was so choked with traffic that at times we were stood at the roadside for hours. We all finished up more or less on our knees, and were glad enough to take advantage of the cold comfort of the leaky huts. The next morning we were out in the village on fatigues, doing scavenging work, cleaning roads, not sweeping them, but removing a coating of about six inches of filthy mud. There was a pioneer battalion in the village but they appeared to be doing anything but work. We weren't allowed out of camp except on fatigues and there was no chance of a drink.

On the 20th two of our companies went up the line, but only on a road-mending job. They came back a few less than they went up and said things were in an awful state up the line. Friday night and all day Saturday there was a heavy strafe on the line but the only exciting part of the scrap we saw was one of our aeroplanes making a dart at one of Jerry's observation balloons and bringing it down in flames.

We marched off about 3.30pm on the Sunday, 22 April. Sunday again, always Sunday, when anything big comes off – and made our way to the one-time village of Rochincourt, now hardly recognisable as such, apart from a heap or two of stones where formerly a church and houses had stood. Our temporary resting place was in the old German lines of trenches in front of the village, but even these had been battered out of all semblance of trenches. Every few hundred yards there was a huge mine crater and the sight of these gave one a queer sensation at the pit of the stomach. The havoc that the explosion of one of these mines must have caused must have been enormous. Whole companies of men must have simply disappeared from the face of the earth forever. Men laughing and joking together one second and the next, blown to shreds and mixed up with the churned-up earth of the crater.

Back at St Catherine's and in the military cemeteries of Arras there are huge crosses erected with whole strings of names of officers and men. 'Erected in memory of the following officers and other ranks who were killed in a mine explosion. RIP.' One consolation about it was the fact that there were more and bigger mines in Jerry's lives than in ours. Why the hell weren't we back in the days of Waterloo or Agincourt where fighting was fighting and not wholesale slaughter and wanton murder, where one had the sight of one's enemies and were assured that you would meet him on your own level. Not have him burrowing through the muck fifty feet below you or throwing half a ton of high explosive at you from a distance of five miles or so away.

After hanging about in the shell-shattered no man's land of Rochincourt for a few hours we were eventually stowed away in some of German dugouts about midnight. Jerry kept lobbing 5.9s over, but more to catch the traffic on the Arras-Gavrelle road just on our right. Sleep for me was practically out of the question and I was out on top with the first streaks of dawn. I was in time to see the opening of the barrage by our artillery for the attack on Oppy, Gavrelle and Moncy.

Our 189 and 190 Brigades were to attack the village of Gavrelle and advance their line to about 200 yards beyond. The sight of our guns firing was simply stupendous, one I should imagine will never fade from the memory. The strafe put up for us at Beaumont-Hamel was something, but this far outweighed it. As far as the eye could see, all along the horizon, was one mass of flame and the crash of guns was simply stupefying. Ahead of us, lying just under the ridge of skyline, were the field guns, almost gun wheel to gun wheel. Behind those the 60-pounders, then the howitzers 5-, 6-, 8-, 9-, and 15-inch, bringing up the rear. Amongst the lot was a sprinkling of naval guns mounted on railway trucks. All were blazing away as fast as ever they could go; the sight of it all pictured Hell better than any artist could do it.

The bombardment was by no means one-sided and German shells were bursting amongst our guns with terrible effect. Ammunition dumps were going up in a sheet of red flame in all directions and God knows how many guns were being smashed out of action with their crews blown to bits. It was almost impossible to miss them, they were so close together.

As the light got better we could see events more clearly on the ridge in front. Ammunition limbers going forward at the gallop to feed the guns and lots of them made contact with Jerry's shells, which were dropping in tremendous numbers all over the place. Our vantage point was none too safe but we stuck it. It was a sight worth seeing and was a good parallel to the fleet shelling Gallipoli on 25 April 1915. Scores of planes were in the air, fighting to the death, and several of both sides came crashing to earth, most of them in flames. Civilisation! The sight of this would make a crowd of cannibals sick with disgust.

So much for the part of the picture we could see, what of the infantry creeping and crawling about amongst the crashing ruins of Gavrelle with the fear of death in their hearts.

About 9.00am batches of wounded and prisoners made their appearance and from the wounded we got snatches of news. The attack had been fixed for 4.45am, a most cheerful hour. The first line of attack for our division was, from right to left, Drake, Nelson, 7th Royal Fusiliers and 4th Bedfords with the Hoods under Asquith as close support for 189 and 1st Honourable Artillery Company (1 HAC) as support for 190 Brigade.

There were three objectives: first, the line of trenches in front of Gavrelle; second, a road running north and south through the centre of the village; and third, a line roughly 300 to 600 yards the other side of the village. Drake, Nelson and 4th Bedfords had taken their first objective in ten minutes and with few casualties. The Royal Fusiliers on the left, however, had been held up on the uncut wire and were practically wiped out. The fighting for the second objective had been far more fierce and losses were heavier, but the road through the village had been gained on schedule. The commanding position, however, the windmill on the ridge of the high ground to the left of the village, was still in German possession, and showed no signs of falling. The Germans were in full strength and fighting mad, and pouring in reinforcements by the thousand.

In the rush for the third objective (which by the way was never gained) all our battalions suffered terrible casualties. A mixed lot under Commander Asquith succeeded in reaching the far edge of the village and commenced digging in front of the cemetery, and Asquith took possession of the mayor's house and captured the garrison, most of whom he found asleep in the cellars. On this precarious line they awaited the inevitable counter-attacks. And they came, the first about 1.00pm, and took some stopping too; but that was nothing to the second which came off about 4.00pm on the 24th (the next day). Jerry had been massing all night and morning and his artillery was in mighty strength. So was ours, and after some terrible fighting our two brigades managed to consolidate their guns.

Early on the 24th I was warned off as platoon guide to go with a small party of officers of the battalion to reconnoitre some former enemy trenches on top of the ridge, the trenches we were to occupy during the night prior to going forward to the front. Our way lay across country for a bit, through the heavy guns, all firing away like mad, then into a deep railway cutting which led to the top of the ridge. Walking up that cutting put the fear of death into us. There was no cover of any description and Jerry kept lobbing 8-inch shells right into it every few minutes. Lengths of rail were torn and twisted into the most grotesque shapes and heavy sleepers were smashed into splinters. Dead and maimed men were lying about in various attitudes, one or two with still a twitch or two in their limbs.

We arrived at 189 Brigade Headquarters after a time and a gruesome sight met our eyes. About ten men were lying dead in a group, just where the galley was. The cooks were serving out breakfast just before we arrived and an 8-inch shell had dropped amongst them. Ten killed outright and about twenty badly injured. You talk about a queer sensation at the pit of the stomach. We were all pretty well hardened, all sentiment and feeling for others killed in us by our previous scraps, but yet, after the few weeks away from close shelling, away from the horrible sickening things left by the war, we all felt that sinking feeling, that twitching of nerves and muscles that takes possession of one for a time.

I suppose it's fright, pure fear of death or mutilation, and you feel that you want to run screaming away from it all. I don't think it is cowardice for a chap to feel that way so long as he does keep control of himself. It's a feeling that soon wears itself out. Familiarity breeds contempt. We picked up a guide at Brigade Headquarters and he led us up out of the cutting, for which small mercy we were thankful, and into the trenches on the right of the cutting.

There were two lines of them, sadly knocked about and with none of the deep, safe and comfy dugouts usually associated with Bosch trenches. We walked round our battalion sector and took note of the parts allocated to our respective companies and platoons, and managed to have a look at the surroundings. Field guns were stuck all over the place, hardly any being in prepared gunpits, but sticking out in all their nakedness. Shells were dropping amongst them even as we looked and half a dozen 5.9s dropped right in a battery, knocking out two of the guns.

What happened to the guns crews I couldn't say with certainty, but when we first looked the guns were firing. When the smoke had cleared away, there wasn't a man to be seen. We saw parts of the guns blown into the air and perhaps some of the spokes were wheel spokes and perhaps they were limbs of Royal Field Artillery (RFA) men. It's hard to tell from a hundred yards away.

We stayed in these trenches about an hour then made our way back to the railway cutting. We got to the edge when a terrible rushing sound over our heads made us all pause. Just above us was one of our triplanes rushing to earth. We could see the pilot, even the expression on his face, so near was he. He looped the loop twice in a frantic effort to regain control, then his machine nose-dived and crashed in front of a battery of 18-pounders about forty yards away. The pilot's fate was obvious, poor devil! A crowd of artillery men rushed to the spot but nothing could be done; the plane had burst into a sheet of fierce flame and the remnants of the pilot would never be found.

Several fresh bodies were lying about along the railway track, but things were a little quieter as we made our way back to the battalion and joined them without further incident. I stopped for a few minutes about fifty yards from one of our 15-inch howitzers. Its crew of about fifty men had just got it ready for firing and, as they fired, I could see the huge shell as it left the muzzle and soared its way into the heavens until it was no more than a tiny speck. 'There's a hell of a bump coming for some Bosch,' I thought as I joined up with the others.

Chapter Twenty-Eight

24 April 1917 – Gavrelle and a Few Casualties

The battalion moved up about 3.00pm and took over the trenches on the ridge. We had quite a number of 5.9s amongst us during the day but very little damage was caused by them. The field guns round about us appeared to be the object of the shelling and they must have suffered enormous losses. Battery ammunition dumps were going up in flames all over the place. We had only to stop in these trenches for a few hours until dusk, before moving forward to relieve our other two brigades who were badly in need of rest.

A little stunt was also on the plans, but we could get nothing from our captain, Wanky Mitchell. If ever any man was mad and unfit to be in charge of a company of men, Wanky Mitchell was the man. Lieutenant Hardy, one of our other officers, told us himself that he was mad and he'd thought of mentioning it to the CO. Hardy himself wasn't very happy about things. He used to be as cheery and happy a soul as any in the battalion, but since coming up the line he had been horribly depressed and hadn't mended things much by consuming enormous quantities of neat rum and whiskey.

The night before we moved from Ecouvrie, the officers of our company joined us in the sergeants' mess and we spent a convivial night with the rum jar. Tongues were loosened to such an extent by the fiery spirit that the officers forgot for a time that they were officers and Hardy for one let us see that he wasn't looking forward with much pleasure to our expected scrap. He had won heavily at cards with the other officers and told us that he had at least £50 in English and French notes on him and that whoever found his body was welcome to the money. What a cheerful spirit to start a scrap in. Wanky Mitchell! Well we didn't know what to make of him. He had a tendency for religious mania, but whether it was assumed or not for the purpose of working his passage back before the stunt we couldn't say.

Jock Saunders, platoon sergeant of No. 2 had brought a water bottle full of neat rum with him and, being a typical Scot, drank the lot. I had a stroll amongst No. 2 Platoon during the night and came across somebody grovelling along the trench on hands and knees and making vain efforts to climb over the back of the trench. It was Jock and in one hand he had his rifle with bayonet fixed and all the time he was muttering 'Where are the bloody Germans? Let me get at the bastards.' I talked to him a bit and managed to get his rifle away from him, but off he went again. 'Let me get at 'em.' Just then Colonel Hutchinson came along looking for Wanky Mitchell and, of course, spotted Jock and the condition he was in. 'Get four men, Sergeant,' he said to me, 'and keep this man under arrest.' He told me the battalion was moving forward but I should have to stay there all night and look after Jock; I should hear from them in the morning. As soon as they had gone I found the best spot in the company sector, told one man off as a cook and, after a supper, we settled down for the night. Jock had dropped into a drunken sleep and kept moaning and shouting out all night. Sleep was impossible for me and I kept watch all night while my men slept like logs.

The night was fairly quiet with the exception of a few spasms of shelling down by Gavrelle. Just before dawn Jerry started slinging over gas shells in the dip about a hundred yards to our front. Over they came, six at a time. First came the familiar shriek of the shell through the air, then, instead of the deafening crash and crunch of high explosive, there was nothing more than a slight pop. There was no wind and, as it got a little lighter, I went forward to the edge of the ridge overlooking the valley and could see the gas as it hung like a pall over the little hollows in the ground. About 2,000 to 3,000 yards away I could see the church and village of Gavrelle, both of which looked in a pretty fair state from here.

About ten o'clock in the morning I was on the ridge again when I noticed two men coming towards me. One belonged to the Ansons, the other was a German and in a pretty bad way. I took them both along to our dugout and, as the cook had just made tea and a nice pudding, I gave them both a feed. I made the German understand that he was welcome to anything we had, but he wanted nothing but a drink of tea and that cold. He made signs that he was wounded through the chest and couldn't eat. Just as he was finishing his tea a brigadier and lieutenant colonel of the Royal Field Artillery dropped into the trench and the brigadier asked me what party we were, what we were doing, and what the German was doing there with us. I made him wise and then he started talking in German to the prisoner and got information from him regarding his regiment, etc. He belonged to the 55th Reserve of Guards, the same lot that we were up against at Beaumont-Hamel. The brigadier then wished us a polite 'Good Morning' and took himself off. His colonel stopped behind to whisper a few kind words in my private ear. He said I ought to have called the whole party up to attention when the general came along. I told him I had saluted both when he came up and when he went away and hadn't thought it necessary to bring the whole party up to attention. I told him even saluting in the trenches was not insisted upon in our lot. 'Probably not,' he said, 'but this case is different, now you have a German prisoner with you, and it was up to you to show him that they are not up against a Rag-time Army.' He was awfully nice about it and I gave him an extra-smart salute when he sheered off. They both left me with the impression of being two very pleasant gentlemen and altered my views a little regarding senior officers.

About half an hour later Colonel Hutchinson came along from the front and asked me how the prisoner (meaning Jock of course) was. I told him he was sober enough and sorry enough now. 'Have your party all ready for moving in half an hour,' he said. He was just going over to Brigade Headquarters and when he came back he would show us the way to our company. We moved off as soon as he came back and he led us at a fair old pace across open country which was in full view of Jerry. He kept away from the communication trench for about a mile, past derelict German field guns in concrete emplacements and ammunition dumps, past groups of dead men as they lay rotting on the ground. After a time he dropped into a communication trench of sorts that had been renamed Thames Alley by our troops. It was in a badly-battered condition with dead men lying about in all attitudes and various stages of mutilation and rottenness. Lewis guns, German machine guns, trench mortars, ammunition and bombs were scattered all over the place. I noticed that, although there were dead Germans in plenty lying about, our own dead far outnumbered them.

Thames Trench ended at Battalion Headquarters and the Colonel stopped there and told me to report at my own company HQ. He pointed out the way, and it lay over open ground as far as the support trenches and he advised me to run as we were very liable to get sniped. We were! Bullets were soon zipping amongst us and the advice to run was superfluous. With all my experience of warfare I had not acquired that pitch of courage or foolhardiness to walk calmly through a hail of bullets. In fact, I never have seen anyone like that yet, although I have read about them. I think that spirit is only acquired by the aid of other spirits, say a canteen of rum, or a bottle of whiskey.

Poor old Jock's spirits had evaporated and he was quite as eager to run as the rest of us. We had about 300 yards to go to the nearest trench which lay along the near edge of the village, and I think we all made it in record time. We had an audience of a crowd of our men in the trench for the last fifty yards and they were splitting their sides at our frantic efforts to join them. We did join them and without mishap and I made my way to my platoon which was in a bit of a trench leading up to the front line.

I found Billy hard at work on a funk hole for Jim Hearne and himself, and I straightway joined him in making it big enough for the three of us. I scrounged some iron sheeting and logs of wood and we soon had a shelter that would stand anything up to a direct hit from a 5.9.

We had a busy time at night with the wounded men of 189 and 190 Brigades. Just by our trench was the uncut German wire, not like ordinary wire but like saws about half an inch wide and there were great masses of it, yards wide. Scores of our men were lying out in it and had been for three days. No one had made any attempt to see to them before and the poor devils who were alive were in a terrible condition. One poor lad had had a leg shot off above the knee and the stump was one mass of sepsis and gangrene. Nothing for him but morphia, and plenty of it. How the devil he had kept alive for three days and two nights I can't imagine. Others died as we got them into our trench; just a few had hopes of life but very slender hopes. We made no attempt to tackle the dead; we left them for the pioneer battalion.

Our C and D Companies were in the line in front and some were holding the ruins of the village and both they and the Germans were inclined to be windy. Time after time the SOS lights were sent up, to be replied to immediately by both our own and Jerry's artillery.

The night was pandemonium and the dawn was greeted with a terrific barrage put down by both sides. Sleep was absolutely out of the question and the dugout on which Billy and I had spent several hours of hard labour was only used on a few occasions when the shelling got too intense.

We were having a good few casualties and there was a steady stream of men from the front line. Just after dawn on the 26th a sniper from somewhere in Jerry's line had picked off two or three of our chaps and we had a good look for him. Joe Woods spotted him at last in a tree on the Gavrelle-Arras road and four of us got on to him. He was pretty well covered with the leaves and branches but we had the satisfaction of watching his body crash to the ground. Some of us had got home on him. We accounted for a few more too before the morning was very old.

The Bosch was as badly off for communication trenches as we were, and his men had to nip over the ground in full view of us. It was just like shooting rabbits. There was Billy, Jock Baird and myself at the game and if one missed one of the others was sure to hit. We couldn't help but laugh at the efforts of the Bosch. First he would nip over the back of his trench and start off over the open ground at a trot. A bullet from one of our rifles would make him sprint for dear life; another ten yards and he was down, most probably a dead German. It was coldblooded murder, but still it's the same for both sides and some of the Germans managed to get back.

We got news along that Company Sergeant Major Milne of C had been killed by a shell during the night. He was digging some of his men out of a fallen house when he got it. Damn it all, there is good in the worst of 'em. There was none of the rejoicing at his death that might have been expected from the old Portsmouth crowd. With them, the men who knew him on the *Gloucester Castle* and Gallipoli, he was the most hated NCO who had ever been made. I remember the time on Gallipoli, at Backhouse Post, the rejoicing throughout the whole battalion when word flew round that Sergeant Milne was wounded, and the genuine regret when we knew that it was only a very, very slight wound in the neck from a very tired bullet that had travelled at least four miles. Poor old Milne, gone at last, and gone like a soldier.

The Bosch concentrated most of his artillery on the village during the day and the amount of stuff he dropped into it was simply tremendous, nearly all 8-inch shells, and what was once a solid, square-towered church was very soon a heap of powdered stone.

We had to shift our position during the day to a trench no more than knee deep that lay close behind the church and we had a terrible time. We soon got it deep enough to give us head cover and we needed it too. Lumps of 8-inch shell casing kept whizzing down amongst us and several of our company were badly hit. A 5.9 right in the trench where No. 2 Platoon was accounted for seven men, four blown to bits and three terribly wounded.

What with the heavy shelling, poor cover, no sleep and plenty of hard work, nerves began to fray a little at the edges and some of the men began to be a bit jumpy. It's always a bad sign when men crowd together in a trench and we had all our work cut out to keep them in their places. Several kept on about having no water, Kelly Clayton being one of the most persistent, so I sent half a dozen off under Willet, now lance corporal, to the village where there was a decent well. Jerry had been fairly quiet for half an hour but they had no sooner got to the well than he opened up again with a score of guns right on the village. Lance Corporal Willet, Clayton and another chap came back, the others had been killed outright at the well. Needless to say, no water came back and we had to sit on Kelly to stop him from bolting.

Our aeroplanes had been getting it hot all day and we saw four driven down in flames in less than two hours. They were our artillery spotting planes with open fuselage and petrol tanks in a conspicuous position above the pilot and observer. They were patrolling over the Bosch lines about 800 feet up, not caring a damn about the anti-aircraft shells which were bursting in scores about them, or about the countless rifle and machine-gun bullets that were fired at them from the Bosch lines. All at once a German fighter would drop out of the blue, get behind our man's tail and let fly with about half a dozen tracer bullets into his petrol tank. Poor devils, they hadn't a chance, the plane was a mass of flames in less than a minute and in three instances we saw the pilot and observer jump from the plane about 500 feet up. Their fate was obvious. In the fourth case the two men stuck to their machine and managed to get it to within a hundred feet of the ground when it crashed just behind our support lines. The Bosch straightaway sent over a salvo of shrapnel and got a few of our men who had dashed over to help the two airmen. These little incidents got our blood to boiling point and we would cheerfully have dashed over the top for a smack at the Bosch. As we couldn't do that we took to cursing him and our own fighting planes, not one to be seen anywhere. Then we cursed the men who were responsible for sending out such old-fashioned and out-of-date planes. They should have been scrapped ages ago, or in any case they should have had a few of our fighting planes to protect them.

Just as dusk drew on we observed a German aeroplane flying very low over our front line and the ruins of the village. Of course, we all opened up on him with our rifles but he took no heed and presently he dropped two red lights and a green one. It was obviously a signal for his artillery and we had to crouch down for a full hour. The amount of shells those hellhounds sent over was simply overwhelming and for long into the night we were all more or less dazed.

If we had to take any ground off Jerry with his present strength and attitude we would need far more men than there appeared to be round there, and a lot of luck too. There appeared to be nothing wrong with the German morale; if we could hold on to what we had we would be jolly lucky.

The night was a repetition of the previous night, alarms and excursions on both sides, a terrible ghastly night of sudden spasms when every man stood to and the imagination of one windy individual would set the guns of two corps firing like mad. Dawn came and with it another intense barrage by both sides, but after another hour things quietened down to normal. I think both sides were pretty well exhausted.

About 10.00am on the 27th, after a meeting of our officers with the CO, Wanky Mitchell sent along for platoon sergeants to go to him to get plans of the attack. Jim Hearne went but after about half an hour he was back and the expressions he used about our worthy officer are really not fit to print.

He took the sergeants out over the open into the village and got them all seated in a newly-made 8-inch shell hole. There, instead of telling them about the attack, he started preaching to them, 'Were they prepared to meet their God?' It's much he didn't meet his there and then, but Mr Hardy kept them quiet and, after about ten minutes, sent them back to their platoons. They left Mitchell in the shell hole, protesting for all he was worth that he wasn't mad, but Mr Hardy said he was going straight over to the CO to report him.

We knew the attack was to come off about dawn but that was all we did know. Colonel Hutchinson came along and had a talk to Mitchell and took him back to Battalion Headquarters to see Jimmy Ross. They decided to keep him there, which was a big relief to us all.

No doubt we should want every man we could get hold of to carry us through, every tooth and nail, but we certainly didn't want a blithering lunatic in charge. We pottered about during the day, improving the trench, but what for God only knows; very few of us would ever see it or want it again after that night.

Jerry kept at it all day, pounding the ruins of Gavrelle into the dust, and the only place that had any walls standing at all was the mayor's house, standing right in the front line.

Our aeroplanes were very conspicuous by their absence and Jerry certainly ruled the roost in that respect. Only twice did our spotting planes try to get over and, in both cases, they were chased to the ground. One was fortunate and dropped to earth behind our own lines; the other was unlucky and came down behind Jerry's supports. We watched the two airmen scramble out of the plane and nip off for the nearest trench; they had no sooner left the plane than it burst into flames, probably fired by the pilot.

About four o'clock in the afternoon Jim Hearne said he was going to see Mr Hardy. He wanted more details about the stunt, but he never reached Hardy. He was back in about five minutes, his face livid and his right hand shattered by either a rifle bullet or a piece of shell casing. He was in terrible agony and Billy took him back to Jimmy Ross after we had put his first dressing on it. No more fighting for Jim and I was in charge, absolutely in charge, of No. 1 Platoon A Company 2 RM.

When Billy Hurrell got back I went along to inform Hardy of what had happened and on the way back practically the same thing happened to me. A lump of red–hot casing from an 8-inch shell struck me on the back of the left hand and I turned nearly sick with the pain and shock. My hand was badly cut about, but I felt certain that nothing serious had happened to it. I got back to Billy and told him what had happened, then on to Jimmy Ross. I had to wait about half an hour before I could get near him; he was going at it as hard as he could go with casualties. If things carried on in this fashion, no one would be left to attack at dawn.

Jim Hearne was still there and awaiting a favourable opportunity to go back down the line to 1st Field Ambulance. He was in a terrible state of exhaustion and could hardly summon enough interest in things to ask what was wrong with me. When the time came for my turn I felt a lot better and after Jimmy Ross had bandaged it up I felt ready for the line again. I told him so and he said I had better go down to Field Ambulance with the next batch. 'No thanks, Doctor,' I said, 'give me a drink of hot tea and I'll go back to the company.' He let me go at that, but I couldn't help thinking what a damn fool I was. Chance to get away to hospital and wouldn't take it. Maybe I would have lost the chance by morning.

I wasn't feeling very happy about things and hadn't that confident assurance of getting back out of it all. For one thing I'd missed my usual 'Good luck mate' and for another thing I didn't like the way the Germans were taking things, not a bit like a beaten army. To me they seemed as ready to attack as we were and their artillery was every bit as powerful as ours. Then again they certainly had the upper hand in the air.

I expect it was the failure of the French offensive in Champagne and the withdrawal of several divisions of German troops from the Russian Front. Anyhow, whatever it was, Jerry had his tail up.

About half past six we received orders to move forward to a section of trench just behind the firing line. From there we should move forward about midnight to the tape which the Royal Engineers would lay out at dusk. We got in the trench but I never thought anybody would get out of it alive. Billy, three men and I got in a fire-bay, the traverses of which were filled in with very recent shells. After about ten minutes Jerry started lobbing 8-inch shells over. He must have had three guns working on a stretch of trench no more than fifty yards long and he did everything but hit us. We were all simply terrified for half an hour, dashing about from one spot in our little bit of trench to another in a frantic effort to dodge the shells. I don't think I've ever been in such a state of funk before and the five of us were too helpless to curse after about ten minutes of it. By then Jerry had missed us with so many shells that we felt certain that one of the next was almost bound to hit us.

No one, who has not been through a similar experience, can have the faintest conception of what we felt like. And all the time I couldn't help but think that if only I had taken Jimmy Ross's advice I should have been well out of it all. All good things come to an end and Jerry piped down a bit and shortly after our heavies retaliated with 6-inch and 9.2s all in the German wire and front line. We were watching them burst and giving forth curses of satisfaction when our people happened to drop one in his trench. One 9.2 dropped short, right in our own front line, and we soon had word up that it had accounted for twenty of our men, mostly killed. We had word along about 11.00pm to stand by to move over to the tape and we moved at midnight.

Just as I put my hands on the parapet of the trench to pull myself up some stumbling nervous fool stepped back with his hobnailed boot right on my gammy hand. My curses brought up Mr Hardy who was checking us over and when he saw the blood dripping from the bandage, insisted on me going back to Jimmy Ross. I said I'd carry on, I could still hold my rifle but he wouldn't hear of it. 'My God, Sergeant,' he said, 'if I'd half your chance I'd take it and be thankful.' Bob Bayliss was standing by and whispered fiercely 'Get back out of it, you bloody fool.' I'd very little heart left with which to tackle the fight and I was nearly all in with the pain from my hand and with the fatigue and nervous strain of the past few days, but still I didn't like packing up. However, like a good soldier, I obeyed the last order and got back, and the boys went over to the tape, where they had to lie shivering with cold and fear until zero hour at 4.30am.

After much searching I found the doctor's dugout, the entrance of which had been filled in two or three times during the evening with the shelling and the surrounding trench battered out of all recognition. He was having a bit of a stand easy, having just got a batch of wounded away to 1st Field Ambulance. He looked to my hand, cleaned it and put on a fresh bandage and then told me I had better wait until the next batch was ready to go down. We had a chat together about Gallipoli days and then he advised me to get a bit of sleep. I found a corner but, although I was nearly dead with fatigue, I couldn't sleep a wink. My thoughts were with the boys and zero hour.

I was dozing when, at 4.25am, with barely a streak of light in the sky the battle began. With a soul-splitting crash, our barrage opened up and the Bosch straightaway put down a counter barrage and the whole front was a mass of flame, smoke and lumps of flying metal.

The very earth shook and we all expected our dugout to fall in on us, but we daren't go outside. Shells were falling in scores and, by the sound of things, mostly 5.9s and 8-inch. It would be as well here to give a few details of the attack and the objectives to be carried out. The front stretched from Monchy on the right to Arleux on the left. On the left were the Canadians, then 2nd Division at Oppy, then the RN Division, and on the right XVII Corps.

The objective of 2 RM was the ridge of high ground just on the left of the village, the tit-bit of the whole position being the windmill, nothing like a windmill now but a strong fortified position held in full strength by the Bosch.

First Royal Marines were to attack on the left of our battalion; and their main element was enfiladed from a strongpoint on the single line of railway just beyond the windmill. The windmill was attacked by Lieutenant Newling and a party of men who captured it, killed every Jerry in it, and held it against three or four vigorous counter-attacks. Owing to the attacks on both flanks failing, the main body of our battalion had to fall back and by noon the attack had failed. Only the windmill held out and if ever a man deserved the VC it was Newling.

The Bosch was running reinforcements right up the Douai–Arras road in motor-buses and sending them against the windmill, but Newling and his little band of thirty men never budged an inch. He stood up on top of the trench and flung Mills bombs at them as fast as the men could pass them to him. For that he got the Military Cross and two Honourable Artillery Company officers, Lieutenant Pollard and another, got the Victoria Cross for taking a strongpoint on the railway. Petty Officer Scott and fifteen men of the Ansons on the right were isolated during the night of the 28th/29th and had to fight their way back in the morning, bringing in with them 250 German prisoners. Had he been an Australian it would have meant the Victoria Cross. There is no doubt that when a Naval Division man got the Victoria Cross he more than earned it.

Hardy's presentiment proved to be only too correct. The poor devil was shot dead somewhere round the windmill and, as far as we knew, his body was never found; the money he had on him too is still going begging.

Sergeant Major Chapman was killed, Bob Bayliss was taken prisoner, or so Billy thought, and that brilliant soldier Hobson walked straight over the top as soon as it was light with his hands above his head. I hope the swine got killed!

Joe Woods, the first man in Sedd-el-Bahr castle was killed. Billy told me that he fought like a tiger. Good old Joe, the finest soldier that ever went over the top and the biggest damned nuisance down the line that ever worried an NCO.

Jimmy Ross sent me down to the Field Ambulance about 9.30 am on the 28th with the first batch of walking wounded, but I may as well finish with the attack before I carry on with my own troubles.

During the whole of the 28th and well into the morning of the 29th the Bosch counter-attacked time after time against the village and all the sick-bay men and even the doctor had to turn to with rifles and fight the Bosch in the village. He got as far back as Battalion HQ and things looked very serious for a long time. It was not until about midnight on the 29th that he was pushed back away from the village and his last line of defence.

Very, very little had been gained, except that our hold on Gavrelle had been strengthened by the taking of the windmill position. And the losses were out of all proportion to the little that had been gained.

Our battalion alone lost in killed ten officers and 200 men and the total in killed, wounded and missing was over 600. The 1st Royals lost their Colonel Cartwright and six other officers killed and over 500 other casualties. The casualties for the division in the fighting from 15 April up to the morning of the 30th, when they turned over to the ill-fated 31st Division were: killed forty officers, and 1,000 men. The total killed, wounded and missing was 170 officers and 3,624 NCOs and men.

On being relieved, the division returned to the comforts and luxury of the battered dugouts and trenches of the Rochincourt area.

Chapter Twenty-Nine

28 April 1917 – The Pleasures of being Wounded

I made my way down to Rochincourt with a party of walking wounded and reported at the 1st Field Ambulance. After a bit of waiting we were all told to bare our chests and, after a painting with iodine, were inoculated for tetanus. The syringe they used for the job was like a young garden syringe, and the sergeant pumped pints or nearly pints of the stuff into me. It made me feel as sick as a pig and I almost reeled over from the effects of it. Then came examination of wounds, then cleaning and dressing and, as soon as we were finished with, bundled into waiting ambulances and rushed off to the 20th Casualty Clearing Station (CCS). I did nothing there but have a feed and scrounge around and begin to feel sorry that I had come away from the line.

About teatime we made our way down to the railway siding and settled down in the hospital train for Étaples where a lot of us were sent to the 26th General Hospital. There the usual procedure had to be gone through: strip, have a bath and roll into bed. I didn't waste much time before getting off to sleep.

First thing next morning I was down at the stores hut for a new uniform, but I was so early that I upset the Royal Army Medical Corps (RAMC) sergeant in charge and he went off alarming at me. He must have taken me for a full private, but I soon disillusioned him. I told him I wanted a nice-fitting tunic and three neat chevrons to stitch on the right arm so that people would know I was a sergeant and then three gold stripes[1] for the left arm. He even fished out needle and cotton for me at the finish so that I could sew them on.

---

1. These were wound badges, worn on the lower left arm.

I am going to skim quickly over my short period in hospital; there was very little pleasure attached to it. Our chief recreation was reading the newspapers, usually the articles dealing with the splendid time the wounded Tommies had in England. They drew pictures of these charming nurses, angels of mercy. They want to come out here to draw their pictures. The only way to fetch a smile to the surface is by doing most of the slushing in the ward and by doing everything for yourself by yourself.

Two days in the 26th and I was agitating for a move to details, but got sent to No. 6 Convalescent Camp. Saw the doctor there and told him I was fit for the line again, so he passed me A.1 and told me I should have to go to the detail camp first and then to the base at Calais. Entrained at 7.00am on 4 May for Calais and arrived at about noon. Not exactly express but it got us there.

Colonel Mullins (old Joe) was in charge of the base and there appeared to be more men there than we had up the line. Dropped across Rimmer and Coulter just out again from England. I tried all ways to draw some money but without success. I was absolutely stony broke. Saw Joe Mullins and told him I wanted to get back up the line as soon as possible. He said he was sending a batch away on Tuesday and I could go with them or I could stop there and take charge of a squad on the Bullring. I told him the line was good enough for me, got rigged out on the Monday and took train on the Tuesday for Étaples again and stayed there the night, then away to Pernes, to another detail camp, in the morning.

There all Thursday and on the following morning set off on the march to Béthune. It was a blazing hot day, so hot in fact that the officer in charge (a HAC man), who happened to have a humane touch about him, begged a couple of limbers from someone, to carry our packs. A march to Mont St Éloi the next day and on the 13th joined up with my own battalion. It felt like being home again – almost.

Chapter Thirty

13 May 1917 – A Little Fighting and a Lot of Digging

I found the boys in reserve just in front of Rochincourt and their time was pretty well occupied with working both up and down the line. Very few of the old boys were left and a new crowd of NCOs was out. I found out I had lost my lance stripe for the time being, but I wasn't unduly distressed about that. A few weeks would soon thin down the ranks of the new NCOs; meanwhile I was a bona-fide corporal so I couldn't dip those two. Billy was made full sergeant, so for once he was my senior. Dick Howarth was acting Company Sergeant Major and he had a job for me as soon as the working parties were out: digging and wiring in Renjal trench.

We had rather a long rough walk to get to the trench and every now and again Jerry would send over a bit of shrapnel or a 5.9 or two. It was amusing to watch the antics of some of the new chaps, a lot of them out for the first time. I was with Billy bringing up the rear of the party, and every now and again we should have to fetch back one of two of the 'windy' souls. We were moving along at a fair pace but evidently not fast enough for them. One lad in particular, 'Young Price', a Welsh lad, with no heart or stomach for war, would gradually work his way forward from man to man until he was nearly leading the whole party. It was a kind of fear of the open and a desire to get to a trench as quickly as possible that urged them forward. Billy told me that a lot of the new lads had already gone back with 'blighties', most of them caused by the point of a pick during digging operations. Somehow, either intentional or otherwise, they had got in the way of their opposite number's pick. It must want a hell of a lot of pluck though to willingly get into the path of a pick. I'm afraid I'd be a coward at that game. Two men were hit that night in our party but it was about the finish of that kind of work. A battalion order was issued the next day to the effect that any man being wounded by a pick-axe would be court martialled and treated in the same way as others with self-inflicted wounds.

Back at 4.00 next morning and were allowed to turn in until 10.00am, then out for drill. The same routine carried on until the Saturday when we moved up to Maison Blanc, some old German trenches by the Arras-Gavrelle Road on top of the ridge. We relieved the West Yorks there (31st Division). The Bosch strafed the road both frequently and effectively and there was plenty of evidence about to prove it, in the shape of broken lorries, GS wagons and limbers. We were out digging all night and the brilliant officer in charge of the party lost his bearings coming back and kept us wandering about in the open until nearly dawn. All the next day the Bosch was banging our line with 5.9s and things got very unpleasant. One of our stretcher-bearers was killed and a few men wounded.

We were very interested spectators of a splendid air fight during the afternoon. Six Bosch fighting planes came over our lines and, regardless of the anti-aircraft barrage, had reached a position above our reserve line. Dropping straight out of the blue came one of our Bristol fighters right into the midst of the Bosch formation and the prettiest fight I have ever seen took place right above us. In less than a minute two enemy planes were out of action, one to come crashing to earth, the other making a downward dive for his own lines with his tail a mass of flame. He was followed shortly after by another whose obvious desire was to get to ground as soon as possible. That left the odds at three to one, enormous odds still, but our chap still stuck it. Down came another Bosch, absolutely beyond all hope, and then we thought our man's turn had come. Down he came in a terrific spiral nose dive and we all thought he was done; then, when still a couple of hundred feet above us, the cheeky blighter flattened out and made for home.

The two Bosch planes that were left made straight for home; they had no more stomach left for the fight and two more of our planes coming along then made the Bosch put on speed. I really think the reason our man packed up was because he had no ammunition left. What a spirit! What a nerve! – without a second's hesitation to plunge into a fight with odds of six to one against him. There was no room in the RAF for a man with a conscientious objection to fighting.

We had a glorious night. It started raining hard about dusk and we were soon wading in about a foot of water and had to turn out and do a bit of digging. Our job usually happens to be getting down the first three feet from the top, but there is always an incentive for the fellows to dig. They get down as quickly as possible for cover, and it's necessary; all sorts of things come over, shrapnel, 5.9s and crowds of machine-gun bullets, and even if you haven't a very great fear of being in the open it's nice to think there is a hole to drop into if anything heavy is coming anywhere near

The officer in charge was obviously at a loss about which way to get back home. I expect he had turned round about three times and didn't which way our trench lay. Anyway, he started off in the wrong direction altogether, and about a dozen of us let the rest go on with him. I made straight for the Arras-Gavrelle road, just on our right, and straight up it to the ridge. We were home then and had turned in two hours when the others came cursing their way back.

Each day to 29 May was a repetition; out every night from dusk until four the following morning on the infernal digging. During the day we did a bit of drill, just to make the troops realise that it wasn't exactly a holiday we were on. I think I'm safe in saying that it rained on an average fourteen hours out of every twenty-four, so that it won't be difficult for anyone to make a guess at our condition. We were filthy, we were lousy, and we were sore, but no one had a cold. True, one or two went back to Field Ambulance but only because they were worn out body and soul.

Casualties? We had a few. One night when we were out digging B Company had nine men badly wounded. Two men were left in the trench because they were sick one night, but were both dead when we had dug them out of their funk hole. They had both turned in in one hole and the thing had collapsed on them when they were asleep. Owing to the continuous rain, most of the trench was in a similar condition and great chunks of it would gently subside into the quagmire at the bottom. The Bosch never failed to shell it and managed to register a few hits at least every day. And when he got the trench he usually got a man or two.

The 29th (Whit Tuesday) brought a change. We were to move to the support line just behind the village of Gavrelle and relieve 1 RM. Set off at about 10.30pm and the relief was complete about midnight. Things had been pretty quiet but the 1st Royals told us the Bosch was always dropping heavy stuff in the trench. I could quite believe it too. The trench was in a shocking state, in parts nearly battered flat, and, for all its length, about knee deep in mud and water. It was an old German trench and had formed part of his third line of defence before the Battle of Arras.

I hadn't been in long before the platoon was warned off as water and ration party, and we had to go to a dump on the Arras road. Lieutenant Buckley was in charge of the party and Billy and I followed close behind. We had just reached the road where the trench ended when the Bosch opened up with terrific strafe. Every conceivable size and weight of shell was hurled at us and hundreds must have dropped within a space of a couple of minutes just around the road. Buckley had vanished, the carrying party had vanished and there was only Billy and me left, and we were both frantically striving to get our heads and as much of our bodies as possible into a small undercut in the trench bottom. We were almost smothered with the showers of earth and stones from the bursting shells and every second I expected would be my last, but the spasm died away and we stood up and prepared to look for our carrying party.

Buckley came back from across the road where he had found a decent dugout, but the others were nowhere in sight. I had to go back to the support trench for them. Some of them said they felt sure we had all three been blown to bits. The trench we had sheltered in was blown in in about a dozen places. We got the water and managed to get back without further incident.

Pretty quiet the following morning and we had orders to fill in all the funk holes as they were dangerous owing to the soft state of the ground. Billy and I set about making a fine shelter on the fire-step. We scrounged sandbags, corrugated iron and logs and had just managed to finish it when a thunderstorm came on and with it a downpour of rain that put two feet of water in the trench in less than ten minutes. The officers had a lovely deep dugout, but in a few minutes they had to dash out to save themselves from being drowned; the water reached the roof in those few minutes.

Billy and I stuck it in our little shelter. Both of us had taken our packs off and we were watching huge lumps of trench as they slid with a squelch into the muddy liquid at the bottom. All at once I felt a movement in our shelter and I scrambled out and yelled to Billy to get out; we had only just got out when the whole affair collapsed in a heap. The fire-step had given way and our rifles, packs and food were hopelessly buried in the mass.

Then we had a tottering time for three days clearing the trenches round about. Most of the time we were wading about up to the thighs in mud and water. One or two men were nearly drowned through dropping in sump holes. To make things better Jerry started slinging over 10-inch *Minenwerfers* and our only rations consisted of sodden biscuits, bully beef and water. The weather cleared and turned awfully hot.

The Bosch was bluffing a bit, and our people didn't know what his intentions were, whether he was going back to a new line, or going to counter-attack and push us back. We were all standing by to move forward at ten minutes' notice, either to take up the chase or to repel an attack. We were in the support line until 9 June, twelve days, not a bad spell, when you consider the weather and the conditions in brigade reserve before that.

Artillery on both sides had been very active and hits had been registered on our trench almost every day with the usual casualties. Ration parties had suffered badly and so had rations. I went one night with a party to the ration dump at the bottom of Thames trench and had just picked up the rations when the Bosch opened up with one of his terrific strafes. Hundreds of shells burst in about two minutes, then everything was still again and signs of life began to appear again on the face of the earth. My party were all right, but three of the men on the dump were lying in mutilated heaps on the trench bottom.

The people on our right carried out a stunt about 8 o'clock on the night of 5 June and we were 'standing to' all night, and got badly shelled in the trench. On 8 June the people on our left made an attack on Oppy and the artillery put four barrages down on the place. The Bosch replied in a like manner and kept it up for two hours after our people had piped down.

Our relief turned up about midnight on 9 June and we made our weary way down to the old German trenches of East Rochincourt. We set about getting ourselves clean as soon as we arrived, ready to move again.

Left at 5.00pm on the Sunday, 10 June, and reached Maroeiul, a partly inhabited village just behind and to the right of Arras. We were duty platoon and I touched for corporal of the guard for the night. The next day was a stand-off and my twenty-fifth birthday and, thanks to the good, dear people from home, I had a good time.

Started drill on 13 June; we mustn't stand easy too long, we might get too contented, and contented troops are no good to anybody. Sports were arranged and we were paid, so could indulge a little with the fiery wines of pleasant France. Everybody cleaned up and hot baths were provided, so that in a day or two we were all looking like new soldiers.

On 19 June we were inspected by Admiral Lord Charles Beresford. Paid again on 21 June and received orders to get ready to move up again, so, of course, everybody got as much beer or wine down him as possible. Money is no use up in the trenches except for play at brag or pontoon.

Moved to East Rochincourt on 22 June. Being the first day of summer it poured with rain all day and, on arrival, we were shoved in bivouacs. Our clean, smart appearance had vanished and we were soon caked in mud and chalk. There was a big raid on at night on our front and forty-seven prisoners were brought in. Three companies went up digging in Thames trench at night – our turn tomorrow.

We played cricket during the day amongst the old trenches and shell holes. Our company were crack cricketers and beat all the others. Dick Howarth, our Company Sergeant Major, was a good all-rounder and a new lad in my section, Brown, was a fine bowler and could do very near what he liked with the opposing side. I missed the night digging but had to go up to Thames trench at 5.30am for three mornings on a revetting job. And just at the murderous spot where Jerry dropped most of his stuff.

We were expecting an attack to come off in a few days' time but we were only to prepare the trenches for 31st Division and the 5th, who would attack from the left of the windmill to the left of Oppy Wood. My party had a pretty quiet time in Thames trench and only on the third morning were we shelled at all badly. We got it hot for about ten minutes but fortunately no one was hit.

Wednesday 27 June was a stand-off as far as forward work was concerned, and on the 28th the 5th and 31st Divisions went over and took Jerry's front line from him, thus making our position far more secure and comfortable. As far as we could gather neither division had many casualties and very few prisoners were brought back to the fold. XIII Corps' commander came and said a few kind words to us about the Gavrelle stunt and the splendid way we had wielded the pick and shovel since. He was Lieutenant General Congreve VC and a fine fellow and made no fuss about coming. He just walked over to our company bivvies with the CO and had the company fall in just as we were. We looked proper veterans too.

Up in the deep railway cutting for two days for a new kind of work, repairing the railway track and banks of the cutting. Meanwhile 190 Brigade had been practically washed out; 10th Dublins had gone north to provide reinforcements for 16th (Irish) Division, who had suffered heavily in the new scrap at Messines; the Artists Rifles were to take the place of the HAC who, I suppose, would join up with something more aristocratic than the RND.

The 5th King's Shropshire Light Infantry were to take the place of the Irishmen when they had all been fitted out with leave to Blighty. The Artists Rifles were short of active service training and would have to get a bit of instruction from the marines before being fit to take over a section on their own. They seemed a similar crowd to the HAC, what one might term the 'pampered of London', but that won't matter a hang so long as they could fight and not let the RND down. As a fighting division we gave place to no other on the whole front.

On Monday 2 July we were paid and told to get ready for a three-week spell in the front line. We relieved the 18th West Yorks (31st Division) about midnight on the 3rd and went in support behind the windmill. Things were pretty quiet and we had a decent trench but it started raining as soon as we got in and things were soon in a filthy condition. We had fairly quiet conditions until the Saturday (the 7th) when we went up in front to relieve 1 RM. The poor souls had been a bit windy for the last three days, sending up needless SOSs at night. A Prussian regiment was holding the German line and were all as keen as mustard and always active; some of the new hands of 1 RM, seeing a wiring party or a patrol near our wire, would straightaway put up the SOS, thinking an attack was coming off. That would mean a bad ten minutes of strafing, for both sides' artillery would put down a barrage.

The Bosch was very active in the air and scores of his planes were over every day. We saw fights every day between their planes and ours and I am sorry to say the Bosch obviously came off best.

As soon as the relief was complete, about 11.00pm, we had a terrible thunderstorm with a perfect deluge of rain that very soon swamped the trenches. We weren't so badly off as the Ansons, as our trenches were on the slope of the high ground by the windmill and the water soon drained off into the Ansons' trenches. We spent four fairly hectic days in the line round the windmill before we were relieved again by our 1st Battalion. We only had a few casualties in our company but, on the Tuesday night, just as we were going over for a wiring job, Jerry sent over a couple of nasty black shrapnels that burst on the parapet just where we were getting over. Two of my men were killed outright, and three more wounded. It was as near a thing as I'd had for some time. Needless to say, the wiring party was cancelled. Jerry was active all night and, when he wasn't blazing away at us, he had strong patrols out in no man's land.

I touched for a weird job on the Monday night; with three men I had to get out about twenty yards in front of our wire, get down in shell holes and act as covering party to the wiring party. Eighty yards away in the semi-darkness of the July night we could see the Germans working on their own wire, could hear them as they worked on their own trench with pick and shovel, and at times could see the shadowy forms of their fighting patrols as they made their cautious way up and down the front. I might mention that they kept well on their own side and very close to the wire. I was itching to fire but knew I dare not, with our own wiring party just behind me.

The relief on 11 July passed off very quietly and we were back in the support line just after midnight. The next day was hot and dry and we had a chance to clean up a bit. I had a very pleasant shock during the day: I was warned off for a six weeks' course at the XIII Corps School at Pernes. I was to go on the Saturday; meanwhile my only hope was that I shouldn't run into anything hot up to then.

Friday was pretty hot and Jerry sent over no less than 150 8-inch shells just on our left. For us he sent over a decent amount of 5.9s, but no one bothered to count them. We heard the next day that not one man had been hit with all those shells, and we expected at least a battalion to have been wiped out with those 8-inch shells.

A whole stretch of ground on our left was in a constant state of upheaval. Saturday came and with it orders to get ready to relieve 1 RM again at the windmill. It appears that they wouldn't trust the windmill position to anyone but our brigade. It was the tit-bit of the whole corps front.

Orders for me to clear off to the transport lines at Rochincourt. Got down about three in the afternoon and was paid 50 francs, then served out with new clothes. A hot bath, and everything clean and new on. What a luxury. Yesterday seemed like a horrible nightmare. Just imagine, after all the filth and horrible conditions of the past few weeks, the incessant shelling, the constant fear of death or even worse, of lingering mutilation, to feel clean, almost safe and with a bundle of notes in my pocket and to know for the next six weeks I should be in pleasant company amidst lovely country. What more could a chap wish for? HOME!

Chapter Thirty-One

15 July 1917 – A Pleasant Interlude

Away by 10.00am on the Sunday in a motor lorry to Pernes where I joined up for a general course for officers and NCOs of XIII Corps. We were in a fairly pleasant building and the NCOs were a very decent crowd, so that I looked forward with pleasure to the six weeks. We were told off in syndicates and banded together by divisions. Work started on the Monday and, although it was hard, it was interesting. It was a case of cramming into a few hours the study of years. We had most nights off and could do pretty much as we liked. The CO had put us on trust and I don't think anybody abused it.

Our syndicate (63rd Division NCOs) won the shooting competition easy and the same day, 7 August, we drew in the semi-final of the football competition. On 12 August the syndicate were runners up in two prize shooting competitions and we had about 100 francs to share.

On the 13th we had another competition and I was leader of the 63rd NCOs. We had to start off from a trench, attack an enemy position, dummies in the trench representing the Bosch which we had to bayonet, then another similar trench, then to shoot at the retreating enemy represented by tiles in the ground about thirty yards away. My team was easily top with a score of 265 out of a 300 possible, but 5th Division won the competition owing to our syndicate of officers letting us down. The next morning was taken up with the final exam and I passed well up, both in theory and practical, which should mean the other stripe at least on my return.

The six weeks had simply flown by and I could have stuck another six easily. At the same time I felt a desire to get back to my own battalion. Away from the pleasant little market town of Pernes by 10.00am on 15 August. Joined up with my battalion in the railway cutting next day and found to my satisfaction that I was made full sergeant, backdated to 28 April in place of Jock Saunders who was taken prisoner in the attack. Good old Jock, he did me a good turn, but then I earned him his Military Medal at Beaumont-Hamel.

Chapter Thirty-Two

August 1917 – Odds and Ends at Gavrelle

We were in the railway cutting three days until 18 August, working every night, digging a new reserve line, or else carrying up the line. Things were fairly quiet on our part of the front but over in the Lens district it was Hell. For two nights the whole sky was a blaze of light and we had word along that most of the town was on fire.

Sunday night we moved up to the line just by the windmill and had things fairly easy, except for a few rifle grenades and a few 'flying pigs'. We had one man pretty badly wounded with a grenade. The following day we were witnesses of one of the queerest sights I ever saw during the whole war. Two of our planes were patrolling the front just above us when all at once three Bosch planes darted down on them. One of our planes went down straightaway out of control with the first burst of firing. The other continued to fight for about a minute when he dropped to within 200 feet of the ground, and we thought he was done, but he flattened out and turned his nose towards the German lines. The German planes followed him down, switchbacked all over him and then quietly escorted our chap into their own lines. I have often wondered if any more planes were ever captured in the same manner. I put the cause down to our man getting wounded and taking that way out to save his own skin.

Things were very quiet in the line with not much activity from the Bosch and I passed my time potting at various objects on Jerry's trench, tins he had thrown over the top, loop-holes and low spots in his parapet. I had my head over the top for every shot, but not one German was enterprising enough to take a pot shot at me.

Our latest platoon officer was a Mr Downey, a mild, pleasant-mannered man and most obviously unsuited for this life. He had been the pianist at Queen's Hall and on two or three later occasions we had evidence of his skill with the piano. The most interesting part of Downey though was his field-glasses, the finest pair I've ever looked through. He lent them to me practically all through the few days we were in the line and I had some good views of the Germans in the back areas. I also spotted several trench mortar positions just behind his support line and passed the information on to the Intelligence Officer with the necessary map references and had the satisfaction later of seeing them badly strafed by a couple of our guns.

At dusk on 21 August we were badly shelled with 8-inch shells and things were very unpleasant for an hour. He managed to knock our beautiful trench to bits with two of the big foul brutes. It was a nightmare of a night, the weather turned and we had a wet drizzly night; the Bosch started a trench mortar strafe, most of the bombs filled with a new gas, and we were in gas helmets most of the night. Among the gas-filled ones were several 10-inch *Minenwerfers* that burst like the crack of doom and blew our new sandbags to blazes.

To make matters more pleasant our people shelled Jerry's front lines with gas shells and what little breeze there was drifted the whole lot back onto us. Some of the chaps got fed up and took their gas helmets off; the consequence was several needless casualties. Dawn came with a change in the breeze that drifted the gas that had hung over us like a pall over to Jerry. I hope he enjoyed it.

The day following was fairly spasmodic, Jerry trying very hard to smash in the cellar of the windmill with 8-inch. He didn't manage it, but at the same time things were very uncomfortable and we were continually shifting our position. With no deep dugouts in our company sector we had no alternative but to stick it in the trench. The night was a repetition of the previous night, one continual strafe from dusk to dawn; we had several men badly knocked about.

The Howes on our right just by the cemetery got fed up with being shot at and a party of them went over and bombed the Bosch out of a portion of his front line, then came back, or rather some of them came back. We had just one man killed. Dawn brought a little relief and for two hours we had peace. Then our heavy Stokes started on Jerry and for two hours we had the satisfaction of seeing Jerry's trenches blown up in lumps, and had the added pleasure of a few pot-shots at some Bosch who were looking for a better hole.

C Company had a little job on at night, just a matter of connecting up the three isolated posts in front of the windmill. They were getting on fine when a pick wielded by a hefty C Company man found a billet in a buried dump of German bombs and a score of men were killed and wounded. Our CO, Major Wainwright, happened to be somewhere near and received a slight scratch on his arm. He fairly ran down to the Field Ambulance and when he came back next morning his face was covered with smiles; his right arm was in a sling and on his left was a beautiful narrow gold stripe. I wouldn't have bothered.

Friday the 24th was fairly hectic; the shelling was spasmodic but still it never ceased for many minutes on the battalion sector. The news that the Howes were to relieve us at night helped us through the day. The relief was complete about 10.00pm but on the way out via the new Foxy trench I nearly got caught by a whizz-bang. The thing burst only a yard over the top and I was almost buried with earth and stones.

We were down in Wakefield Camp at Rouchincourt just after midnight and the next day we went into billets at Marouil and spent a fairly decent week down there with a few trips to Arras at night where we managed to get rid of a few francs. I developed trouble with my teeth and when the battalion went up the line on 2 September I had to stay behind in the Transport Lines. Next morning, I went down to Field Ambulance and had three teeth out and one drilled ready for stopping next week. I went up with the rations after dusk and found the boys in the Red Line, a lovely new support line. And it ought to be lovely. We dug it. Things were very quiet so far as we were concerned, but the work was frightful. We had dug and dug in this sector until we had made it such a stronghold as the Germans made Beaumont-Hamel.

Wherever you looked you saw nothing but new trenches, belts of wire, new gunpits etc., but still the Heads aren't satisfied; they must have us out every possible hour of the night digging more, putting out more belts of wire, burying cables six feet deep, and in fact doing anything so long as we weren't idle.

The days were passed snatching sleep at short intervals, in between sitting on top of the trench, hoping that a shrapnel ball would oblige us by hitting us in a soft spot and so put an end for the time-being to the awful monotony of life. Air fights were pretty common and our guns were continually shelling the Bosch planes above us and the contents of the shells kept coming down with an angry zip amongst us, but not one of the damned things would hit us. Just excepting one lad, a new reinforcement who had come out prepared with all the latest lifesaving apparatus, a beautiful steel body-shield, light as a feather, but strong enough to stop a Bosch bullet at close quarters. This lad was writing a letter in his funk hole when somebody shouted out there was a lovely air fight on above. He popped his head out of his hole, minus his steel helmet, and got a shrapnel ball straight on his brain box.

Relieved by the Howes on the 6th and went down to the Black Line, where all the mud from the sector seemed to gather. We were covered in it from head to foot, slept in it, worked in it, ate in it and ate it too.

The Ansons were in the front line and carried out a small raid at night, bringing in three or four prisoners. We didn't hear the cost, but it's easy to imagine what those four Germans cost the Ansons.

The battalion moved up again, this time in the windmill position, on the 8th. I went down again to St Cathcrinc's to have my tooth filled and had a fairly dizzy time. The Bosch aeroplanes were over all day dropping bombs and one got home on a big shell dump, causing immense havoc and a terrible loss of life.

I went up the line again with the rations and found my company in close support to the other three who were in the front line. Our job was carrying and wiring again and we were at it nearly every hour of the day and night. We carried and wired until both our hearts and hands were sore and bleeding. The Bosch was fairly quiet and our trenches were in splendid condition. We relieved C Company on the morning of the 13th and had word along that the smug-faced hypocrite, Horatio Bottomley, was making a tour of inspection of the line. We saw nothing of him but were very interested spectators of an incident that occurred and which no doubt *John Bull*[1] made great profit from.

---

1. Bottomley, a former MP, was editor of the popular magazine *John Bull*. In 1922 he was convicted of fraud and imprisoned for a Victory Bonds scam.

Two of our planes were just making their way over our lines, about 2,000 feet up. Jerry opened up with his anti-aircraft guns and one of his first shells smashed right home on one of our poor chaps. His plane was smashed to bits and we watched the various parts as they came to earth. Some came down with a rush, the pilot more slowly, turning over and over; we could only hope that the shell had killed him; then came wings and tail fluttering down gently to earth. I've seen millions of shells fired at planes but that was the only plane I have seen hit by one. Everybody was shocked at the sight, it had all been so sudden and unexpected, but still war is like that. It's always the unexpected that puts us out of gear.

We expected some retaliation from our people but nothing happened, except that the sky was full of nothing but Bosch planes and our futile shrapnel. The day was brilliant sunshine but towards evening the rain came on, first a miserable drizzle then a steady downpour. From 9.00pm to midnight we were out in front wiring and, at various intervals, were treated to spasms of shrapnel, which caused a few casualties, two of the wounded being corporals of No. 2 Platoon. We had the impression that the Germans were only holding their front line with a few odd posts and patrols, relying as much as anything for defence on the machine-gun posts in their third line. There was very little firing from them but every now and then they would send up a few Very lights which showed us all up in alarming distinctness. We stood like statues until the blackness of the night covered us again.

We carried on work in the trench after the wiring had been finished, improving funk holes, revetting the trench, anything in fact to keep the men on the move. Everything was in a sticky state with the rain and mud and the men were fagged out. More than that, they were fed up and as soon as the order 'stand down' was passed along after dawn every man, except the few on watch, got down to it. I started shaving and was about halfway through when one of the men on watch in the next fire-bay dashed round the traverse and in a hoarse whisper said 'the General' was coming up the trench. I glanced wildly round the trench and there, on the fire-step in front of me, was a bunch of rifles, thick with mud and with the metal red with rust. I snatched up a waterproof sheet and threw it over them and had just got busy with the lather brush again when the general came in the fire-bay. I expected our brigadier, but it was no other than General Laurie, our Divisional Commander. 'What's happened to all the men, Sergeant?' he said. 'Just stood down, Sir,' I replied. 'Where are your officers?' he asked me next, and I told him they had a dugout down the communication trench. All the time I was hoping he wouldn't catch sight of an awful rifle I had missed. However, the next thing he did was go to the waterproof sheet and pull it away from the bunch of rifles. 'Very pretty,' he muttered, and I noticed the backs of his ears turn a nasty tinge of red. However, he went off up the trench and I saw him no more.

I roused the men out to clean their rifles and sent one chap away for the company officer. Mr Hardisty came along and I told him what had happened and he could hardly believe his ears. 'Get things straightened up, Sergeant,' he said, 'we shall have the Colonel round in a few minutes blowing us up.' We had too, and he was like a bear with a sore head, but things were more shipshape and all the men were busy either on their rifles or washing and shaving. One result of the GOC's early morning stroll was that the officers had to give up their comfy dugout in Foxy Trench and take up their abode in the firing line along with their men.

The Bosch was nasty all day and succeeded in smashing in our line and new Foxy no less than nine times. We had no casualties but some men got a bit jumpy. Some never seemed to get used to a bit of a strafe, and it needed a lot of good cursing to keep them from bolting.

Billy and I went with Mr Downey on the Saturday, finding out a new way out; we were to be relieved by 31st Division in a day or two and had to go down via the railway cutting. This was a new route for us and we had to smell out the way first.

Sunday morning 16 September came and with 'stand to' just before dawn came the first rum issue of the winter season. Just after 'stand down' I turned in for a little sleep, but was soon roused out. Billy came dashing up and told me that Corporal Bill Marsden of the Machine Gun Section was out beyond our wire and the Germans had just shot him. It appeared that the hog had drunk a canteen full of rum and had made up his mind to go over to the German trenches and have a scrap on his own. He went over, dropped in their front trench and prowled round a bit, but saw no Bosch. He came back but still wasn't satisfied and went again. This time he went as far as the support line and obviously again had the whole trench to himself; and some of the men saw him walking back with his arms full of souvenirs. However, the Bosch was awake and got home on Bill Marsden with a machine gun; he dropped halfway through no man's land with a bullet or two through him. Some of the men who were watching him got the wind up then and told Billy Hurrell who explained things to me. We dashed up just in time to see the end of things as far as Bill Marsden was concerned. We could see him crawling along towards our wire, then he managed to get up and make a rush. The Bosch was waiting, though, and Bill got another bullet through him, this time through the spine and he collapsed like a pricked bladder just on the wrong side of our wire.

I sent for the officer of the watch, Mr Hardisty, then got the whole of the platoon up on the fire-step and gave them orders to keep up a steady fire on the German second and third trenches. Then Billy and I and the ever-ready Puggy Willett dashed over and got Marsden in. And we'd a hell of a job too. It was bad enough getting through our wire without his body, but it was a terrible struggle coming back. Perspiration was pouring off us and our clothes were almost ripped off. Our hands and legs were bleeding where the barbed wire had got home. Jerry kept popping away at us, but I think the fire from my men must have put him off his aim because none of us was hit. Marsden was just alive when we got to him, but by the time we passed him over the parapet he was dead and when we rolled over into the trench we were very little better. Curse the bloody rum! Those were the sentiments of the three of us until Hardisty gave us a swig from his flask to revive us a bit. Wonderful stuff!

He said that whatever happened we mustn't let it get to the Colonel, or there would be serious trouble about it; Marsden's wife might lose her pension through his folly. Not only his wife, but the mad idiot had five kiddies too. Curse the bloody rum!! There was one certainty about this stunt as Hardisty said. There would be no medals.

I turned in after that for two hours but sleep wouldn't come. For one thing, I was too exhausted; for another, I couldn't get Bill Marsden's wife and kiddies out of my mind. The whole thing was like a horrible nightmare. The day passed off fairly quiet and, with finding the men plenty of work to do, I managed to shake off the memory of the morning.

We were out wiring again at night but it was a scrappy job. Our guns put up a strafe at 9.00pm and the Bosch retaliated, making both a mess of our new wire and our trenches. Luckily there were no casualties. We managed two hours' wiring between 10.00pm and twelve midnight when the Bosch opened up again with 5.9s and a bit of shrapnel. We could find no reason for it whatever, but then the Bosch was a very uncertain beast and his ways were very strange and sometimes passeth understanding.

I have an idea that Jerry was holding his first and second trenches with only a handful of men, especially in the daytime. At night I think he had pretty strong patrols working up and down the line, and these sudden strafes from his guns were just to give the impression that he was all about and in good strength.

Two more hours wiring between 1.00 and 3.00pm and then a rest until 'stand to'. Orders along to get ready for moving down as soon as we stood down and the Hoods relieved us about 5.30am on 17 September. Billy and I, along with Billy Black, were bringing up the rear of our company when, halfway down new Foxy, the Bosch sent over a whizz-bang which burst in the trench just behind me. The force of the explosion lifted me off my feet and sent me with a crash into my two chums; we finished up at the other end of the traverse in a tangled heap of cursing and very scared humanity. It might have been a horrible catastrophe for the British Army, and a feather in the Germans' cap: three of the smartest sergeants in the Army nearly out at one smack. If the German High Command only knew how near it was, they would give that gun's crew Iron Crosses as big as frying pans. Three very frightened sergeants ran like hell when they untangled themselves and found out they weren't hurt. Fancy getting almost laid out when we were off for a rest.

We were some time catching the company up and Mr Downey was just ready for coming back with a party to gather up the pieces. He said they'd look well in Kensington Museum. We thanked him nicely for his kind solicitations on our behalf and made our way steadily down to St Aubin, near Arras.

Chapter Thirty-Three

September 1917 – Now for the Salient

Billets at St Aubin, any sort of billets, but very acceptable after the open trenches. We slept like tops, but I woke up in the morning feeling stiff and sore with great bruises all over my body from the effects of the shell. We had hot baths, clean clothes and a good spruce up, then Captain Ligertwood, who had only recently taken over our company paid us all and with 50 francs in my pocket I felt like facing a few of the terrors and pitfalls of the Arras estaminets. I formed one of a very jolly party that night and we almost shook the ruins down with our songs.

The next day was a stand easy and we began to look like soldiers again. Clean buttons and badges, boots shining and clothes brushed as clean as we could get them. Marched to Ach on the 20th and then on to Frevilliers the next day to some decent billets, with plenty of decent straw to bed down on. Found out we were only about four miles from Ohlain and set off for a walk after drill had finished to see if the old place was still there.

It was a beautiful evening, visibility good for miles, and all the woods around were showing their autumn tints, every conceivable shade of brown and green. A more peaceful scene it would be hard to find. I watched four of our fighting planes take off from one of the aerodromes and fly calmly on their way to the line for a spell of dirty work. They looked like four huge birds of prey sailing majestically along with the bright blue of the sky all around them. I stood still for five minutes drinking in the beauty of it all. One couldn't imagine trouble, but it was there.

Suddenly one plane dropped out of line and turned his nose round and made for earth. All at once his nose dipped and he crashed into the corner of a field and almost at once burst into flame. The sense of peace was shattered, and one realised again the horrors of war. Sudden death, and, perhaps for the two poor devils in that plane, worse. Lingering death, but nevertheless, death, far better than getting smashed up body, mind and nerves and then not to die. That's the only thing I feared, to drag on year after year in that horrible condition. Away with such horrible thoughts. A horse and trap came driving up to me and the only occupant was a French girl. She pulled up when she got to me and wished me a polite 'Bon soir, Monsieur.' 'Bon soir, Mademoiselle Jeanne,' I replied. She stared hard at me and I could see recognition come to her. 'Ah. Le petit Corporal Harry,' she said and motioned to jump up beside her. I felt quite honoured, to be recognised by Jeanne after all these months. Hadn't poets of two Armies sung her praises, colonels and brigadiers fought over her, Jeanne of Ohlain!

It was a pleasant ride to Ohlain and we carried on a conversation as well as we could. She wanted to know how Monsieur Billy and the big Charlie were. She was quite touched when I told her about poor old Charlie and some of the others. Ohlain was full of Canadians, most of them French-Canadians, and they were a noisy crowd and Jeanne's place was crowded with them. There were cries of delight when she came in and I came in for a few curious looks from some of them. She took me to see her mother who clucked over me like an old hen, and I had to give an account of myself and the others. All this over a bottle of their best champagne. Wonderful stuff, and I soon felt all aglow. I didn't stay long because I had a long walk back and the night was pitch black.

I hadn't been walking long when I thought I heard footsteps behind me, but could hear nothing when I stopped. There they were again though as soon as I started and they kept pace with mine whatever speed I kept at. My nerves weren't very steady and the champagne had gone to my head a bit and I began to imagine things. All sorts of weird thoughts kept flashing through my head and I gripped my loaded stick tightly by the thin end. The footsteps were still there, getting no nearer but keeping pace with mine. An empty and forsaken village loomed up out of the blackness and I glanced nervously about me. Not a light about, not a sound but the steady tramp, tramp of the footsteps behind me. Just on my right was a graveyard and just beyond, looking huge and ghostly in the blackness, a church with a big square tower. Suddenly, a horrible bloodcurdling shriek rang out, and the marrow in my backbone froze and I stopped dead. Any second now I expected something to grip me and beads of perspiration stood out on my forehead.

I managed to look up at the church tower and, dimly, I saw the figure of a large bird fluttering around, which, in a second or so, gave out another horrible shriek. An owl! I took off my cap to wipe my forehead and felt something jingle in the cap. A small piece of chain with a steel ball on the end. I remembered then taking it off a dead German and pinning it on the lining of my cap. This thing had been banging on the leather band every time I put my foot down and accounted for the following footsteps. I stood there for five minutes and cursed myself. I called myself everything I knew about and then made a few more up. When I reached my billet I sat down and wrote home for a bottle of Phosferine tablets.

The days following were now full of drill, discipline and red tape, and I was busy for several hours trying to knock a bit of shape into my platoon. And it was a task. Most of the men had forgotten all their drill and discipline; up the line and down are two different and distinct things. I hadn't much help from my platoon commander, Mr Downey. He looked all right certainly, and had a lovely pair of light-coloured breeches, but his knowledge of drill was practically non-existent. Our captain was keen though on getting the company up to concert pitch for the next stunt, somewhere near Ypres as rumour had it, and, as Captain Ligertwood was liked by everybody, we all went to work with a good grace and the company was fairly happy.

At drill on 26 September when Dick Howarth came along and told me that the captain had put my name through to the colonel for a commission. 'Would I go?' the sergeant major asked. 'How long does it mean in Blighty, Dick?' I asked. 'Oh, about six months,' he said. Needless to say, I was on it like a shot. I had to go along to the colonel, who talked to me like a Dutch uncle and told me it depended on the brigadier. I should have to see him and satisfy him that I was fit to be an officer. I was all excitement and eager to be off, but of course had no idea when I should have to go.

On the 27th we started a musketry course to qualify for our good shooting allowance and I managed to get 89 out of a possible 100. Made sure of my penny a day at all events; dated back for nearly three years it meant a nice little sum in reserve.

I filled in an application form for a commission on the 27th and the following day passed the doctor and saw the adjutant, Captain Newling. On 1 October I had to go to Chelers to see the brigadier, but there was nothing very terrible about it. He was very human and nearly nice. He had all my particulars down on a paper and only asked me a few questions. Then he told me I would have a hard task to pass the exams at the Cadet School as they were very severe but that, according to my reports, I should have very little to fear from the practical side, but must swot up on infantry drill, and King's Regulation, etc. And then, with a 'Good luck, Sergeant', he dismissed me. There was only one other man there on the same errand, a Corporal Cutmore of the 1st Battalion.

Rumours of a move on the 2nd and we were busy packing gear. Set off about midnight on a short march to Tingues where we entrained at 4.00am on 3 October. Arrived at Poperinghe about 5.00pm and marched about six weary kilometres to Brown Camp behind Ypres. There was every evidence to show that a big battle was raging in front. On the train we had passed four trainloads of wounded and round the camp the roads were crowded with traffic of every description, from staff cars full of brass hats to heavy lorries full of shells for the guns in front. Our new home was a canvas camp in a sea of mud. Mud that even the mud of Ancre had little in common with. Life there is going to be absolutely terrible and I was praying for my call to come. There was nothing to see where we were, no landscape, nothing but mud, tents and filthy figures crawling about in khaki.

Each tent was surrounded by a three-foot wall of double sandbags and we soon felt thankful for the protection they afforded us. As soon as night set in the Bosch came over in his bombing planes and stayed with us all night. Bombs were dropping with a crash all around us, nasty things that burst on concussion and spread a hail of shrapnel along the ground or rather a foot above it. The battalion had several casualties during the night, one bomb making a direct hit on a tent in C Company and wiping out of existence the twelve men in it. All their remains were buried in one sandbag.

It poured with rain all night and the wind was blowing a gale and we had to keep dashing out with the mallet to knock in the tent pegs. In conversation with some troops the next day who had been round those parts for several weeks, they told us that every night was the same. As soon as darkness came the Bosch planes came and stayed until nearly dawn. Luckily our stay was very short, as our brigade had been picked for the next attack and we had to go back for special training.

On 6 October, 189 Brigade relieved us and motor lorries took us back to Herzele, about thirty kilometres away. We were shoved in the usual class of billets, cowsheds, barns and pigsties, but, nevertheless, a very acceptable change from the tents of Brown Camp. The division was now attached to XVIII Corps commanded by General Maxse, a corps, and a general, famous for hard deeds.

Training started in earnest on the 8th and we had to forget all our previous knowledge and assimilate new methods for attack. I'm afraid my interest in things was very lukewarm. The weather was simply vile, rain practically every day and the state of the ground even so far behind the line as this was simply terrible. We had a special training ground, everything set out as near as possible to the ground over which we should attack. Every German pillbox and machine-gun post was marked, every semblance of a trench or breastwork, every ruin, was there, marked either by a flag or a mound of sandbags. The attack was to come off somewhere about 26 October and was to be made by our brigade, 188, somewhere on Passchendaele, to the right of Poelcapelle.

Captain Ligertwood was red hot about the company coming out with every distinction. He presented each platoon with a beautiful silk flag made for us by his wife; he would carry one for the company. These we should take with us to the battle. He was as fit as exercise could make him and had won all the prizes at the racing meetings on his own nag. He'd made the horse get him there and he intended the company getting him there too. He talked to me one day as we were marching back from a pretty strenuous day and told me he was attaching another sergeant to my platoon who would go over with them. If I received no orders for England before the fight he would see that I hadn't to go up. The new sergeant was a real acquisition to our Sergeants' Mess and proved himself a proper scrounger. He went out one night and came back an hour later with the body of a fowl. He had plundered some poor Belgian's fowl-house. 'It's a young cockerel.' It wasn't, it was a young cockerel's great grandmother I would say, and the thing was wasted. We couldn't get our teeth in it. However, that was only once; on other occasions we fared better and he proved himself a real handy lad in a fowl pen.

Chapter Thirty-Four

18 October 1917 – Blighty and a Commission

Orders along from Brigade Headquarters on the morning of 18 October, special orders for me to proceed to England. Did I dance for joy? Did I throw my steel helmet through the billet window? I did not. Neither did I kiss the sergeant major when he brought me word. I took the news as I took everything else, as some sergeants I know take the whole rum issue. I felt a keen regret at having to leave the battalion, at leaving the friends I had made, lads who had fought with me time after time. I had to leave them now to fight on, while I lived cushily in England for months perhaps.

I had to leave at 6.00pm and walk about fourteen kilometres to the railway station at Arneke. After a whip round the boys and a few hearty handshakes, I set off on my lonely tramp, a cold cheerless night in the station of Arneke, then a painful journey to Boulogne. From 8.00am to 6.00pm. What a journey. I dropped across Cutmore from 1 RM and we chummed together.

Taken to a leave camp at Boulogne, a huge schoolroom where hundreds of men going home on leave were waiting the night for the leave boat in the morning. It was a cold night and our bed was the bare floor with no blankets, just a case of getting down as we were.

Lights had been out about an hour when the anti-aircraft guns boomed out all over the town. The Zeppelins were over and very soon two or three huge explosions testified to the fact that he was getting rid of his load of bombs. There is no question about it: I was terrified and was shaking the whole time like a leaf. To get so near to home and safety and then there's still the chance of going sky high. About two hours that spasm lasted, and after that I managed about an hour's sleep. Wasn't I glad when morning came and with it orders for the boat?

A very uneventful passage across the Channel and a quick run to London. Report at Parliament Street in the morning for instruction. That night I slept at Buckingham Palace Hotel, shorn of all its former gilt and glory. After hours of waiting at the office in Parliament Street I got my papers and warrants for fourteen days' leave. It was too late to leave London that night so caught the train on 22 October 1917 and arrived home in time for dinner.

So we draw the curtain on another act of the thrilling drama.

Chapter Thirty-Five

Odds and Ends

Before I carry on with my own new troubles and trials I will give an account from the *Official History* of the RND concerning the doings of my company in the attack at Passchendaele shortly after I left them.

One of the finest exploits of this second stage of the attack was the crossing of the Paddebeek (a flooded stream) by Captain Ligertwood's A Company 2nd Marines. The platoons of this company had gone into action under their own flags, solemnly blessed by the Battalion Chaplain, Father Davey, and taken into action with honour and reverence. These flags were carried through the battle. Captain Ligertwood, three times wounded, led his Company to within sight of their goal, when he fell mortally wounded to rise only once to direct his men to their final objective. This Company, staying on its objective throughout the entire day, were powerless to lift a finger to assist the main battle.

The loss to the RND in three days' fighting amounted to thirty-two officers and 954 men killed or missing and eighty-three officers and 2,057 men wounded. The division remained in the sector until 6 December, when they received orders to entrain for the Cambrai front and Third Army.

Now to carry on with my own affairs. Fourteen glorious days at home, every minute full to the brim, too full to write about. Then came my orders, report at Rugely on 6 November, then next day to Ripon where I was posted to a cadet camp and attached to the 5th Battalion Argyll and Sutherland Highlanders. We were merely waiting there for vacancies in the cadet schools and the biggest job we had was killing time. Stayed in Ripon about five weeks, then sent to the 20th Officers' Cadet Battalion, Fleet, near Aldershot. There I had to start soldiering all over again from the very beginning, but it was easy. Every man in my company was active service and knew his job. We had several exams, both for theory and practical work, and the third paper exam. I did very well, finishing third from top with a total of 139 marks out of a possible 150. The final exam, set by the War Office came off on 30 April and I did it easily. No marks were available though and we only knew whether we had passed or failed. We had still another month to drag on though before getting our regiments.

I had applied for a commission in my own corps, the Royal Marines. The War Office allowed us £50 towards our kit allowance and I had got most of mine together. Left Fleet on 28 May 1918 and went home to await my papers.

Received a telegram on 21 June to report at once at the Marine Barracks, Plymouth, and went off the next day. I had to wait until the Monday morning to see the commandant who, after a few kind words and a keen scrutiny, sent me off to the adjutant who presented me with a copy of my commission. I was gazetted to the Royal Marines from 29 May 1918, a fully-fledged officer. The adjutant hardly knew what to do with me. He had a crowd of young subs, dug-outs from different departments of the War Office, Admiralty etc., who were going through their first schooling as soldiers under crusty sergeant majors. He said it was no use putting me with those people, so sent me away with an old sergeant for several days' rifle shooting and revolver practice over at Mount Edgecombe.

I met several of my old friends in barracks. Poor old Jim Hearne, pottering about with only one decent hand, Sergeant Osgood, with one good arm, the other withered beyond all possible use. He told me then that I had saved his life on 13 November 1916. Several more of the old boys were there, too.

Off for a course of field training on 8 July to Tavistock. Under canvas at Whitchurch, but I got decent digs in the village for Mary and myself, and the colonel (a wreck from Jutland) gave me permission to live out. There I spent the most pleasant three weeks of the whole war, three glorious weeks of July in the heart of Devon. It came to an end all too soon and orders came for me to report at Plymouth again before proceeding to the RND Depot at Aldershot.

Back at Plymouth on the 30th and next day but one, 1st August, went to Aldershot. After reporting at Salamanca Barracks to RN Headquarters, Colonel Findlater, I spent about six hours with Mary trying to get rooms. It was a terrible job; the people who had rooms didn't know what to ask for them as soon as they saw the officer's uniform – as much as four and five pounds a week for a bed-sitting-room. We managed to get fixed up for the night about 11.00pm and the next day Mary managed to get rooms where, for a week or two, we were twisted right and left. Bloodsuckers. Later we found a home from home and were comfortable and happy for the rest of our stay in the town of armies and Army followers.

Work started for me the day after arrival and our second in command, Major Coode, the man who really mattered, was one of the most difficult men I have ever met. He was efficient, terribly efficient, and would have nothing but the best from all the subs under his wing. I passed him one day after I'd been there about a fortnight; he was walking across the barrack square with two more senior officers and, of course, I gave him, as I thought, an extra smart salute. 'Mister Askin,' he called, 'just a minute.' I walked smartly up to him. 'How long have you been in the Royal Marines, Mister Askin?' he asked. 'Four years, Sir,' I replied. 'Well, I've been in them about twenty-four years and I have never seen a Royal Marine salute like that before.' Then he gave me a demonstration of correct saluting and I felt like a piece of the gravel on the parade ground.

My time at Aldershot was spent doing course after course, Lewis gun, Vickers machine gun, trench mortars, bombing, grenades, musketry, gas, platoon and company drill etc., etc., until I too became terribly efficient.

The first exam was on 14 August, and I finished up fourth in a big class with a score of 168 marks out of a possible 200. I came across my old chum Billy Hurrell there; he had come home for a commission but had failed in the preliminary exam at Ripon and was now waiting for his demob papers to come through. He was a miner and so many of them were being released from service for work in the mines. He had got safely through the fighting of Passchendaele, Welsh Ridge, the big retreat, in which Billy Black had been taken prisoner, and had fought his way well up in the new advance before coming home.

I managed to get a downing with the flu while in Aldershot, and Mary, myself and our landlady were all down together with it. Troops and civilians were dying by thousands all over the country from the disease, and work was practically at a standstill in Aldershot.

My warning for a draft came on 1 November. Ten days' leave at home and back in Aldershot on 10 November.

Chapter Thirty-Six

11 November 1918

rmistice Day, and I couldn't possibly express my feelings on paper. All drafts cancelled for the time being, but my call came on the 16th. Three days' draft leave, then report at Dover on the 22nd for a little more service in France. I could do it on my head!

A decent crossing to Calais and then on to Douai, a town I'd gazed at from our trenches at Gavrelle for months. I managed a ride through Gavrelle on a lorry one day while there, but there wasn't a vestige of the place remaining. No one could imagine that a solidly-constructed village had once stood on the spot. Absolute desolation, and a lump came in my throat as I raised my hand to salute the memory of so many fine comrades lying dead there.

I went one day with Cutmore and another fellow from Douai to Lille just to see what the place was like. We walked part of the way and did a bit of lorry jumping in between, and managed a few hours in the place. My impression of the people there was that they had got so used to the Germans they were sorry they had gone. We had to walk about half the distance back in the pouring rain. Every car that came along we tried to stop but they were mostly full of brass hats.

Eventually we managed to stop a major of the ASC with his two mechanics in a Rolls-Royce. He was very obliging and told us to jump in. The night was pitch-black, and he was in a terrible hurry. We were doing at least 50mph. All right on the straight but the mad man tried to take an S-bend without slowing down. He would have done it but for the fact that a railway track ran across the road halfway through the bend. Round we went, first on two wheels, then two terrible leaps in the air and round the other bend on the other two wheels. We finished up all in a heap on the left bank of the road. It took one of the mechanics over an hour to get the car in running order again. The major was stamping up and down the road spitting out fire and brimstone. We finished the ride back to Douai at a more reasonable speed.

My next trip was the result of the non-arrival of our mail for three weeks. Not a line from home had anybody received since leaving England and we were all fed up. I knew the battalion was somewhere around Mons and I thought if I got up to them I should get the mail. I happened to be orderly officer for that day but, as duties were non-existent, thought I wouldn't be missed.

I caught a lorry going to Valenciennes and had a pretty bumpy journey, going through Denain, a fair-sized town. Halfway between there and Valenciennes, I noticed a motor car coming towards us flying the Royal standard on its bonnet. As it passed us I gave a smart salute and saw the King raise his hand in return. Just past there we came to what once had been a sizeable village and a huge factory used by the Germans for making big shells. The factory was nothing but a heap of broken brickwork and twisted metal, the village just a shell. Not long before the Armistice our airmen had paid it a visit and had got home with a direct hit on the factory. Hundreds of Belgian girls were killed as they lay in bed.

I got a decent feed in Valenciennes and, after a time, managed to get another lorry that was going to Mons. I got off about nine miles from there and commenced my search for the battalion. I walked from Bousso to Dour where they were supposed to be, a matter of four kilometres. Part of 189 Brigade was there and I was told that my battalion was at Eugies, another nine kilometres away. I arrived there tired, hungry and splashed with mud about 4.30pm. I went to the battalion postman first thing, but he informed me that he had only re-addressed the letters that morning and sent them on to Douai. B Company Mess was nearest, so I went in and found Pilgrim and two more officers just having tea. I shared tea with them and had a spot of whiskey and then a wash and clean up. They invited me to stay the night but I wanted to get back to Douai. I decided to walk on to Mons, another six miles away and set off at 6.00pm. Pitch dark and only a hazy idea of the direction. Got there eventually and found it a fine place, full of light and life and fine women. I had no use for them though, and so made my way to the Grande Place to pick up a lorry or car going to Valenciennes or Douai.

I found a lorry and got to Valenciennes about 11.30pm, almost dead beat. There I had to start hunting round for something to complete the journey. About midnight a very nice car passed me on the Denain road and I yelled out 'Douai?' The car pulled up and I asked one of the two officers in it if he minded giving me a lift. 'Jump in the back,' he said, and off we went and in a few minutes I was fast asleep. I was awakened in the midst of a terrible, godforsaken village. 'Here we are,' said one of the officers. 'Where?' I asked drowsily, 'This isn't Douai.' 'Oh, my Lord!' said one of them, 'we thought you said Iwuy.' They were very sorry, of course, but couldn't get on any further as they were out of petrol. They were billeted in the village and offered me a shakedown for the night, which kind offer I turned down. Where was I and how far away from Douai? They told me if I carried on for nine kilometres along the road I should get to Cambrai. Another nine kilometres and I thought I should get to a far, far better land, for I was about all in and the rain was coming down from a pitch-black sky in a steady downpour.

Off I stumbled in and out of rain-filled shell- and pot-holes along one of the most dreary roads in France. All this part had been the scene of some of the hardest fighting of the later stages of the war. Bitter fighting and, on the part of the Bosch, deliberate destruction of everything useful. What few houses and villages I passed were shelled or shaken into ruins, while along the roadside I could make out derelict and broken German tanks and other implements of war. I was almost on my hands and knees when I reached the outskirts of Cambrai and the first object I clapped eyes on was a military policeman. 'Is there an Officers' Club anywhere about here?' I asked him. 'Twenty yards up that street on the left, Sir,' he answered. I could have kissed him but hadn't the strength to struggle. To hell with Douai tonight, I thought and asked for a whiskey and a bed. They put me right until morning and about 9 o'clock, after a good breakfast and another drink, I found a lorry going to Douai.

As a companion I had a Wesleyan padre and his language would shame any old marine I ever knew and his repertoire of filthy tales was unlimited. I was glad when the Grande Place of Douai was reached and I had wished the holy man a polite good morning. He left a nasty taste in my mouth. A dirty piece of work!

As soon as I got back to billets, Cutmore told me the adjutant wanted me at Orderly Room. He had been asking for me all yesterday, the first time while I had been at Douai that the Orderly Officer had been wanted. Just my luck, and I went there prepared for the worst. In any case I expected a real dressing down for being absent from duty. Not a word though. That HAC captain was a gentleman. 'Oh! Mister Askin,' he said, 'all details are moving to their battalions today and I want you as Entraining Officer, here are the details for trucks.' That was my punishment and I heaved a sigh of relief as I made my way down to the siding. I got every man on board without a hitch and the adjutant complimented me on my work before the train steamed out. A perfect gentleman as I said before! Personally I would sooner have a chap who would have cursed me up and down and then let it drop. For all I knew this chap may have sent a little confidential report up to my own colonel. Curse the post, the postal authorities and all those people who conspire together to keep the troops and their letters apart.

Reported at my own Battalion Orderly Room on arrival and was told off to A Company, my old lot, but not one familiar face did I see. I think there was one other man in the battalion who had landed on Gallipoli with me, and he was still a private and quite content. Just about two men out of nearly 5,000. Where were the others? Others come, others go, but I go on forever.

Lieutenant Tully was in charge of the company, and with Butler-Porter, Donaldson and McCleau made up the complement of officers of A Company. They all made me welcome to the mess and I was given my own platoon, No. 1, in which I had had so many stirring times.

Major Clutterbuck was our OC, an old marine with a liver, unapproachable until after lunch. Donaldson told me he once walked into the mess at headquarters in the early morning, and wished the major a polite 'Good morning, Sir.' 'Is it? the OC asked, 'and what the Devil's that got to do with me?' A sweet man! I thought that the less I saw of the old man the better it would be for me.

The second day we moved on a few miles to fresh billets in a decent-sized mining town, la Bouverie, and I was billeted with some genuine, kindly, Belgian people. They put the best of everything at my disposal, even fetched the bedding out that had been hidden from the Germans throughout their long occupation of the place.

Artillery Employed for V Corps Attack in Battle of the Ancre

13 November 1916

18-pounders	364
4.5-inch howitzers	108
15-inch howitzers	2
12-inch howitzers	1
9.2-inch howitzers	28
8-inch howitzers	16
6-inch howitzers	56
6-inch guns	4
4.7-inch guns	8
60-pounder	46
Total	**633**

In addition several guns were lent for counter-battery work. There was one gun for every thirteen yards of front.